MW00387201

SID GILLMAN
FATHER OF THE PASSING GAME

Josh Katzowitz

Foreword by Dick Vermeil

CLERISY PRESS

Sid Gillman: Father of the Passing Game

Copyright © 2012 by Josh Katzowitz
All rights reserved. No portion of this book may be reproduced in any fashion, print, facsimile, or electronic, or by any method yet to be developed, without express permission of the copyright holder.

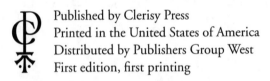

Published by Clerisy Press
Printed in the United States of America
Distributed by Publishers Group West
First edition, first printing

For further information, contact the publisher at:
Clerisy Press
306 Greenup Street
Covington, KY 41011
www.clerisypress.com

CATALOGING-IN-PUBLICATION DATA IS AVAILABLE
FROM THE LIBRARY OF CONGRESS

ISBN 978-1-57860-505-7

Edited by Jack Heffron
Cover designed by Scott McGrew
Interior design by Annie Long
Cover photo credits: *Main photo:* courtesy of the San Diego Chargers. *Top left and right:* courtesy of the Gillman family. *Top center:* courtesy of the *Los Angeles Times*
Photo insert credits: Page 5, top: courtesy of the *Los Angeles Times*. Page 5, bottom and page 6: courtesy of the San Diego Chargers. Page 7: Courtesy of the Tennessee Titans. All others images courtesy of the Gillman family

For Julie, Bella and Jonah—
the three great lights of my life

This book is dedicated to the memory of
Conrad Fink (1931–2012). I'll take your
teachings with me forever, you rascal.

TABLE OF CONTENTS

ACKNOWLEDGMENTS

I was sitting in Terry Hill's basement in San Francisco, leafing through Sid Gillman's mother's scrapbook, and I was almost finished. Nearly done with my research for the day—I actually was on the very last page—I came across a plain white envelope.

Postmarked Dec. 27, 1933, from Minneapolis (with a two-cent George Washington stamp), the letter was addressed to "Sidney Gillman, c/o General Delivery, Palo Alto, California." Gillman, at the time, was playing in the East-West Shrine game, which is why he was on the West Coast after his senior season at Ohio State was complete and why this particular letter was traveling halfway across the country to find him.

Then, the typewritten letter:

Dear Sid:

This, I imagine, will be something very unexpected to you, but nevertheless, I can't help but say that I have been one of your admirers for the past three years or more and want to say that your picture, which is shown in the "San Francisco News," is even more than handsome. . . .

Maybe I am wishing for way too much, but then one's heart but cannot help but flutter. Then again, I suppose competition would be far to (sic) keen for one of my "Standing." Aaah! How I wish I were even nearer to San Francisco. . . .

I'll be looking for more of your pictures and I will travel right along with you but Please! *Remember* I am one of your everlasting admirers.

(Signed, in cursive) Florabelle

Needless to say, I had many questions about this supposed secret admirer letter. I walked upstairs to ask Terry—Gillman's youngest daughter—about it, and she had no idea. Could anybody alive today know the origin of this letter? There was nobody I could call on the phone or write to in an e-mail. As far as I could tell, it was impossible to know who sent the letter. Was it a joke? Was it real? What did Gillman think about it? More importantly, what did Esther Berg, his future wife, think about it?

And why had the letter been kept in the family album? Why was the name of Gillman's sister, Lillian, written on the envelope?

Why, why, why?

When you write a book on a man who's no longer walking in this world, the challenges are mighty. You don't get to feel the grip of his handshake, to hear the tone of his voice, to view the gleam in his eye. He doesn't have a chance to explain his life, to defend himself, to counter your preconceived notions, to talk about those he loved and hated, to talk about himself.

And you can't ask him about a 70-year-old secret-admirer letter.

Mostly, you have to rely on the words of others to paint the picture of the man you never got to know.

That said, I highly doubt I could have written this book without the help of Sid's kids—Lyle Gillman, Bobbe Korbin, Terry Hill, and Tom Gillman. Also, many thanks to Bill Korbin and Larry Hill. Lyle was the first kid I contacted, and it immediately felt like we had known each other for years. She traveled many hours from her home in the mountains of Arizona to Los Angeles to meet up with Bobbe and me and spend two days talking about Sid and Esther and what life was like around them. They answered questions that could not be found in research materials—old newspaper clippings or 50-year-old magazine stories. They took a two-dimensional Sid off the ink print of the newspapers and breathed life into him, giving me a three-dimensional sketch.

We met at the Sheraton Four Points at LAX with handshakes and exited with hugs and kisses. And, from me, a lifetime of gratitude.

Terry, in San Francisco, gave me a great gift—a look at the dusty, deteriorating scrapbook Sid's mom kept of all his high school athletic exploits that is nearly a century old. Terry also happened to stumble across five videotapes of interviews of Sid and Esther—who in the hell owns a VCR these days, anyway?—that were a lifesaver in helping me piece together their childhoods in Minneapolis.

Tom, though we never connected in Los Angeles, allowed me to pester him on the phone repeatedly during a three-day span, answering questions that were incredibly personal and that opened another side of Sid I never would have seen.

One of my biggest regrets was that Esther died in February 2010, a few months before I started this journey. Lyle, throughout our conversations, kept saying, "If only Mom were still alive, she could have written the book for you." Esther's kids did a pretty good job, themselves.

I also would be remiss if I didn't give much praise and thanks to the following kind souls: My CBSSports.com colleagues Mike Freeman, Pete Prisco, Clark Judge, Will Brinson, Ryan Wilson, and Andy Benoit for their help; Bob Hunter of the *Columbus Dispatch*; Tim Sullivan and Nick Canepa from the *San Diego Union-Tribune*; the *Houston Chronicle's* John McClain for, upon my request, telling me the same story twice five months apart in cities 800 miles apart; Jon Kendal with the Pro Football Hall of Fame, who let me hang out in the basement bunker all day and make what felt like about a thousand copies; Brandon Standafer of the San Diego Hall of Champions for loading me up with a decade's worth of newspaper articles in dusty binders that probably haven't been touched since Sid left the Chargers in 1971; Mike Pearson of Miami University who introduced me to Paul Dietzel on that beautiful autumn day in beautiful Oxford; the ladies in the Ohio State University archives; Bob Schmidt in the Miami University archives; Jack Brennan and P.J. Combs with the Cincinnati Bengals; Jennifer Rojas with the San Diego Chargers; Patrick Smyth with the Denver Broncos; Todd Tobias for having such great material on and such great interviews with Gillman; Mike Patton, David Gilmour, and Greg Graffin for the soundtrack; Sheila Weiss of Hillside Memorial Park and Mortuary; Margie from riflemanconnors.com; Allen Brown for key photo identification; and Nick Shundich (a University of Cincinnati team co-captain in 1951) and his son Steve for mailing me various clips and videotapes.

Many thanks to my editor, Jack Heffron, who began to believe in this project as we ate macaroni and cheese across the street from the Clerisy Press offices. I'm glad he thought enough of it to continue working with me after he moved into the online world. Thanks also to Richard Hunt, Donna Poehner, and Ronnie Kutys from Clerisy.

I have so much gratitude to Trent and Michelle Rosecrans (Cincinnati), Brent Duersch and Jennifer Depalma-Duersch (Delhi, Ohio); Diana, Joe, Mak, Charlie, and Alexa Pasquarello (San Diego); Mariko Miki and Brent Fitzgerald (San Francisco); and the Rev coffee shop (Smyrna, Georgia) for extending to me your warmest hospitality during this process.

—⚋—

Another word about Trent Rosecrans. More than just giving me a place to crash, Trent has served as an editor, an idea-giver, and one of my best friends. This book wouldn't have been the same (it would have been much, much worse, in fact) without Trent's input.

Many, many thanks to my parents, Joel and Ellen, for their everlasting love, and my in-laws—Victor and Susan Alonso—for providing huge amounts of support whenever we've needed it.

The first time I wrote a book, I had no kids and, for all intents and purposes, had no job. This time around, my house has been inhabited by a pair of twins, and I have a full-time gig with CBSSports.com. I couldn't have finished this book—spending all those hours burying my head in library books, flipping through online archives and bleeding on my computer keyboard—without the person who's closest to my heart.

With that, I thank my wife, Julie—who, while supporting this endeavor, managed to complete her triple-board residency at Cincinnati Children's Hospital, finish her psychiatric forensic fellowship at Emory University in Atlanta, pass her medical boards, and land a pretty sweet job in Austin, Texas.

And most importantly, she's the mother of my Bella and Jonah, who came into our lives three minutes apart in February 2010 and teach me new things each and every day. They are my inspiration. With them, I am the Florabelle.

FOREWORD
by Dick Vermeil

Sometimes it's not about who were or are the best NFL coaches; sometimes it's more about who has coached a winning Super Bowl team. People know Vince Lombardi's name because the NFL media continues to promote Vince Lombardi, as it should! He was one of our best. Paul Brown's name is still remembered because he not only coached teams, he owned one as well. But sometimes the National Football League media does very little to promote those coaches who contributed even more than a Super Bowl win, such as Sid Gillman.

Sid Gillman never won a Super Bowl, and that is one of the reasons why many people, especially the younger generation of NFL fans, don't even know who he was, let alone talk about him in the same vein as a Lombardi or a Brown. I was fortunate to work with Sid. I got to know him very well and one of his greatest assets, that transcended his technical and offensive scheme brilliance, was his teaching ability. Sid broke down and analyzed the fundamentals of all of the offensive positions better than had ever been done before, and his success may not have been duplicated since. Let me explain.

Before I hired Sid in 1979 to come and help coach me and my offensive coaches in Philadelphia, I called around and visited with people with whom he had worked or coached to see how they felt about me bringing him out of retirement at 68 years old. All but two people told me to stay away from him, stating that he was way too opinionated and stubborn. Only Al Davis and Jack Pardee said hire him! Realizing I was also very opinionated and stubborn, I knew we would make a good team. Here is what he did for me, and here is what he did for my offensive staff. He made us all better coaches, better teachers. He challenged our thinking in every phase of offensive football, especially the fundamental technique side of the game. Over his career, Sid had built a film library of all the truly great offensive players executing their specific techniques at game-day speed. Those films directly related to each specific position and each individual thing a player would have to do to execute the fundamental techniques at the highest level. Not only did he challenge us to open up our minds and evaluate the techniques we were all teaching, he taught us a better way to teach these fundamental techniques.

These action film clips of all these great players executing their specific techniques at a Pro Bowl level were great teaching aids as well as a great way to convince us there was a better way to do some of the things we were teaching. From there, Sid proceeded to show us how to better utilize the skills within the offensive scheme.

We had been to the playoffs in 1978—the first playoff appearance of an Eagles team in 18 seasons—so we were going in the right direction. But I really felt that hiring Sid would help us all get to where we wanted to go much faster. There is no substitute for the wisdom that only years of research and experience can bring, and believe me when I say, Sid brought wisdom to my staff that I doubt anyone else could have, even if that other coach had already won a Super Bowl.

Sid was what I needed, Sid was what my staff needed, and I'm sincere in saying I don't think we would have won the 1980 NFC Championship and advanced to Super Bowl XV without Sid's guidance. As a result of all the time we spent together, we became very close friends. It was like working with my father. We shared a lot of time outside the office, off the field, doing what good friends do together. We shared great home-cooked meals, backed and supported by good wines, though I must say Sid was not a wine connoisseur. I'll never forget watching Sid mix different varieties of red wine in the same glass. Wine was about the only thing he didn't know a lot about. What a piece of work!

The only mistake I made was not filming and/or recording our meetings. I felt like I was in graduate school, working toward a PhD in offensive theory, concepts, schemes, and game fundamentals, all being taught by the leading professor of his time. Wow, what a difference from my first exposure to NFL coaches. Now, I'm not trying to be critical by inserting a direct opposite impression when I insert my Stanford experience. While working as a young assistant coach at Stanford in the mid-1960s, I, along with the rest of the staff, was invited to lunch with a visiting pro staff that was in Palo Alto preparing to play the San Francisco 49ers on the following Sunday. It was midweek, so it was an obvious preparation day, but it didn't stop the pro staff from drinking martinis along with their lunch before heading back into staff meetings. Not a Sid Gillman approach in any way!

I realize everybody has a different personality as to how they approach the game. I was my own worst enemy; way too intense, way too emotional, and too much of a workaholic. Sid used to tell me all the time, "Vermeil, you work too damn hard trying to make four yards. No matter how many hours you study opponent films, there's only going to be 11 players on the other side of the line of scrimmage. You would be better off getting more sleep." Sid was smart enough to know when to turn off the projectors and get some rest.

Sid was always looking for or trying to create something for the offense that hadn't been done. He loved to be the first coach to do something new, something creative. If he got a good idea from someone else, with very little effort he would improve on it, install it in one of his packages, and begin teaching it as soon as possible. He never lost his thirst for knowledge. He was continually working on expanding his offensive concepts and packages, even after he retired for the last time.

Sid taught us all: the Bill Walshes, the Don Coryells, and many of the other great coaches of that era and beyond. Sid's greatness isn't all based on his wins and losses; no, it is more about his overall contributions to the hows, whys, whens, and wheres of the game. He researched what to teach like a mad scientist, then broke it down and defined what to teach, how to teach it, and when to teach it. From there, he proceeded to coach coaches how to best coach it themselves, how to fit it into their scheme and get it executed at the highest level on game day.

You really had to be there to appreciate Sid. You had to be with him. Sid Gillman touched the entire National Football League, just like Vince

Lombardi did with his leadership greatness and his Green Bay Sweep. The concepts, schemes, and techniques are ingrained somewhere within the 32 offenses running in the NFL today, though there are only a handful of us left who can watch a game on Sunday and recognize where that specific concept originally came from. The 18-yard comebacks, the shifting, motion, the multiple formation packages, all either were originated by Sid Gillman or came across his desk for improvement. It all started with Sid!

Like any great scientist, his mind never rested. He was still thinking X's & O's the very last time I talked to him on the phone a couple of weeks before he passed away. Thank God he is in a place of honor, in Canton, Ohio's NFL Hall of Fame, among so many NFL greats whose careers were enhanced by Sid Gillman's contributions to the game they all loved to play and/or coach.

INTRODUCTION

The stadium rises from the side of Interstate 30 like a spaceship that just happened to crash-land in north Texas. The behemoth cost Dallas Cowboys owner Jerry Jones and the citizens of Arlington, Texas, a cool $1.2 billion, the most expensive sports construction of all time, and, in turn, the stadium looks like it was built on a different planet.

This immense structure is a symbol of what the NFL is today. Like everything else in Texas, it's humongous, and no expense was spared to make the stadium's patrons as comfortable as possible. At the same time, Jones reaches as deeply as he can into those same fans' pockets.

The stadium sits off the interstate named for legendary Cowboys coach Tom Landry, but this is not the kind of football stadium he would recognize. Inside, the centerpiece is the video board that hangs like a Boeing 747 over the turf. It's the biggest TV in the universe, and with its high-definition capability, it's like watching real life above what is, in fact, a real, live game.

Actually, it's tough to decide where to look when you're watching a game at Cowboys Stadium—the field or the video board—because they both look so spectacular. Do you look at the gorgeous sun setting over the Caribbean Sea, or do you focus on those beautiful blue waters that shimmer underneath? Same problem here. The entire viewing experience is almost too eye-popping to comprehend.

Today is Media Day for Super Bowl XLV, and with Jones serving as the maître d', this event is as big as big can possibly get. That's the way he's lived his life and the way he's built his team. Going bigger than humongous is a way of life in Texas, and it's a way of life in Jerry World.

Before the game, Jones talked about his desire to set an all-time Super Bowl attendance record (for the record, he would fail), and he sold expensive tickets to those who wanted to stand *outside* the stadium and watch the game on large HD screens.

Yet, by God, Cowboys Stadium is a magnificent structure, light years away from Super Bowl I, which was played in cavernous—not to mention,

1

old—Los Angeles Memorial Coliseum in front of a 60 percent-full crowd and which featured a halftime show with a trumpeter named Al Hirt and two college marching bands. (Super Bowl XLV, by contrast, featured the Black Eyed Peas, tragically one of the most popular bands in the world.)

Five days before the championship game, I stood on the turf at Media Day, the largest TV in the world precariously hanging above my head, and all around me, the worst part of the modern game was on display. The part where the clowns rule the afternoon, where entertainment means more than the game.

On days like this, knowing it's hardly ever a good idea to bring your laptop to the circus, you can forget about getting any work done.

Put Sid Gillman in a scene like this, and it'd be like putting a football coach on the moon.

During Gillman's era, mostly during the heyday of the American Football League when a band of upstart owners and players tried to break through the NFL's monopoly in the 1960s, teams desperately tried to draw attention to themselves. But their ideas weren't usually insulting to the viewers.

Many aspects of Super Bowl XLV week were exactly that, and though Packers quarterback Aaron Rodgers outdueled Steelers quarterback Ben Roethlisberger as Green Bay won its fourth championship, the winner these days is really a secondary issue. For fans—and, let's face it, the corporate sponsors and bigwigs who fill the stadium to watch two teams they most likely care very little about—it's all about the experience.

This is the NFL of the 21st century. Money rules all. Sponsors and advertisers are worshiped. The fans pay exorbitant ticket prices, especially if they're forced to buy on the secondary market. Hell, they pay ridiculous prices just to stand outside. Everybody but the owners gets shortchanged.

The game is different from the time Gillman coached, and most who play the game today wouldn't recognize Gillman's contributions.

Since I started this project, one of the most interesting obstacles I've run into is the lack of name recognition for Gillman, one of the game's most important coaches. Most fans of my generation who were born after Gillman's head coaching days were behind him wouldn't have ever heard his name. To be honest, I knew nothing about him before I started researching my first book, *Bearcats Rising*, but the more I read about him and the more I talked to people who played for him, my fascination grew.

Simply put, Gillman was an innovator. On the field, off the field, in preparing for games, in preparing for a season, on social issues, and on rule-bending. He's the most important person in professional football that hardly anybody remembers.

I'll give you an example.

During Super Bowl Media Day, I asked 10 offensive players—5 from the Green Bay Packers and 5 from the Pittsburgh Steelers—if they had ever heard of Gillman. I asked offensive linemen and running backs and tight ends and wide receivers. I asked stars and scrubs. Nine of them said no, they'd never heard Gillman's name.

The one player who said yes is a Packers tight end named Tom Crabtree. He happened to play at one of the colleges where Gillman once coached. I asked him if he knew anything about Gillman, and his eyes lit up. "He coached at Miami Ohio, didn't he?" Crabtree asked.

Among other places, I responded. You know anything else about him?

"Um, that he won a lot of games?" Crabtree said in less than confident terms.

Yet if I'd asked those players about Gillman's more famous contemporaries—say, Vince Lombardi or Paul Brown or Woody Hayes or Bill Walsh—a lot more than one of them could have given me a usable answer.

So, I ask: Why has Gillman fallen through the cracks of NFL history? Why do we lose sight of him in the glare of today's ever-flashy Super Bowls? Gillman was just as innovative as any of the coaches I mentioned above (hell, Gillman helped tutor Lombardi, and Walsh's West Coast offense took much of its inspiration from Gillman's teachings), so why isn't he as well known?

Theories abound from those who knew Gillman well.

Some say it's been many years since Gillman coached on the sidelines, that he's simply a man forgotten.

"There's been a little separation in time," Super Bowl–winning coach Brian Billick said. "But within the profession, the regard that Sid Gillman is held in is second to none."

Some say it's because Gillman never won a Super Bowl title of his own.

"There seems to be an inordinate focus by the media, which then contaminates the football public, that the only measure of a player and a coach is, 'Did they participate in a Super Bowl or did they win a Super Bowl?'" said Hall of Fame offensive tackle Ron Mix. "That is such nonsense.

"I know this is a silly example, but it's somewhat reflective of that attitude. If I meet somebody new and the person who's introducing me says, 'You know Ron played professional football, and he's in the Pro Football Hall of Fame,' the question almost immediately is, 'Oh, did you play in a Super Bowl?' My response is, 'Look, there are about 5,000 Super Bowl rings.' Then I show them my Hall of Fame ring, and I say, 'There are only about 200 of these rings. Why would I need to participate in the Super Bowl?' They seem to measure coaches by asking if he won a Super Bowl."

Some say it's because he didn't seek out the spotlight, and therefore, the spotlight didn't shine on the memory of Gillman after he died in 2003.

"Dad always refused—and we yelled at him and cajoled him—to have an agent," said Lyle Gillman, Sid's oldest daughter. "Never had one. He would have a local TV show or a local radio show, but he didn't want to ever put himself in the spotlight."

Some, though, are brutally frank.

"I don't know. I don't know. Maybe it's because Sid . . . well, I don't know," longtime Dallas Cowboys personnel director Gil Brandt said.

What we do know is this: Gillman's influence lives on in today's game. Those who know Gillman and understand his impact refer to him as the father of the modern passing offense. Today's players might not know Gillman's name, but they're intimately familiar with some of his groundbreaking concepts.

Five days after my failed "Do you know Sid Gillman?" experiment at Media Day, the Packers led the Steelers 28-25 midway through the fourth quarter. Green Bay had built an 18-point lead, but Pittsburgh had regained momentum and if the Steelers forced the Packers to punt, Ben Roethlisberger—who had willed his team to victory so many times in the past—could be counted on to, at the very least, tie the game.

The Packers faced a third-and-10 with six minutes to play, and they desperately needed to convert the first down. As center Scott Wells snapped the ball to Rodgers, three Packers receivers, including Greg Jennings as the inside man (the one closest to Rodgers) lined up to his left. Tight end Jordy Nelson was the lone receiver on the right side of the line.

Rodgers took the snap, and the play unfolded. As Rodgers took his five-step drop, three defensive linemen rushed the Green Bay offensive line, and all of them were engulfed by the Packers. Two linebackers stayed in the middle of the field to ward off any short or medium crossing routes. Six Steelers defensive backs chased the Packers' receivers.

Lined up against Steelers cornerback Ike Taylor, Jennings curved to his left as if to cut into receiver Brett Swain's path, and then, like a plane circling the runway in preparation for landing, Jennings moved toward the middle of the field where Rodgers found him, skimming the ball over Taylor's outstretched hand and into the comfortable embrace of Jennings's arms.

It was a seam route, a common path taken by modern-day receivers trying to advance the ball down the field. Today, every offense runs a seam route—when the receiver lines up in the slot position (between the outside receiver and the offensive line, near the hash marks) and runs straight up field. It hardly looks like anything that's innovative.

In Gillman's day, though, this was pioneering, because wide receivers didn't line up in the slot and because tight ends weren't a big part of most team's offensive passing attacks.

"Most teams did not run down the seam," said Greg Cosell, who has worked at NFL Films since 1979 and coauthored the book *The Games That Changed the Game.* "Basically, back then, you played with two receivers, a tight end, and two running backs. Sid's big innovation was that he took [running back Keith] Lincoln out of the backfield and made him his third receiver. He'd line him up in the slot. The whole idea of seam routes, which Sid strongly believed in, was that if you controlled the middle of the field, the area between the hash marks, you could win in the passing game. That stands today."

Back in the Super Bowl, Jennings had made his move, emulating the type of route that Gillman had worked so hard to develop. The ensuing catch gave the Packers a 31-yard gain, a first down, and allowed them to take more time off the clock in their eventual triumph.

It was a result that would have made Gillman smile.

Keith Lincoln, sitting at his home in Pullman, Washington, could recognize the importance of the route and what it meant to a league when virtually nobody used more than two receivers at a time. Lincoln doesn't spend too much time watching football these days, and if you really want to talk about the minutiae of route-running, he points you to other former players, other people. But even though most of the players actually participating in the Super Bowl had no idea where and when the seam route was born, Lincoln knows why Gillman's theories—35 years after his last head coaching job—were so important to the game.

"Sid was one of the first people to lengthen the field, and he worked hard at that," Lincoln said. "You have to remember that back in the 1950s, it was black and blue football. You ran the ball. But Sid was the guy who really, really believed in covering the whole field. Against us, the defense couldn't have the damn safeties three or four yards off the line of scrimmage, like they could before, because we'd throw it over their butts."

Gillman's ideas made the game of football different than it had ever been before. He shifted the paradigm and transformed the sport into the kind of football you see today, the kind that has made it the most popular spectator sport in this country. You might not know about Gillman. But you know his ideas. And you know his essence.

In the end, it doesn't matter much why Gillman isn't recognized by today's fans in the same way Lombardi, Brown, and Hayes are remembered. He didn't coach for more than a half-century to be canonized after his death anyway. He stayed involved in the game for nearly every day of his 91 years on Earth because he loved it and because he never could find a way—or a need—to part with it.

After the Packers completed their Super Bowl XLV triumph, Rodgers was named the game's MVP and, as such, he did the annual "I'm going to Disney World" commercial spot. Jennings, meanwhile, was lost in a sea of confetti. If Rodgers was the one showcased on that enormous HDTV inside that spaceship of a stadium, Jennings was the one in the supporting role in the background. If Rodgers was the star, Jennings was still stuck in the shadows.

Much like Sid Gillman—the coach who has fallen through the cracks of history but whose impact on the game should not ever be forgotten. Because he was an innovator, because he's the only coach in the Pro Football Hall of Fame *and* the College Football Hall of Fame, because his concepts are still used today more than ever.

Because they still work.

one CHAMPIONS

On his way to the biggest game of his career and the biggest game in the history of San Diego, Chargers running back Keith Lincoln felt lousy. He felt like he was coming down with the flu, and his legs felt heavy. Considering he was about to play in the 1963 American Football League championship game, this was a rather unfortunate occurrence. It wasn't just because San Diego would compete for the league title for the third time in four years, but it was also a game—and the team recognized this at the time—that their coach needed like he needed oxygen. It was the game of Sid Gillman's life, the moment he had prepared for ever since he gave up playing football to coach it.

And here was Lincoln, who would be counted on so heavily to beat the Boston Patriots as one of the most important pieces of San Diego's outstanding offense, driving his car to the game. And feeling sluggish. And crappy.

"I didn't feel," Lincoln said, "like I wanted to feel going into a championship game."

Gillman had waited 30 years for a moment like this. He had waited three decades to showcase his offense, the evolution of which had made him the foremost expert in the art of the forward pass. He had waited so damn long to prove that his crazy ideas, inspired by a maniacal Ohio State coach from the 1930s named Francis Schmidt and expanded upon by Gillman throughout his career, would work.

The AFL championship game was not quite the biggest platform Gillman could have wanted, though the upstart league finally was seeping into the country's consciousness and pushing against the NFL's monopoly. But Gillman thirsted to show a national TV audience, and those who had denied and derided him because of his Jewish heritage, and

9

those who always picked somebody else to coach their team, that his Chargers squad knew how to score. That they knew how to win. That *he* knew how to win.

After AFL championship game losses in 1960 and 1961, after losing the NFL championship title in 1955 when he coached the Los Angeles Rams, and after a 1962 season in which Gillman presided over his worst year as a coach, Gillman needed this win. He needed this validation. Needed it like he needed food in his belly. He needed Lincoln.

And Lincoln needed an aspirin.

—∞—

In 1963, San Diego was still new to the pro sports scene. The Chargers had moved from Los Angeles two years earlier, and it's not like a longtime, historically successful NFL franchise had suddenly burst into town. No, the Chargers left L.A. because they were never going to be more popular than the L.A. Rams. They were never going to be more popular than the Rams because the Rams were a longtime, historically successful NFL franchise that drew crowds of more than 100,000. But the Chargers were as exciting as they were fresh-faced. They were AFL upstarts with a growing fan base and an eclectic group of players and coaches who showcased a different brand of football.

Before the Chargers arrived, the city of San Diego was a curiosity to much of the country. To an outsider who hadn't ventured that far south before, San Diego was a Navy town, a town in which you stopped briefly before heading to the Mexican playground 20 miles away.

The only athletic teams in town to which anybody paid attention were the minor-league baseball Padres and San Diego High School—the latter of which consistently was the biggest sports story in the area. Hardly anybody cared about San Diego State athletics, and Balboa Stadium, which was built in 1914 and now held low-level car races and prep football games, was crumbling.

Until Chargers owner Barron Hilton left L.A. for San Diego, the town's sporting events sleepwalked through the city's consciousness. It was, as *San Diego Union* sports editor Jack Murphy wrote, "the Rip Van Winkle of American cities."

Or as the wonderful *Los Angeles Times* columnist Jim Murray put it, "There's always a lot of suspense going to San Diego these days because you never know when President Johnson might order it closed or mothballed—or transferred to Newport News. But I guess they're afraid of a serious dislocation of the tattoo industry."

"San Diego was kind of in the doldrums in this period," said longtime San Diego sportswriter Jerry Magee. "The period through World War II was a very active one here, because we had people making ships and doing things like that to aid the war effort. After the war ended, San Diego went into the doldrums. San Diego needed a catalyst. It needed something that people could rally around in the community. The Chargers became that entity. It represented San Diego's ability to really become big league."

That's why the Chargers' fans became so entrenched in the team so quickly. It's why, although the metal seats at Balboa Stadium were awfully uncomfortable, fans suddenly had a new reason to attend games there. It's why the Chargers knew their decision to leave L.A. for a washed-up Navy hub, which was in the middle of a near-fatal case of sleepy-town blues, was the right one.

Because when the Boston Patriots came to town for the 1963 AFL championship game at Balboa Stadium, the fans were going to experience what Gillman felt. That the Chargers *had* to win the game.

—w—

Before they could get to that title game, San Diego needed a quarterback. Oh, the Chargers already owned a 23-year-old second-year Kansan named John Hadl, but even though he started 10 games in 1962, his reign as a rookie quarterback was disastrous. His passing was inaccurate and inconsistent. He threw 24 interceptions against 15 touchdowns. The team went 1-9 in the games he started. It was clear Hadl wasn't ready to lead the Chargers anywhere but to the AFL's basement.

Though Hadl eventually would find his mark, earning six Pro Bowl berths in his 16-year career, Gillman needed a veteran to run the team while Hadl learned how to become a successful pro quarterback. Gillman needed a player who could integrate the team's passing game into the offense and mesh it together with two of the best running backs in the league. He needed somebody who could inspire.

Gillman found the perfect guy in Canada. He was Tobin Rote, by then a 35-year-old quarterback with not much football left in his body. He already had a long career, winning an NFL championship in 1957 with the Detroit Lions before moving on to the Canadian Football League with the Toronto Argonauts and becoming the best quarterback in that league.

"Tobin Rote is about as great a quarterback as ever took the ball from center," Gillman said after the 1963 AFL title game, clearly in love and full of hyperbole. "He has a great mind, has all the ability in the world, and is a great leader. As a balanced runner, passer, blocker, leader, field general, he has no superior."

He also was pretty special when playing with a pounding hangover. For one night game in Toronto, after he had been out until 7 a.m. that day and had slept only three hours, he set a CFL record with 38 completions. He couldn't stop his hand from shaking a few hours before the game, but still, he managed a feat that would have impressed Mickey Mantle.

The man's tolerance for booze must have been off the charts, because, even though teammates could smell Rote's beer breath in the huddle whether it was an 11 a.m. practice or an afternoon workout, he never appeared drunk. In fact, Tobin could down a dozen beers, guzzle a few more while marinating steaks for a barbecue, and then bet anybody that he could drink another dozen Molsons in the span of three minutes. That was a bet Rote would win, and the respect shown by his Argonauts teammates those years was nearly as high as his blood-alcohol level.

Yet, in mid-January of 1963, Rote was available for the Chargers to sign him, and immediately, Rote proved his leadership capabilities. An example: During the 1963 season, Chargers guard Pat Shea was fined $250 by the San Diego police after he went berserk when a traffic officer made what Shea considered rude remarks to Shea's pregnant wife. The very next day, Rote campaigned to his teammates to get everybody to kick in some money—$5 here, $10 there—to help Shea pay off the fine.

Rote could sit there shirtless in the locker room, a swath of hair on his chest, belly, and arms that made him look like he was wearing a tank top of black fur, and he could make his teammates believe—in him and in themselves.

"He was the greatest guy in the world to be around," said Tom Bass, then a Chargers assistant coach. "He just brought leadership qualities that were completely unique. Players loved him and would do anything for him."

Plus, he was tough. On the second play of the Chargers' first exhibition game of 1963, a defender tore one of Rote's ribs away from his sternum, an injury that could have kept him out months. Five weeks later, he was starting San Diego's first regular-season game.

"Tobin Rote had all the stuff," fullback Keith Lincoln said. "John [Hadl] had a learning curve. Tobin had leadership skills, he could rally the troops around him and his arm still had life. He did a really good job of tying it all together. He taught a lot of people how to be a football player."

That was what Gillman wanted for his 1963 season. If this was going to be the season his team won it all, Rote was the quarterback that would be in charge. And Rote rewarded Gillman. He would end the season throwing for 2,510 yards, meaning that Rote, during his career, led the NFL and the CFL in passing and, in his final year as a full-time starter, finished third in the AFL.

Probably first in beer consumption, though.

—⚬⚬⚬—

The Chargers—led by the passing of Rote, the running of Paul Lowe and Lincoln (1,836 yards and 13 touchdowns combined), and the receiving of Lance Alworth (61 catches, 1,205 yards, and 11 touchdowns)—were, suffice it to say, a very good team that season. They were unquestionably the best in the AFL and perhaps the best in the NFL as well (there's little question they also were tops in the CFL). They were the AFL's No. 1 in points scored, offensive yards, yards per pass, rushing yards, first downs, touchdowns, defensive scoring, and rushing defense. Sid Gillman's forte was the pass offense, but that year, his team finished third in that category in the eight-team league, slightly better than average.

But San Diego's run game was spectacular, and the defense, with Earl Faison (four-time All-Pro) and Ernie Ladd (three-time All-Pro and future World Wrestling Entertainment Hall of Famer) as half of the Fearsome Foursome, was fantastic.

Entering the final regular-season game of the year, San Diego was 10-3 but needed one final victory against the atrocious Broncos—who went 2-11-1 but somehow crushed the Chargers earlier in the year—to win the AFL West and qualify for the title game. Denver's coach, Jack Faulkner, had known Gillman for 25 years. Faulkner had played for Gillman at Miami (Ohio) in the late 1940s and then had been Gillman's assistant coach at the University of Cincinnati before moving west with Gillman to the L.A. Rams and south to the Chargers.

He finally had landed his first head coaching job the season before, and after beating the Chargers twice in 1962, he metaphorically slapped Gillman in the face during the fourth game of 1963, calling timeouts in the final minutes to try to score just once more in the 50–34 Denver win. Gillman and his team hadn't forgotten those slights.

San Diego, after taking a 23–17 lead early in the third quarter of the final game of the year, showed no mercy to remind Denver of its early-season decision. And to insult the Broncos once and for all, San Diego, after scoring again with only seconds left in the game, attempted a two-point conversion, got it thanks to a touchdown catch by Faison, the defensive end, and then attempted an onside kick. It wasn't a slap in the face. Gillman had metaphorically punched Faulkner in the gut and then slugged him in the jaw.

"How many points did you want to score, Sid?" a furious Faulkner asked as the two met on the field for a post-game handshake. Silence from Gillman. "Sid, how many points did you want to score?" Faulkner asked again. Gillman walked away without a word, his revenge complete.

Added Faulkner, "Thanks a lot, Sid, you son of a bitch."

Afterward, Faulkner was still too stunned to answer questions from the press. So, he asked questions instead. "How many points did he want to score, anyway?" He never got his answer. But the Chargers weren't done scoring points yet. Not by a long shot.

—⁓—

In the championship game, the Chargers would face the Boston Patriots, who had performed only slightly better than average in winning the AFL East. Still they would be tough opponents, because the key to the Patriots' good fortune was a defense that blitzed more than anybody else in the league. The two teams had played twice during the regular season—the Chargers had won 17–13 and 7–6 while being held to 108 rushing yards combined—but San Diego still hadn't quite figured out Boston's blitz packages. In reality, nobody in the league had determined how to shut down a defense that, as Gillman said, could stop water.

"Hell, we blitzed a lot because we could get away with it," said Boston defensive line coach Marion Campbell. "We blitzed our way to the championship game."

Gillman had to come up with a plan to stop the Patriots from constantly chasing and sacking the middle-aged Rote, who, to make matters worse, was suffering from bursitis and who nearly needed to take a Novocain shot before the game just to get out there and play.

The Chargers, though, had a couple of advantages. The Patriots had to beat the Bills in an extra playoff game in order to qualify for the championship contest, but that additional 60 minutes wasn't the real problem for Boston. The real problem came in the following days when, after the team flew to San Diego to prepare for the title game, the Patriots partied a little too heartily.

Though Patriots defensive end Larry Eisenhauer was in the middle of three straight All-Pro seasons, he couldn't escape his reputation as a wild man. In an attempt to save himself from himself, Eisenhauer had his dad room with him at the Stardust Inn in San Diego in the days before the championship game. Still, Eisenhauer couldn't help himself around dusk one evening. The two sat in the pool, and as the sun was about to knock off work for the night and the air began to cool, Eisenhauer confided to his father, "They've got another pool that's heated. It's private. I think you'll like it."

What his dad didn't know was that this was the pool where girls in skimpy swimwear—mermaids—performed underwater ballet for the patrons who watched them through the glass tank in the hotel bar. The audience enjoying refreshments that night included some of his teammates, and they watched aghast as Eisenhauer appeared in the tank and then pulled down his shorts to give the customers the first full moon they'd see that evening.

Boston backup quarterback and punter Tom Yewcic and starting quarterback Babe Parilli were eating at the bar. Out of nowhere, Eisenhauer's smiling mug appeared next to them behind the glass, almost assuredly disrupting the mood of the meal and, assuming he turned around with shorts at his knees, positively ruining their appetites. Eventually somebody called the police and Eisenhauer hustled out of the pool.

Another problem for the Patriots: coach Mike Holovak was considered a sweetheart of a guy, but he was also naive and gullible. The week before the game, Holovak received a phone call from Gillman. "I've got it all set up for you," Gillman said. "You're going to train at a Navy base. They're going to have everybody ready to help you."

Holovak was touched by Gillman's sporting gesture, especially since it came just before the two teams were to play for the title. What Holovak didn't realize was that several of the men in Navy uniforms who observed practice were not Navy men. They actually were Chargers personnel. Another advantage for Gillman.

But the biggest obstacle against the Patriots in claiming a championship was the mind of Gillman. He wanted this game badly, and he spent countless hours with his assistants trying to work his mind through Boston's blitz packages and personnel. Eventually, Gillman finalized the game plan. He thought it was a good plan, maybe even a work of art.

He had no idea how right he would be. He had no idea everything was going to go perfectly for the only time in his career.

—⁓—

Once Gillman finalized his team's game plan for the AFL title game, he gave it a name. "Feast or Famine," he called it, because he knew either the Chargers were going to eat Boston's lunch or San Diego was going to starve. Boiled down, the key to the game was the Chargers' offense beating the Patriots' blitz. Make those rushing defenders irrelevant, and San Diego was going to celebrate a championship.

What Gillman accomplished was brilliant. He took the Patriots' biggest strength and made it their biggest weakness. And what he did was quite simple. He put a man in motion. That was the big revelation. Starting a man in the backfield and then having him to run to a wide receiver position. That was it.

Suddenly, the game for the Patriots was no longer familiar. Suddenly, it was confusion and hell blended together in a chaotic mess that smothered Boston's chance to win. Suddenly, the Patriots had no idea how to play defense.

"What one man in motion does to this defense is changing the responsibility of practically all the linebackers and all the secondary men," Gillman said many years later. "By putting one guy in motion, with this (blitz) setup, it disrupted their entire system of coverage. We hit them lucky at the beginning of the ball game, and we went on and on and on."

Lincoln could see how effective the game plan could be the week before, sitting at his locker and listening to Gillman work himself into a frenzy. "Look," Gillman said to his team, "if you get in this formation and he gets that goddamn read, you're going to be there and I promise you it's going to be a touchdown. This is going to happen. Then, if they continue to show this, we're going to give them a false read. It's going to work."

Gillman was absolutely right. It worked, and it worked better than he could have imagined.

In the first series, San Diego exploited New England safety Ron Hall and made him cover a speedy receiver as opposed to the slower tight ends he usually shadowed. Gillman did this by lining up tight end Dave Kocourek next to left tackle Ernie Wright on the opposite side of the line of scrimmage where receivers Lance Alworth and Don Norton positioned themselves. Hall had to shift over to help on Alworth and Norton. Meanwhile, Paul Lowe, the halfback, and Keith Lincoln, the fullback, were split in the backfield. On the first play of the series, Rote could see that a blitz was coming, and while the Patriots came hard after Rote, he faked a toss to Lincoln and faked an inside trap to Lowe. Two Patriots weren't fooled by the first fake but went for Lowe on the second fake. Instead, Lincoln slipped away and found himself open for an easy 12-yard catch (early in the second quarter, the Chargers ran the exact same play and gained 24 yards).

Twelve yards was a great way to start the game, but Gillman wanted the big play. He wanted the Patriots to overreact and overpursue—exactly what they did in blitzing and trying to tackle Lowe, who did not have the ball.

On the second play, the Patriots brought Hall closer to the line of scrimmage and made the defense an eight-man front (four linemen, three linebackers, and Hall, the safety). With Alworth and Norton still split right of the line of scrimmage, Lowe went in motion toward the right side to overload it. This was a huge problem for the Patriots, who were not ready for the extra movement. Rote then handed the ball to Lincoln on an inside trap that went to the left side, where there were no linebackers or defensive backs. They all had been shadowing Alworth and Norton and, then, Lowe in motion. Lincoln ran for 56 yards.

During the course of their two meetings in the regular season, Gillman had used his running backs mostly as blockers to stave off Boston's blitzers, but the motion and the fake handoffs upset the equilibrium of the Patriots.

"The whole game plan was [centered] around [eventual Hall of Famer Nick] Buoniconti and blitzing," Alworth said. "When he moved one way or the other, it was wrong. It wasn't his fault. It was strictly Sid's design."

Said Lincoln: "We showed them motion. That's a half-step we had on their linebackers, but it was enough. How brilliant is that? Sid saved that. He could have used it earlier in the year."

But he didn't. Instead, Gillman waited for the perfect time to spring his brilliance. And four minutes into the title game, Lincoln had 123 rushing yards on two carries, and the Chargers led 14–0. It's a good thing Lincoln's legs had felt heavy beforehand. If he felt completely healthy, he could have *really* hurt the Patriots.

—⁓—

Two years earlier, Lincoln wasn't sure he would be in this position in the first place, because after finishing his college ball at Washington State, he was a man headed to defense. "I'm just about convinced the boy is a pro misfit," Gillman had said. "I don't believe he runs good enough to play halfback, he's not big enough for a fullback."

Those comments came before he actually watched Lincoln in person at Chargers practice. Before, Gillman's scouting report was based on his filmwork of Lincoln in a Washington State uniform and what he saw of Lincoln in the College All-Star game in Chicago where Lincoln played as a defensive specialist and didn't receive especially good reports from coach Otto Graham. But what Gillman witnessed firsthand changed his mind.

Then, suddenly, Lincoln was "a tremendous prospect" who could "run against the wind." Lincoln even got Gillman to admit, "I was completely wrong."

The Patriots didn't have to look at Lincoln on film to know how effective he could play. The ass-kicking they were receiving at the hands and feet of Lincoln in the title game was proof enough.

On the third series of the game, the Patriots finally got the Chargers into a third-and-long. Boston knew Gillman was going to call for a pass because that's what Gillman *always* did on third and long (and first and 10, on second and short, and on and on). This was why the Patriots had game-planned the way they had—to stop the ability of Rote to pass. The Patriots blitzed but kept four men in the secondary. Lowe went in motion and one of the defensive backs had to follow. Lincoln ran an inside trap, and he hit the hole right where that defensive back had been stationed. It went for 11 yards and a first down.

Perhaps that's when Gillman knew there was no chance the Patriots could stop his team. On the next play, the Chargers called for a "Toss 78 Y-Man 0," a pitch to Lowe running behind tackle Ron Mix. Patriots cornerback Bob Suci was the unfortunate soul who was blocked by Mix twice on the play—10 yards apart, mind you—and Lowe went around the end for a 58-yard touchdown. For San Diego, it was the third score in 10 plays, only three of which were passes.

The man in motion addition was only part of the game plan's genius. It was also the way Gillman and his longtime line coach Joe Madro had devised at least three different ways to attack every hole at the line of scrimmage, meaning the team could run its base plays over and over again without any of them looking the same.

"Let's say we were going to run off tackle with Mix leading," assistant coach Tom Bass told Ron Jaworski for his 2010 book *The Games That Changed the Games*. "We could double-team block it and kick out with the fullback. That's one way. Another would be for Ron to block down along with the tight end, then pull for the kick out with a guard. Or we could block down with the tight end and pull Mix for the kick out. It's all the same play, going to the same area, but with three totally different looks. It was confusing as hell for the defense."

After the game, Larry Eisenhauer admitted the Chargers had embarrassed the Patriots defense—and Eisenhauer clearly was not a man who embarrassed easily. What was even worse was that Boston had no idea what was coming and no idea how to stop it. The offense didn't fare any better against San Diego's defense, meaning the Patriots defense kept taking the field without getting any rest.

Still, Boston never abandoned their game plan. According to the calculations of Jaworski and his co-author, Greg Cosell of NFL Films, the Patriots blitzed on 14 of San Diego's first 26 plays. On those 14 plays, San Diego averaged 14.6 yards gained. Still, the Patriots couldn't stop themselves. They kept blitzing and blitzing and blitzing.

Though Gillman never let up on Boston—in fact, he tried two on-side kicks in the final minute of the game with his team leading by 41 points—he didn't mind cutting his halftime speech short. At that point, he knew Boston had been flambéed, and since the always-entertaining Grambling marching band was playing halftime, Gillman stopped talking, walked out the door to the field and muttered, "I want to watch the band."

In the second half, the Chargers continued stomping the Patriots all over the field, finishing with 51 points and 610 total yards. Lincoln carried the ball 13 times for 206 yards, caught seven passes for 123 yards, and scored two touchdowns (a performance that inspired the *Los Angeles Times*' Jim Murray to write, "alone, it almost equaled the two-year rushing total of the German army in 1939–40.").

"The 1963 AFL championship is a game any coach or fan should study to see what perfection is on a football field," Bass said.

As the embarrassed Patriots trudged off the field following the destruction, linebacker Tommy Addison, the team captain, looked at *Boston Globe* reporter Will McDonough and said, "I've never been on my knees so much in my life. I got knocked down on every goddamn play." Holovak—who had been dominated by Gillman's wile at his Navy base practices and then by his coaching in the game—was reminded of the day 21 years earlier when, he, as Boston College captain, had been decimated by Holy Cross 55–12. After this latest embarrassment, there was nothing for Holovak to do but smile, shrug his shoulders and say, "We just got the hell beat out of us by a real fine football team."

Nearly 40 years later, Mix thinks back to that day. He remembers the immense thrill he felt by how perfectly the game plan and the execution had come together. He marvels at something he never experienced before or since.

"Everything we did was perfect," Mix said. "It was unusual. Sometimes some players—two or three or four players—have great games that result in the team victory. But in this instance, it was freakish in that *everybody* on the team had their greatest game ever up to that point. It was just amazing how we ran up the score."

It also gave Gillman a pretty good idea.

—⁓—

George Halas had finished watching the Chargers dominant the Patriots 51–10 in the AFL championship game, and soon after the Chargers celebration had begun, he received a phone call. On the other end of the line was a La Jolla, California, businessman named Bob Smith, who introduced himself and said he was a Chargers fan. Smith asked Halas, by then in his 41st season coaching the Chicago Bears and coming off the 1963 NFL title-winning game, if he had seen the game (apparently, in those days, it wasn't all that difficult to ring up a Hall of Famer and get him on the line).

Indeed, he had, Halas said. And he had been impressed.

Smith then asked how he would like to play the Chargers to determine which team was the best in pro football.

"A fine idea," Halas said before disconnecting the call. "I'd very much like to play Sid's team."

Easy for Halas to say, of course, because it couldn't ever happen. The AFL and the NFL wouldn't merge for another three years, and the first Super Bowl—a title game between the best AFL team and the best NFL team—wouldn't occur until January 1967. Safe and sound at home, Halas could say whatever he wanted about playing Gillman's squad, as he knew he would never have to back up his statement.

But Gillman really wanted the game. Even though Gillman must have known it was an impossibility, he sent NFL commissioner Pete Rozelle a telegram the day after the victory, asking for Rozelle to schedule an immediate contest between the Bears and the Chargers. Gillman, in essence, wanted a Super Bowl before anybody knew what a Super Bowl was.

In the note, Gillman referenced the recent decision by Pope John XXIII to declare that Jews should not be presented to the world as rejected by God. Gillman, himself a Jew, pointed out to Rozelle, "Pope John was a great man because he recognized the 'other league.'" Responded Rozelle soon after: "Yes. But it took 2,000 years."

So, no Halas. No Bears. No worldwide acclaim for the Chargers. Instead, they had to be content with the $2,498.89 extra they received for the win and an AFL championship ring on which Gillman inscribed: "1963 AFL and World Champions."

Said Gillman: "If anyone wants to dispute that claim, just let them play us."

So many decades later, there's only this reality. January 5, 1964 was Gillman's day, and nothing—not the Patriots' blitzers, not Lincoln's immune system, and certainly not Halas—could take away his biggest triumph. The game was the culmination of Gillman and his offensive genius (the 610 yards was the most any of Gillman's teams ever amassed). He needed this championship. He needed it so bad that he was willing to take a huge risk in making the passing game a secondary thought and temporarily reinventing his team in the process. He would do whatever it took to win, because that's the kind of coach—and the kind of man— he was.

People think of Gillman as a passing guru—and there's no question that he was—but the 1963 championship game raises interesting questions. Here was a game where the Chargers killed the Patriots with the run, mostly because the Patriots were expecting the pass.

Many years later, when Gillman was an assistant coach to Dick Vermeil with the Philadelphia Eagles, he used to tell Ron Jaworski during Eagles quarterback meetings, "You've got to be able to pass to be able to run. When a coach says he's got to establish the run first, he's full of shit." And while the Eagles' offensive line coaches went through the base running plays for that week, Gillman would wait until they left the room and exclaim, "I don't know why we waste all that goddamn time trying to gain three yards."

But in reality, without the rushing attack of Lincoln and without the man in motion by Lowe, decoying as a receiver, there's no telling how the AFL championship game would have changed. Maybe the Patriots, who blitzed 47 percent of the time in that game, would have knocked out Tobin Rote. Maybe John Hadl wouldn't have had the experience to run such a new offense in such a short period of time. Without Gillman's reinvention, the Chargers wouldn't have gained 352 yards and scored four touchdowns on those 28 Boston blitzes.

But Gillman had made the changes, and in the process, he had captured his elusive championship.

"I think it meant the world to him," Lincoln said. "It had to have, because that stuff isn't guaranteed. For him to make that commitment for all those years and all those things he brought to the table, it meant an awful lot to Sid."

Gillman took immense pride in that game for the rest of his life. He needed to win on this day, in this game, and his team had performed spectacularly. His only son, Tom Gillman, remembers a magical day and a showcase of what his father was all about.

"That was the game," Tom Gillman said, "that opened the eyes of other people."

Fifty-two years after he took his first breath, Gillman, for the only time in his career, stood high atop the world of football and looked down at those who would worship at his feet in the years to come. He was a guru with a championship. And by God, he had earned every bit of it.

two   EARLY LIFE

David Gillman lived a long, fruitful life, and he eventually would pass those survivalist genes down to his son, Sid. David was born in 1885 in Austria, and after he immigrated to the United States, he lived in New York, working as a police detective. He was a strong man with a well-built body, and he was just as strong in his principles (for instance, he refused to let his mother, who lived into her 100s, move to America because he was worried about her traveling in her old age). He would eventually pass all those traits down to his son as well.

David Gillman met his wife, Sarah Dickerman, while in the big city. He was an immigrant marrying a native New Yorker, and he eventually swept her away to Minneapolis. By then, David had left law enforcement, dabbled a bit in the grocery store business, and years after he made his way north, he operated movie theaters. As it turns out, love of movies might have been the most important characteristic David bestowed upon Sid.

David was a friendly sort, and he made many friends when he and Sarah moved to the upper Midwest. Up and down the street, David was well known and well liked. He was basically a politician, shaking hands, slapping backs, and making himself a popular figure in the northern part of Minneapolis.

As a detective, he taught himself how people would act and react in certain scenarios. As a grocer, he taught himself how people wanted their lives organized. As a theater owner, he learned how to separate people from their money and then keep him coming back for more. He knew how to make people happy—or at least happy enough so he could keep food on his table—and that, sadly, was not necessarily a gene he passed down to his son. It was a gene Sid, in his later life, could have used.

Sarah hadn't finished school and couldn't read or write, so she'd often bribe family members to read the letters sent to her by letting them scarf down poppy seed cookies as payment. When the Gillmans moved to Minnesota, she was the housewife and the caretaker of the family she helped produce.

First, she gave birth to Irving in 1905, and soon after, she bore Leonard, who died as a child. Nearly a decade later, she finally got her baby daughter when Lillian emerged from the womb.

But on Oct. 26, 1911, two days after Orville Wright flew a glider for almost 10 minutes in North Carolina, the father of the modern passing offense breathed his first breath and screamed his first scream. His parents named him Sidney Gillman—they decided against burdening him with a middle name—and they bestowed upon him the Hebrew name of Yisra'el, the same name given to Jacob after he wrestled God's angel.

Sarah spent the rest of her life, which cancer cut short at 52 years old, as a homemaker and the spiritual head of the household. Like the vast majority of families of the time, David earned the money while Sarah made the family run smoothly at home. She went through many low points— her father, Louis Dickerman, deserted the family when she was a young girl; she suffered through the death of Leonard; and she experienced the anti-Semitism that plagued Minneapolis like a horde of locusts—but she had strength and she had wisdom, and she made sure the family was well cared for at all times. "She was a doll," Sid said. "A sweet lady."

The Gillmans weren't overly religious, though they belonged to the Beth El temple, where the men sat downstairs and the women were segregated to the balcony. The Gillmans acknowledged the Jewish holidays, but in the end, he didn't think much about studying Torah or listening to the rabbi's sermons and the cantor's prayers.

Instead, he was into sports. *Really, really into sports.* For Sid, life was about athletics and very little else. From the time he was a little boy and discussed his future as a baseball player with Irving as they slept in the same bed until the time he graduated from North High School, his spirituality was tied to a baseball, a football, and a basketball.

"I didn't belong to the French club," Gillman said. "I didn't belong to the debating club. I was a football, basketball, baseball player, and didn't care about anything else except North High rah."

His mother, Sarah, didn't accept that. She didn't want a boy who cared only about the crack of the bat in the spring and of the shoulder pads in the fall. She preferred a more well-rounded son. A son who could read the books she could not and one who could fill the house with beautiful music in which she could bask.

—∿—

When Sid was 7 years old, he was introduced to the piano and to classical piano lessons, and for the next 10 years, he dutifully practiced on the family spinet. An hour a day, oftentimes mind-numbingly dull, the grandfather clock near him ticking away ever so slowly. Eventually, he became quite a good player. Good enough to earn him plenty of money in high school and college, thanks to well-paying gigs, and to keep him as one of the best-dressed students at North High.

He was the ringleader of a small combo of jazz players. Sometimes, five players. Sometimes, four. Sometimes, six. They called themselves Sid Gillman and his Red Hot Chilis, and they'd play your bar mitzvah, your Sweet 16, and the reception after you made your marital vows.

"We played practically every wedding in Minneapolis," Sid said. "If you wanted to get married, it was to our music."

Music was a passion he'd hold the rest of his life. His collection of jazz records was legendary, and until his hands and old age forbid it, he continued to play the piano whenever he wasn't studying football. Yet, while his mother wanted to instill the arts in him—keep him as well-rounded as possible and take sports off the brain for at least some of the time—Gillman resisted. As Gillman got older, he practiced the piano, and afterward, he rushed out the door to play football with his buddies. The arrangement, though, didn't always work for Sid. So, he turned devious, and one day when Sarah wasn't looking, he set the clocks in his house ahead 20 minutes.

"One afternoon, the gang wouldn't wait, so I cheated," Sid said. "Mother let me go after that. She figured anyone who wanted to play that rough game of football that badly should have the chance."

Never again would there be a conflict between music and football. Football, in Gillman's mind, was always No. 1. His Red Hot Chilis were No. 2.

But life changed for Gillman one day when, while playing a Sweet 16 party, he glanced over from his piano and gazed at the pretty brunette who had just arrived with a suitor. That's the day his priorities shifted. Football was still No. 1—more or less, it always would be—but his Red Hot Chilis were about to fall to No. 3 on his priority list.

—⁂—

Isaac Reisberg was born in the Ukraine in 1895, and he immigrated to the U.S. not knowing what he could or even wanted to do. He learned one thing very quickly, though, upon his arrival at Ellis Island. Americans liked to make it as easy as possible when it came to foreign surnames.

When Reisberg showed the customs agent his documentation, the agent took one look at the Reisberg moniker and proclaimed, "You don't need that much name." The man standing in front of him now would be forever known as Isaac Berg, and that man slowly emerged into his new world.

Berg eventually met and married Regina Frankenstein—the two were wed at the Polish childhood home of David Ben-Gurion, Israel's first prime minister—and they made their way to Minneapolis, where Isaac worked at a dry-cleaning plant with some friends.

As influential as Sarah Gillman was in Sid's life inside their house at 1008 Sheridan Avenue, Regina was just as dominant in the raising of her daughter, Esther Berg, who was born in Minneapolis on June 12, 1912, and grew up two miles from Sid.

"She was a beautiful person," Esther said by the time she, herself, was an old woman. "She was a little person with a big mind. She was one of the smartest women. She had a wonderful philosophy about life and about people that has carried on to us. She always thought there was something good in everything, and my kids say the same about me, that I'm a Pollyanna. But that's the feeling she imbued me with. It made it easy for me to love."

While Sid thought about little else but sports, Regina and Isaac opened up a world of culture for Esther, a world with limitless horizons. Isaac, whom Esther described as a dreamer, introduced the family to the arts. They attended lectures. They took in the theater, where one day, they watched future Academy Award winner George Arliss star in *The Merchant of Venice*. Regina dragged Esther to ballet lessons, though this was an interest that soon faded away. Her parents, though, tried to make her well rounded, and she loved them for it.

"They filled us with that," Esther said.

Esther remembers herself as extremely shy, and whenever a stranger approached, she hid behind Regina's skirt and whimpered until she had been left alone. But by the time she reached kindergarten, she had asserted herself as the official "teacher's helper," and her personality bloomed. No longer would she hide in her mother's clothing. Instead, she sparkled.

By the time she reached high school, the outgoing girl already had played the lead of Mimi Mayflower in *The Return of Hi Jinks*, participated in another play that was performed solely in French, taken over the French Club presidency, and made her mark on the debate team. Because the family didn't have much money and because she was so petite, she could wear greatly discounted sample clothes, and eventually, she learned to knit and sew (many years later, she created the wedding dress for her oldest daughter). Every Sunday, her family of six (she had two brothers and an older sister) would pack lunch, climb into a streetcar headed for Lake Harriet, and spend the day attending band concerts. "There was," Esther said, "always something with music."

Esther, though, loved her sports. Really, really loved her sports. She got that from her mother, who would sit next to the radio and listen to baseball games every day. Sometimes during the evening, Regina would board the streetcar with Esther and her brother Ted, and they'd set sail to watch the Minneapolis Black Hawks play hockey. On the weekends, Regina and Esther listened to big fights on the radio, like the night of September 23, 1926, when Gene Tunney beat Jack Dempsey for the heavyweight championship before 120,000 spectators in Philadelphia.

"I cried for days when Dempsey lost," Esther said. "He was my all-time hero."

Naturally, Esther read the local paper's sports page, and every once in a while, she'd flip past an article about Sid Gillman, who was fast becoming a star athlete at North High. She'd turn the page and move on to other items and other subjects.

Then, one day, she accepted a date to a family friend's Sweet 16 party. In the middle of the living room was a piano player in front of a baby grand, providing the soundtrack of the day, and she glanced over and saw the handsome athlete. Esther remembered that sweet music for the rest of her life.

—⁓—

When the Jews first immigrated to Minneapolis, it was after the Civil War when whites had begun to spread to the Midwest and beyond in an attempt to develop the smaller towns and make them into strong, blue-collar cities. While St. Paul already had established two synagogues by 1878, only about 100 Jews lived in Minneapolis by 1880. The Jews came from Germany and were attracted by those industries the Anglo-Saxons had already begun to build. The unique immigrants began opening stores that sold clothes and other goods to the lumberjacks and workers around the area.

By 1900, the Jewish population had grown to 6,000, and a decade later, it had more than doubled to 13,000. By the time World War I ended, farming around the area was an endangered career, the labor industry and sawmills were dying off, and the opening of the Panama Canal was negatively impacting the Midwest's railroad industry. As a result, the unemployed infiltrated Minneapolis and St. Paul, looking for work. And they were angry.

Minneapolis's culture of anti-Semitism became a real problem with the influx of unemployed citizens (though, curiously, the citizens of St. Paul were much more tolerant). Religious leaders invoked hateful language when referencing Jews, and those in the community forbid them from taking part in civic and social organizations—that meant no entry into the Kiwanis Club, the Rotary Club, or Toastmasters International. They couldn't buy houses. They couldn't take certain jobs.

"The telephone companies, the banks, they never hired a Jew in their lives," said Budd Guttman, a first cousin of Gillman's who was about a decade younger and grew up in Minneapolis idolizing him. "You couldn't sell your house to a Jew. That was in the real estate guides."

Writes Laura E. Webb in a 1991 edition of *Minnesota History* magazine: "The post–World War I years were marked by a continuation of the 100 percent Americanism brought on by the war, but without an external enemy, these xenophobic feelings were directed inward at recent immigrants and their families. . . . Historian John Higham wrote of this period: 'The Jews faced a sustained agitation that singled them out from the other new immigrant groups blanketed by racial nativism—an agitation that reckoned them the most dangerous force undermining the nation.'"

Jewish gangsters in Minneapolis during the 1920s didn't help their standing in the community either, especially when people read in the newspaper rags that gangsters like Isadore "Kidd Cann" Blumenfeld and Mose Barnett had been linked to the police department and the mayor in a sleazy web of corruption and crime. The editor of the *Saturday Press*, Jay Near, went on the attack in 1929, writing, "I simply state a fact when I say that 90 percent of the crimes committed against society in this city are committed by Jew gangsters . . . It is Jew, Jew, Jew, as long as one cares to comb over the records." This was at a time when Jews made up less than 5 percent of the state's population, making Near's assertion a little hard to believe.

That didn't stop Near from getting even more vicious: "I have withdrawn allegiance to anything with a hook nose that eats herring. I have adopted the sparrow as my national bird . . . until [the Ku Klux

Klan] hammers the eagles' beak out straight." At the time, Near was seen as extreme, but that doesn't mean he was alone in his views, particularly when an area evangelist named Luke Radar spewed some of the same hateful rhetoric for a quarter-century and gathered a rather large following.

Guttman remembers the anti-Semitism well. He remembers racing down the alleys between houses after school because if his xenophobic schoolmates caught him, they'd give him a beating. That's why he learned to box in seventh grade, so he could teach his peers some respect and so that his legs wouldn't have to carry him so fast if he found trouble. Boxing for Guttman was a necessity, and Gillman surely felt the sting of discrimination as well.

"Growing up," Guttman said, "I thought my middle name was Kike."

The intolerance in Minneapolis lasted until the late 1940s, but the winds began to shift after an article by Carey McWilliams in *Common Ground* magazine shamed the city. McWilliams wrote there was an "iron curtain" that separated the Jews and the Gentiles, and he declared Minneapolis the U.S. capital of anti-Semitism.

"It was a blow to the city's solar plexus," said Hyman Berman, a professor emeritus of history at the University of Minnesota.

Mayor Hubert Humphrey, who went on to serve as Lyndon Johnson's vice president before losing the presidency to Richard Nixon in 1968, appointed a special commission to investigate the citywide discrimination, and he eventually used that successful paradigm shift to fuel the rest of his political career.

But that was many years in the future. Many years after Sid and Esther had left the city. For them, the idea that Jews were lower than the dirt that good, native Minnesotans walked on was still prevalent. For them, the idea of a Jew buying a house or giving him a job was downright offensive. "I did have aspirations," Esther said. "I wanted to be a schoolteacher very badly. I remember discussing this with my senior high school counselor. She said, "You know, Esther. With you being Jewish, they're not going to hire you in Minneapolis. Do you want to go to a small town?' She sort of talked me out of it."

After high school, she got a job with an insurance company as a receptionist and took night classes at the University of Minneapolis, declaring a psychology major. But she never finished her degree. And she never got to be a schoolteacher. Neither Sid nor Esther would ever really break away from the anti-Semitic culture of the Midwest. It followed them, haunted them, and changed the track of their careers. But it also helped shape their personalities and the way they treated others. They learned—independently and collectively—to live with it. But, like Guttman, they also decided to fight back. They just landed their body blows without having to strap on boxing gloves.

"Sid was the first kid that left the Jewish ghetto and became well known," Guttman said. "He was our hero. He was our Jackie Robinson."

—⁂—

With Sid's name appearing more and more frequently in the local newspapers, Sarah Gillman began keeping a scrapbook of all his athletic exploits. At that point Gillman didn't know what he wanted from life—whether he should try to play sports in college or continue to furnish his high-end wardrobe with the dough he collected from his music—but he did know this: sports was still his No. 1 love. And Sarah was destined to record it the best way she knew how: by cutting out the newspaper articles she couldn't read.

At North High School, Gillman made the all-city football team in 1927 as an offensive guard, in 1928 as an offensive tackle, and in 1929 as an offensive end. In basketball, he was an all-city guard who played excellent defense and had a nice touch from outside range, though he later said, "As a basketball player, I would have made a good goalie in hockey." In baseball, he could hit the ball and hold down first base pretty well.

After a stellar sophomore season in 1927, it didn't appear he would play football at all in 1928. One Friday before the season began and just after he had returned from football camp, he had to be rushed to the hospital with an infected arm. He had suffered the infection days earlier from a small cut, probably in football camp, but only when the infection began to spread did he feel it was necessary to take medical precautions. Though it could have been some kind of smoke screen for his future opponents, his coach, Tom Kennedy, said he didn't expect Gillman to play that season. Yet, Gillman started the first game and went on to become an all-city player at his new position.

Gillman battled a knee injury during his senior season and had to sit out a few games. He also was hampered by a charley horse all year, and as one overzealous reporter wrote, "He went into each game only through sheer nerve and grit" and with his "never say die attitude." Before the 1929 season, Gillman was shifted to end (basically, a receiver who lined up near the offensive line) to make good use of his pass-catching abilities, though after catching three touchdown passes his sophomore year, he never scored again in high school. As one newspaper reporter put it, "he came through at his new post in brilliant fashion." He was also helpful in carrying the ball in Kennedy's end-around plays for which the coach was well known. But what really stood out in Sid's game was his jumping ability to catch passes. That kind of talent meant colleges would be interested in securing his services for the next four years.

The year before, Clarence "Biggie" Munn—who played next to Sid on the North offensive line and who Gillman years later called "tougher than a month-old steak"—had committed to the University of Minnesota. Munn, who would go on to coach Michigan State to the 1952 national title, already was showing his potential as the best offensive lineman ever to play for the Gophers, and Gillman was getting plenty of attention from the Minnesota coaching staff. After all, he grew up just across the Mississippi River from campus.

Gillman, though, needed to gain weight. Already, he was a voracious eater, but Gillman weighed a skinny 185 pounds, and in order to play collegiate football, where everyone was bigger and faster, he needed to put on the poundage as soon as possible. So, Sid ate and ate, a habit that never quite worked its way out of his system.

"My brother, Don, used to walk home from school with Sid," Budd Guttman said. "One day, my mom said she was going to make dinner for Sid and Don. Don said, "No, we had two corned beef sandwiches and a malted milk at the deli.' My mother was talking to his mother on the phone, and later, Sarah called back and said that Sid ate a whole chicken when he got home."

But his lean figure didn't mean he wasn't tough. On non-football Fridays, Gillman would try to cut out of piano lessons early and head to North Commons Park to play sandlot football with his buddies. He'd put on a uniform, and by the end of the game, he would be so black and blue that the bruises would last all week. That's how brutal those games were, but it helped build the toughness and stubbornness in Sid that would last throughout his playing days and into his coaching career.

Some of that pluck is reflected in that scrapbook that Sarah so lovingly created and stored. Today, the 85-year-old book lives in the house of Sid's youngest daughter, Terry, in San Francisco. Sid's high school exploits take up about half the pages, and the other half consists of Sid's collegiate career and various diplomas and love letters from his future wife. Eventually, the scrapbook will be placed in the hands of one of Sid's grandchildren, where it will tell some of Sid's story. But only a small portion. Only a small slice of how Gillman played on the field and a tiny portion of what was to come after high school and college.

When Sid would love two things: football, and a pretty girl named Esther.

—⚎—

On a Saturday afternoon in 1929, Esther Berg was invited to a Sweet 16 party, and she arrived on the arm of a long-forgotten suitor. Sid Gillman was already there, playing soft music on the baby grand. Esther undoubtedly knew about his athletic prowess and most likely recognized him, but she also was on a date and probably didn't spend much of her time looking Gillman's way.

Gillman, though, had a different reaction. Said Gillman, decades later as the two sat on the couch in their San Diego home and smiled at each other at the memory: "It was love at first sight. I looked at her and said, 'She is mine.'" Then, Gillman got clever. He tapped a friend named Tom Egan, a fellow member of the all-city football team, to call Berg on the telephone the next day. The purpose of the call: to determine if Berg was going steady with the date she had brought to the Sweet 16 (she was not). Then, Egan, acting as proxy for Gillman, asked Berg out for the next Saturday (she accepted).

By the middle of the next week, Gillman had taken a job at another event and couldn't pick her up for the date. So, Gillman asked if it would be OK if a friend of his picked her up from her house and brought her to the party (it was). After his gig was complete and Gillman's day of work was through, Esther and Sid had their date.

And that, as Esther liked to tell her daughters, was the beginning of forever.

They went out a few times but didn't see much of each other, because she had graduated from high school early and worked a job and because Gillman was busy playing football and basketball. There just wasn't enough time. But something had sparked. By the time Gillman had graduated and was trying to figure out where he should go to college, she knew that he was the guy for her. Gillman also was smitten with the petite brunette.

"I have to tell you, she was the prettiest girl in Minneapolis," Gillman said. "She used to stop traffic she was so pretty."

Still, he knew he couldn't stay in Minneapolis. Even with Esther, he knew he had to get away for college. Though Minnesota courted him, Ohio State had a secret weapon. A man named George Hauser, a former star at Minnesota who was then the line coach at Ohio State, talked to Gillman about enrolling at the Columbus school. It was 750 miles away from home—and from Esther. But Hauser was persuasive. And Gillman figured the only way to move forward with Esther was to move far away without her. Gillman worried that if he stayed in Minnesota then, he might never leave the state.

"I felt that she and I had to separate for a while," Gillman said. "I would have said, 'Let's get married,' and she would have said, 'No, we're not getting married until you get your degree and make something of yourself.' I knew that if I went to Minnesota, I wouldn't have lasted very long. [Going to Ohio State] was the smartest thing I ever did."

Said Esther: "He knew it was most important that he get his degree first. He didn't go into football or any sports education [major]. He was a political science major and a history minor. He was going to be a lawyer. I thought, 'God, that's even better than what I need.'"

Funny thing about Gillman's plans, though. Thanks to an eccentric, most likely crazy coach named Francis Schmidt, Gillman's judicially charged ideas were transformed into something else entirely when his time at Ohio State was finished. Football was his life before he met Esther. It was always priority No. 1. With her by his side, he still couldn't escape that equation. He thought he could be a lawyer, maybe play a little piano on the weekends, build a family and be a regular guy. But in reality, he was destined to spend his waking (and some of his non-waking) hours inside a stadium, inside a film room, inside the locker room.

Football, you see, was still No. 1, and at Ohio State, it would become his career as well as his love.

three OHIO STATE

Sid Gillman never claimed he was a smart man. Not when it came to academics anyway. With football, Gillman wanted to learn, wanted to ingest as much knowledge as his brain would allow. Academics—like just about everything else that wasn't a sport—didn't interest him much. But there was always Esther. She was there to help push him forward, most notably to his high school graduation. Yet, at the same time, to push him away to a city that was a two-day drive away.

"She was smarter than I, honest to goodness," Gillman said many decades later, with Esther at his side. "We had minimum requirements (at North High School), and to this day, I would never have passed those minimum requirements if she hadn't helped me. That's the truth."

Gillman had earned a football scholarship to Ohio State, but he wanted to continue playing baseball as well. That wasn't what football coach Sam Willaman wanted to hear. When Willaman learned of Gillman's plans, Willaman made sure to let his incoming freshman know, "We're going to have spring practice, and I want you there." And thus ended Gillman's illustrious baseball career.

Instead, he prepared himself to play the end position for the Buckeyes, started gaining weight for his transition to the Big Ten conference, studied for what he assumed would become a career in the judicial arts, and found a band that needed a piano player (called the Miserable Five).

Since freshmen weren't eligible to compete on the varsity squad, Gillman played on the rookie team, and since Ohio State rarely threw the ball in those days—it was not the forte of most collegiate squads of the time—Gillman's primary responsibility was blocking defenders on power sweeps.

By the time he was a sophomore, Gillman was ready to make an impact on the varsity team, threatening to overthrow the upperclassmen ahead of him on the depth chart by bursting into the starting lineup as one of the Buckeyes' ends.

The day before the Buckeyes were to open fall practice to begin preparation for the 1931 season, Ohio Stadium was quiet on a Monday afternoon. One could hear workmen banging hammers as they readied Ohio Stadium for the upcoming football season. Student managers, in an effort to obscure the views of those passersby who were desperate to watch a little bit of practice, erected long pieces of canvas around the practice field. They might not have bothered.

It seems hard to believe today, but Ohio State athletic director Lynn St. John had a big problem on his hands with the $1.6 million facility. Simply put, the Buckeyes couldn't fill Ohio Stadium with fans. This was a problem for St. John and his athletic budget, but it was also Willaman's problem. Willaman had been an all-Ohio halfback in 1913 for the Buckeyes, and he had been hired before the 1929 season to replace John Wilce as the Ohio State head coach. In his first two seasons, Willaman had recorded a 9-5-2 record and the Buckeyes had been irrelevant in the Big Ten championship race. He needed better success in order to convince fans to show up to games.

St. John also had big decisions to make. Every night, after his workday was complete, he emerged from his office and walked around the Ohio Stadium track, stepped down the stairs to the practice field, and watched Willaman's team work. While watching, his mind churned, pondering how to convince fans to return. The big question: Should St. John allow a radio station to broadcast the play-by-play from the Buckeyes' games? If not, the only way people could follow the action live was to show up and pay their money, which obviously benefited Ohio State's bottom line. But St. John also realized that radio broadcasts could be a good way to expand the fan base. That also would benefit the Buckeyes. He watched and he pondered, day after day.

As the team set to open the 1931 season, though, there simply wasn't much interest. But the coaches—and the newspapers—were excited about the sophomore class that would begin practice the next day.

While managers inflated 40 footballs on that fall afternoon before the maelstrom of football began, others rolled tackling and blocking dummies onto the practice field. Monday afternoon was calm with the squeaks and the hammer raps. The next day, nearly 90 potential Buckeyes would rip up the grass with their cleats and soak their uniforms with sweat. Tuesday was the storm. Monday was the calm. Tuesday was the beginning of the long, hard journey. Monday was the last day of summer vacation. Tuesday was the beginning of Gillman's football career. Monday was his last day as a nobody.

—∞—

The first day of Gillman's step into manhood was dreary, and rain clouds littered the sky. Occasionally, the sun darted between the clouds and shone on the helmets of the 73 men who actually turned out for practice and the eight-man coaching staff who put them through their paces. If players needed extra motivation, all they had to do was divert their eyes from the practice field in front of them and turn to Ohio Stadium, that most hallowed of places which an incredible football player named Chic Harley had once helped build.

The day's weather was cheerless, but on the flip side, it was extremely and unpleasantly hot. Soon after the whistles began to blow, scarlet jerseys were thrown to the side of the field so the Buckeyes' bodies could breathe through the humidity. The rains came early in the morning and again at noon, but Ohio State managed to practice in between and got in a good day's worth of work before the Buckeyes broke for lunch. The practice had been long but light, and the only time anybody placed headgear atop his skull was to pose for a photo from the newspaper cameramen in attendance.

The cameras were not there to shoot Gillman. No, Gillman was not a star. For one of the few times in his athletic career, he was just another guy on the field. Basically, a no-name who had never accomplished anything. That was proven true when, after a few days of practice in hot, wet weather, Willaman named his initial starting 11. Junius Ferrall and Howard Rabenstein were listed as the starting ends, and not only was Gillman's name nowhere to be found on the depth chart, the September 17 edition of the *Ohio State Journal* didn't think enough of Gillman's chances to list him among the sophomore end candidates who had even a remote chance of winning a starting spot. Not just the end candidates in general. The *sophomore* end candidates.

But it was clear that Willaman saw something in Gillman. Before his team scrimmaged for the first time, Willaman gathered his players in the early evening, passed out the team helmets, and asked a simple question: "How about a little football?" Then, he selected Gillman for the starting team, even though it was clear Gillman was still undersized for the end position. Gillman couldn't take advantage for long. He dislocated his thumb in practice, knocking his chances of starting the season opener against the University of Cincinnati completely off track and forcing him to undergo surgery in order to repair his thumb.

Gillman missed the first game of the season—where Ohio State romped 67–6 against the Bearcats—but he entered his first varsity collegiate game in the first quarter of the October 10 contest against Vanderbilt, which survived a Buckeyes onslaught of 21 unanswered points to hang on for the five-point victory.

Ohio State's next test was against famed rival Michigan, and the Buckeyes would enter the game without Junius Ferrall, one of the starting ends, who fractured a bone in his hand during a midweek scrimmage. Howard Rabenstein, the other end, was not performing up to expectations. He was so bad, in fact, that Willaman didn't even use him during the scrimmages anymore, and Willaman thought Gillman would be a better choice to start. Gillman had been the one to replace Rabenstein early in the Vanderbilt game with the Buckeyes losing 12–0, and he had performed well, according to the *Columbus Dispatch*, which wrote that Gillman "strengthened the end position considerably, in spite of the fact that he was playing his first game of major league football and just over the effects of a bad injury."

Willaman had made up his mind about Gillman early in the Vander-bilt game when Rabenstein, who already was playing poorly, whiffed dur-ing an attempt to tackle a Commodore ballcarrier. That misplay changed Gillman's job status. It meant the starting job was his alone. Though the Wolverines were heavy favorites on that October day, the Buckeyes won 20–7 in a massive upset, and Gillman made a big impact with his aggres-sion on defense, which helped stop the Michigan running attack.

The next week, in true fashion during the Willaman era, the Buck-eyes couldn't sustain the momentum, losing to Northwestern, and by the end of the season, the Buckeyes were 6–3 and 4–2 in the Big Ten, finish-ing fourth in the conference standings. It was only a slight improvement on the 1930 season, but for Gillman, the season was an awakening. On a wet, rainy day in a 20–0 win against Navy, Gillman scored his first col-legiate touchdown, catching a 23-yard touchdown pass from quarterback Carl Cramer that had been tipped, juggled, and mishandled by "Bullet Lou" Kirn, one of Navy's star players. On his way to the end zone, Gill-man sidestepped a defender after an athletic hesitation move and shook off another tackle attempt before ending his run in the end zone.

For a guy who was not expected to contend for a starting job at the beginning of the season, Gillman had played three 60-minute games his sophomore year, scored an impressive touchdown, and won his varsity letter. The next season, his junior year, was even better, as he played five 60-minute games and at least 45 minutes in each of the other contests. He was called an "iron man." He was also beginning to look like a star.

—∞—

Gillman had improved as a student as well. He still planned to enter law school once he completed his undergraduate degree, and he worked harder at studying than ever before. His piano work, though, didn't seem to suffer. During his freshman season, he played piano during lunch and dinner at The Village, where the team ate its meals. The Buckeyes enjoyed music at mealtime, because it kept up their spirit, and it was not unusual for a teamwide sing-along to break out from time to time. The music also kept Gillman's wallet full, but eventually, the undersized Gillman stopped playing at the Buckeyes' training table, because, as he said, "it interrupts my meals too much."

Gillman loved his music, though. When a sophomore named Kenneth Rasmussen was added to the squad before the 1933 season, he was called a "morale builder." Rasmussen would tell stories, sing songs, and play the piano. Sometimes, Gillman would sit down with him on the bench, and they'd rattle off a duet to much applause. Gillman's favorite band was Guy Lombardo and His Royal Canadians, and he was also a fan of Sergei Rachmaninoff because the Russian romanticist's music sounded so big to Gillman's ears. Once, he was asked by a reporter named Harold Davidson if he was glad he had kept up his study of the piano. Said Gillman: "Sure. I am. You bet. The ability to play football and piano gives one prestige around the campus."

He was building his own prestige with the way he played football. And with his car. One June before summer classes let out, Gillman purchased a Model T for the princely sum of $12.50. The automobile wasn't in the best condition, and one newspaper caption writer penned, in a massive understatement, that it was "somewhat outmoded." Gillman drove home to Minneapolis with halfback Jack Greenburg, and the trip home, including gas, oil, food, and one night at a hotel, cost them only $6. On his return trip, a solo venture, he skipped the hotel and spent the night sleeping on the worn interior upholstery of his car. He could get the car up to 65 mph, but it rattled like a baby's toy. He nicknamed the car "Dangerous Dan McGrew," and he was right about one thing. It was dangerous as hell. Just like Gillman on the football field in 1932.

The Buckeyes were on their way to another unimpressive season with Willaman at the helm—in 1932, their final record was 4-1-3 with another fourth-place finish in the Big Ten, and the cries for St. John to fire Willaman were growing louder—but Gillman continued his outstanding play. As one *United Press* reporter wrote, "Sid Gillman, Buckeyes right end, is one of the best all-around wingmen in the west. . . . He was good enough for the all-Big Ten team against Northwestern but they say his game against Wisconsin was the greatest ever played by an end in Ohio's big horseshoe stadium."

Gillman made important fumble recoveries in the Michigan and Pittsburgh games, he caught the second touchdown pass of his career in the Northwestern contest, and in that game, he blocked a punt that was recovered for another Buckeyes score. His defense was noteworthy—he finished with 34 tackles that season, second-highest total on the team—and his pass-catching ability was beginning to raise eyebrows. It landed Gillman on the All-America squad, one of the biggest honors in college football. As one reporter wrote, "He was not only a tower of strength on the offensive line throughout the entire season, but he was a bulwark on the defense, time after time, breaking through to spill enemy runners before they were able to get underway and often throwing them for losses. His play was outstanding consistently."

Would Gillman's play and the Buckeyes' results be enough to save Willaman's job the next season? Even though Gillman's play was constantly improving, the Buckeyes as a team were treading water. Willaman's job was on the minds of St. John, the media, and the vocal fans who were not shy about calling for his head. Willaman had some convincing to do.

—m—

By the time Gillman—who had begun refusing to shave after the Wednesday of every week so he could enter Saturday's game looking animalistic and menacing—was midway through his senior season in 1933, his role had been defined in Willaman's head. Even though he had coached Wesley Fesler—a three-time All American, one of only eight Ohio State players ever to accomplish that feat—Willaman declared in October that Sid was "the greatest end I have ever coached." Along with Joe Gailus, an orphan from Cleveland who gave up grave-digging to become an All–Big Ten tackle, Gillman had been named co-captain of the 1933 season, the first time in school history two men shared the post. But Gillman wasn't a superhero. Gillman couldn't be the only one to save the only college coach he had ever known.

Eventually, Gillman *would* have to defend his coach, but it would be too late by that December. Sam Willaman, nicknamed "Sad Sam" because of his cheerless demeanor and deficit of charisma, was in real trouble before the 1933 season kicked off.

The fans were disappointed in the Buckeyes' coach, and they could do nothing but reminisce about 1929 and wonder about the state of the program if Lynn St. John's first choice had agreed to take the job. The primary choice was one of the titans of the coaching industry, Notre Dame's Knute Rockne. At that point in his career, he was 40 years old, and he had compiled an 11-year record of 86-12-5. Rockne either looked to make a move into the Big Ten or, more likely, wanted to gain leverage against the Notre Dame administration. Rockne and St. John first talked at an American Football Coaches Association meeting in New Orleans in early January 1929, and apparently, the two reached a deal on a contract under the condition he could be released from Notre Dame. That never happened, because Notre Dame convinced Rockne, who died in an airplane accident two years later, to stay in South Bend. Instead, the Buckeyes settled for Willaman.

Up to the 1933 season, Willaman's squads had combined for a 19-9-5 record, the team had never finished better than fourth in the conference, and the din to replace him grew louder after every loss.

Despite beating Virginia 75–0 in the season opener, Willaman felt the pressure. During the Northwestern game, where Gillman scored a touchdown to help win the game before he landed in the hospital with a knee injury, Willaman looked to his bench and saw Ohio State legend Chic Harley. The former Buckeyes star sat on the bench, dressed warmly in his top hat, gray overcoat, and leather gloves. Willaman walked over to Harley, nearly 40 years old by then, and proclaimed, "I wish I could send you in there." Responded Harley: "I wish they'd let me go in."

It might have saved Willaman's job. Instead, the Buckeyes lost to Michigan—the only blemish on an otherwise impressive 7-1 season—and after the 13–0 defeat, the pressure on Willaman and his team grew even more intense. Following the game, Willaman barred reporters from the locker room, and in the emotion of that moment, Grant Ward of the *Columbus Journal Dispatch* wrote the following: "There was a lack of co-ordination and team play in the Ohio ranks, probably due to the fact the Buckeye offensive combination was constantly being changed and heretofore was uncertain regarding its assignment."

The criticism, by today's standards, seems pretty tame—it wasn't all that incendiary in those days either—but it riled up the Buckeyes players. What also might have gotten their attention was Ward's insistence that he would request that the Ohio legislature investigate the activity of the athletic department unless athletic director Lynn St. John fired Willaman. Considering Ward also performed the radio play-by-play duties on WOSU, the players sent a statement to school president Dr. George W. Rightmire demanding that Ward be barred from broadcasting the game over the school's station.

The players did not believe having Ward discuss the Buckeyes during the next week's homecoming game to be "fitting and proper." The statement was issued after Gillman and co-captain Joe Gailus held a secret meeting with the team at noon on the Friday before the game and 18 other teammates—all of them unnamed—decided it was unfair to allow Ward to broadcast the game. Ward had written basically that Willaman was a failure as a coach, and the players wanted him out of the spotlight. Gillman and Gailus intimated the team wouldn't play if Ward was at the mic, but they also made sure to note that it was more a request than a demand.

Rightmire denied the request, but when told that story 80 years later, knowing what was to come in her dad's future, Bobbe Korbin—Gillman's second daughter—wasn't surprised by her father's outspokenness. "There you go," she said. "He was doing it all the way back then."

Even after the Buckeyes commenced winning again in 1933, the stigma around Sad Sam never ceased. The storm of dissatisfaction that eventually would blow him out of Columbus continued to build. Much of the swirling wind was caused by those who Gillman believed should have been the ones protecting the program and their peers who played in it—the writers for the school's student newspaper.

Much of the acrimony came in an October 26 editorial that exclaimed that the Michigan game branded "the season a failure, regardless of the outcome of the remaining five contests." But in December, after the successful 7-1 season, complete with a second-place finish in the Big Ten behind the hated Wolverines, the *Ohio State Lantern* wrote a fiery front-page editorial entitled "Give Us a New Football Coach." Wrote the unnamed editorialist: "We believe (Willaman's) usefulness as a university football coach is at an end despite the statistical outcome of the season. Sam Willaman, we contend, has proved himself lacking the first requisite of a coach: he cannot handle players. The season has been marked by dissension on the team, resignations from the squad, petty jealousies between players and by a general want of respect for the coach. . . . We maintain he lacks a certain type of leadership and diplomacy that are necessary and peculiar to the position he holds."

Gillman, named an honorable All-American, fired back as soon as he read the editorial. He immediately issued a statement that read, "Sam is a good football coach. What do student newspapermen know about a football team or the coaching staff? The squad has the highest regard and esteem for Willaman. This has been proven by the fact that regardless of adverse publicity, we have carried on for him. In the Illinois game we fought for him alone. As far as Sam's ability to coach, we rank him among the best." Gillman also convinced most of the rest of the team to sign a statement that pledged the Buckeyes' loyalty and sincerity to Willaman.

Ultimately, none of it mattered. Sixty-six days after Ohio State ended its season, Willaman resigned and took the head coaching job at Western Reserve (less than two years later, Willaman would die after emergency intestinal surgery). And replacing him would be the coach who had the single biggest influence on Gillman's life. A man who would change the course of Gillman's career, his wardrobe, and his life.

—∞—

While Gillman completed his four years at Ohio State, Esther Berg patiently waited at home in Minneapolis. Sometimes, Esther made the trip to Columbus to see her man, and other times, Gillman made his way back to Minneapolis to visit her. Even when the two were hundreds of miles apart and when long-distance phone calls were a luxury, the two were very much in the other's thoughts.

On a glossy black-and-white photo in the scrapbook that Gillman's mother kept, Gillman scribbled some comments on a scene from the 1932 Ohio State-Northwestern game. Gillman, who was photographed outside the tackling scrum, wrote, "Probably me, doing nothing as usual." He also circled a random spot in the stands—it was impossible to make out faces from that far away—and wrote the name of his future wife, Esther Berg. He couldn't see her, of course, but he could always feel when she was near.

The next week, after Gillman performed well against the University of Pennsylvania, Esther entered a Minneapolis Western Union office at 8:45 p.m. to send a telegram to Gillman's residence at 174 East Woodruff on the Ohio State campus. "Wonderful Sid," she wrote, "every one talking about you[;] you played superably [sic] I love you = Esther."

Even after four years without each other, Esther wasn't going any-where. She had found her piano player at that Sweet 16 party, and she wasn't letting go. Sid couldn't stop thinking about her either, even when he was all the way across the country in San Francisco to play in the East-West Shrine game—an all-star game for the best collegiate players of the day. While Gillman dined on crème of chicken soup reine, grand filet mignon with mushrooms, and a Neapolitan parfait with petit fours at the pregame banquet, he pondered the best gift he could shower upon Esther when he returned home.

That's why, during the week he was on the West Coast, he stopped in Chinatown to buy a pajama set for her. One of his coaches for the all-star game had a petite wife that was about Esther's size, and she tried it on to make sure it would be a good fit for Esther. Back in Minneapolis, when Esther wore it for the first time, Sid thought to himself: "Wow, she looks like a geisha girl."

Once the game was complete and Gillman's East team had lost, he only had one thought on his mind. "After the game was over, all these guys went down to Hollywood to get into the movies," Gillman said. "But I took a train—nobody took the chance of flying in those days—and went home to see my future wife." In his absence, Esther had been well taken care of by Gillman's mom. "She would do everything she could to facilitate Esther staying in her house before they got married," said Tom Gillman, Sid and Esther's only boy. "She recognized that [Esther] was the one for her son."

Luckily, she would follow him wherever he went.

—⁓—

When Francis Schmidt was a senior at the University of Nebraska in 1906, the forward pass—and all the controversy that came with it— was finally deemed a legal maneuver. Up until that point, from the first college football game between Rutgers and Princeton in 1869 through the first half of the Teddy Roosevelt presidency, the game of football resembled rugby (except, perhaps, more violent), and the ball hardly ever sailed through the air. The rules change was hardly impactful, though. New Cornhuskers coach Amos Foster slightly opened up his offense to accommodate the new rule. Pop Warner called it "a bastard offspring of real football," and though Georgia Tech coach John Heisman helped get the rule passed, he didn't use it much. Major Robert Neyland at Tennessee said, "[Fans] want their team to win every game, and they don't want to see it gamble away its chances with a lot of long-shot plays."

With the passing game still in its infancy, Neyland was probably correct. The ball was still too round to make forward passing a winning strategy, and when teams threw it, there was no route-running. It was mostly jump-balls with ends and backs going against the defense. The attitude of the day was that punting was good, because you were playing not to lose. As such, the forward pass was considered a move of desperation, a less-than-macho way to play the game.

But when Robert Zuppke at the University of Illinois began working on gadget plays that implemented the passing game in the post–World War I era, the forward pass received some much-needed credibility. And there was Francis Schmidt, who believed in the forward pass like he believed in his never-ending abilities to invent new plays for it. Schmidt always believed.

As an interview candidate to replace Willaman at Ohio State after the 1933 season, Schmidt was a wonder. He impressed St. John (who had never seen any of Schmidt's teams play) and everybody else who wondered if a no-name coach from Texas Christian University in the Southwest Conference could turn around a Big Ten power that had grown stale under Sad Sam's leadership. After he took the job, Schmidt set off to change the fans' view of the Buckeyes.

After listening to the advice of *Columbus Dispatch* sports editor Ed Penisten, who convinced Schmidt to visit the influential alumni who hung out at Ben Ratner's sporting goods store on High Street, Schmidt charmed the full-throated opinion-sharers (often referred to as the "High Street Quarterbacks"). According to one writer, he "reduced their roars to ejaculations of surprised, vociferous praise." Afterward, the influential Ratner told Penisten that Schmidt was "100 percent OK." Later on his initial visit as the new Ohio State coach, Schmidt met with various campus and city celebrities at the Deshler Wallick hotel, and somebody brought up the subject of the Michigan rivalry. Soon, Schmidt, clad in his three-piece suit and bow tie—the same kind of bow tie that Gillman would wear the rest of his life in homage—dropped to his knees and drew out plays on the carpet, using nickels and dimes as players.

Schmidt was a quick wit, and he had a winning personality. He was self-assured and modest at the same time, and he had a work ethic that put others to shame. While Schmidt was not one of the original members of the Southwest Conference that had used the new forward pass to completely revamp their offenses, Schmidt was a quick study. If most of the playbooks used by collegiate coaches were thin like a magazine, Schmidt's was as thick as *War and Peace*. Many successful coaches had between 20 and 40 plays ready to run. Schmidt's offense included more than 300. He ran a single-wing formation, a double-wing formation, and a short-punt formation, but when asked what kind of system he preferred, he said, "I like the touchdown system best." Simplicity was the philosophy of most of Schmidt's colleagues. Schmidt wanted to make the opposing defenders dizzy with confusion and nauseous with incompetence.

Schmidt and Gillman first met at a luncheon after Schmidt had been hired and Gillman's eligibility had been completed, and Schmidt was immediately impressed by Gillman's smarts and his passion for the game. He offered Gillman a spot on the coaching staff during spring football practices, and Gillman accepted. He saw a mentor in Schmidt—not just with the type of offense Schmidt was going to run but with the way Schmidt never thought much about anything other than football.

Schmidt constantly diagrammed and tweaked plays, and if you visited him in his office, he barely paid you any attention. He worked 18 hours a day, and even when he slept, he hung a pad and a pencil from his bedpost in case he dreamt about a new formation or a new misdirection.

One day, as he got the oil changed in his car, he stayed in the driver's seat so he could continue to study football. Suddenly, he thought of a new play, and with his mind racing, he stepped out of the car to pace off his newfound thoughts. But he forgot his car had been lifted into the air, and as he stepped out, he fell 5 feet to the cold concrete floor. The price of genius—and of forgetfulness.

The new system at Ohio State was a mind-blowing experience for his players and his assistant coaches. His plays used so much misdirection and confusion that on the third day of practice in 1934, two of his assistant coaches, Dick Larkins and Ernie Godfrey, got trampled by a running back because they were watching another player who they thought had possession of the ball.

"He used to come on the field with charts for hundreds of plays," Gillman said. "If someone failed to execute properly, he would start thumbing through his charts, and if he was unable to find the particular play, he'd turn to the boy and say, 'Son, I don't know for sure what you do on that play, but you're doing it wrong.'"

Gillman was hooked on Schmidt. After he participated in the East-West Shrine game in December 1933 and the Chicago College All Star game the following summer—where he infamously was knocked out cold while tackling Chicago Bears legend Bronko Nagurski—Gillman received a bus ticket from the NFL's Boston Redskins. The team had drafted Gillman, and it offered him $125 per game to sign a contact. But Gillman realized early on that Schmidt was one of the greatest minds he'd ever met, and after Schmidt wired him an offer to return to Ohio State and coach the spring practice, Gillman's thoughts about playing pro football—or becoming a lawyer—disappeared.

Said Gillman: "I wasn't interested in anything else after that experience." As he later explained, the coaching bug bit him that spring of 1934, and it bit him hard. He wasn't exactly done playing football, but after one spring with Schmidt, Gillman knew what his mission in life would be. Schmidt had much to teach Gillman about how to coach football, and Gillman had much to learn from Schmidt about how to reach his potential. Schmidt was ready to show Gillman the path. Gillman was just as ready to walk it.

four   ASSISTANT COACH

Sid Gillman didn't have to travel very far to take the first step on the path of his newly realized coaching career. Same city, same university, same expectation of winning. But with a new exciting coach who promised to lead Ohio State out of the pit of mediocrity that Sam Willaman had dropped it off before resigning. It was a new offense and a new sense of purpose—for the Buckeyes and for Gillman.

Gillman had planned to be a lawyer, the same as Schmidt when he was on his way to graduating from the University of Nebraska. Neither expected to be a coach. Both men's plans changed.

After their first meeting, Schmidt blew Gillman's mind with his plans and with his strategy. Gillman impressed Schmidt as well, and though Gillman still planned to attend law school, he agreed to take a student-assistant job under Schmidt for Ohio State's spring practice of 1934. Though he was supposed to use the money made in the spring to help pay for law school in the fall, he realized soon after that he could not escape football's grasp. He would leave the law books to somebody else. He would be a coach, just like his mentor Schmidt. Maybe slightly less crazy and paranoid, but just as hungry for winning and with a penchant for never thinking about anything other than football.

"I haven't seen a law school yet," Gillman said later in life. "I wasn't interested in anything else after that."

He had been drafted by the NFL's Boston Redskins after graduation, and they sent him a contract to sign so he could begin his professional playing career. "Maybe I will," Gillman thought to himself. "Maybe I'll play." He went so far as to sign the contract, but in the end, Schmidt convinced him of his true path. It wasn't the law. It wasn't taking over the family business of movie theaters ("I needed him in the business," Sid's father, David, said. "He wasn't interested."). And it wasn't playing football. Instead, it was coaching college kids for little money in exchange for the many responsibilities, problems, and headaches. That's where Gillman's journey would take him, where he'd really shine.

He performed odds jobs for Schmidt while participating in practices and coaching clinics that first spring at Ohio State, but Schmidt didn't have the money to hire Gillman full time. Instead, he turned Gillman loose into the wild.

Into the arms of Esther, as it turned out. Gillman had graduated in the spring of 1934, and at that point, he didn't have enough money to marry Esther. That would have to wait until Gillman procured a full-time job. "I got paid [as an Ohio State student assistant coach], but very little," Gillman said many years later, turning to his left to address his wife with a smile. "It wasn't enough to take care of you, baby."

That changed, however, when an official from Denison University, a small liberal arts school 30 miles northeast of Columbus, called Ohio State athletic director Lynn St. John and asked for a recommendation. The school needed a third coach for its three-man staff, and St. John spoke highly of Gillman, the All-American who had been one of the top Buckeye ends of all time. Denison called and offered Gillman the job, and he gratefully accepted. The second step had been taken, and it was going to lead Sid and Esther to Granville, Ohio, for $1,800 a year. It was, in Esther's eyes, a princely sum of money. "Isn't it wonderful?" Esther exclaimed to her mother as if they had hit the jackpot.

Even better? It allowed Sid and Esther enough money to get married in 1935, nearly a decade after that Sweet 16 party had brought the two together. They wed in a formal affair at the Curtis Hotel in Minneapolis, and afterward, they set sail on their honeymoon. To Chicago. For the College All-Star Game. So Gillman could work and bask in his loves (football and Esther). You want romantic? Well, Esther received the most romantic honeymoon Sid could have imagined.

"I planned every inch of it," Gillman said. The blissfully wedded couple stayed at the Morrison Hotel, and after attending football practice every day, they went to jazz clubs every night. On the day of the Chicago College All-Star game, the two attended the contest at Soldier Field, and with Esther clad in her powder blue wedding dress, the skies opened at halftime and drenched the field. Esther took refuge under a newspaper and waited out the storm. Not surprisingly, the newspaper wasn't much of an umbrella, and the rain soaked her dress. To make matters worse, she lost her purse that day. But still, the two were together, watching football, and in love (if you visited them at their home more than 65 years later, all three facts would still be true).

After a brief return to Minneapolis following the honeymoon, the two set sail for Granville in a used DeSoto convertible that featured a rumble seat in back (unfortunately, the whereabouts of the Dangerous Dan McGrew, Gillman's college jalopy, have been lost to history). Among their belongings stuffed into the car: a used 35-millimeter film projector that Gillman had bought at a hock shop in Chicago.

At the time, the couple had only $25 to their names. The projector cost $15. The couple couldn't afford it. Even though he had seen himself on film at Ohio State only a half-dozen times during his playing career, Gillman had an inkling about the importance of watching film. He had to have it. He bought it. Esther could have killed him, but she was also intrigued by the new teaching tool. If she was going to be married to a football coach, she wanted to learn everything she could about the game that would keep him up at night. The two arrived at their new home in Granville, and after they took out a loan from Denison head coach Tom Rogers so they could buy groceries, Sid and Esther tacked up a white bedsheet to the wall and turned on the film projector.

Gillman—and Esther, to some degree—never relinquished the habit.

—◊—

While Gillman prepared himself to start coaching by studying film, he also strapped on the pads himself. In order to earn more money and to fulfill a request made by an old friend, Gillman traveled to Cleveland on the weekends to play for the professional Rams. It wasn't the NFL—he had already turned down that chance—and Gillman considered the first edition of the American Football League a rinky-dink startup, but he also wanted to help out his buddy.

The reason Gillman joined the team in the first place was due to an old Ohio State teammate named Buzz Wetzel, who had been a fullback on Francis Schmidt's original squad. Wetzel had tried to draw up enough interest and capital to start a pro football team in Cleveland, and he had recruited Gillman and former Ohio State players Gomer Jones (a 1935 captain) and Max Padlow. But after realizing his idea was probably not going to come to fruition, Wetzel told his former teammates to forget it. Jones went to the NFL's Chicago Cardinals, Padlow to the Philadelphia Eagles, and Gillman to Denison.

At the last minute, Wetzel secured the financing, but with the caveat that the team be built around the top players from the state of Ohio. The financiers, which included a lawyer, a publisher, and an ink manufacturer, realized that the smart way to make back their money was to build a following based on players the Cleveland-area fans knew the best. The more Buckeyes, the better. Gillman didn't have much desire to play pro ball, because there wasn't much money in it and because it wasn't nearly as popular as college football (one advertisement in the Rams program desperately tried to explain "Why pro football is faster and more interesting to watch than college football"). But Wetzel was an old friend, so Gillman agreed.

And what a team it was. The 1936 Cleveland Rams squad featured seven All-Americans, and with talent like that—plus, the ability to buy top-notch seats at League Park at a bargain price of $1.50—the Rams were a popular attraction. In the home opener, they walloped Syracuse 26-0 in front of 5,000 spectators, and the scene convinced one writer to exclaim, "Give the Cleveland Rams a few seasons together and they'll take a place right alongside the best pro teams of the nation."

Gillman was having a wonderful time taking the field with his old Buckeyes buddies. He would play games Sunday, practice with the Rams on Monday, and then return to Denison to coach the rest of the week. The 25-year-old Gillman was learning from one of the great mentors of his life in Tom Rogers, and he was trading sweat and blood every Sunday in the pros. Life was pretty good for the Gillmans with their white sheet tacked to the wall and $1,800 a year filling their bank account.

Life was pretty good for the Cleveland franchise as well, drawing interest from the NFL. While the Rams were successful on the field and at the box office, the rest of the AFL slowly crept into the murky waters of irrelevance. With the franchise's options limited, the monopoly-hungry NFL threw the Rams a lifesaver, and with a strong fan base and a stadium already in place, the ownership group accepted the invite. It spelled doom for Gillman's pro career.

With the AFL on the brink of insolvency (the NFL, once again would be a league by itself after the 1937 season), the NFL decided to punish those who had flouted its rules in order to play for the enemy league. Since Gillman hadn't reported to the Redskins after they acquired his rights and then had the temerity to join the NFL's opposition, the league banished Gillman—along with Padlow and Jones—from playing in the NFL for five years. News reports deemed the decision outrageous and unfair, and nearly 5,000 fans signed a petition of protest and sent it to NFL president Joe Carr and the league's executive council. Homer Marshman, president of the Rams, gave a two-hour speech at a league meeting in which he reminded those there that part of the reason the NFL wanted the Cleveland franchise in the first place was because of the three players it had suspended. The protest fell on deaf ears.

"It's hard to figure out," Jones, a Cleveland native and an eventual College Football Hall of Famer, said after learning of his punishment. "I talked with the manager of the Chicago team and he said it would be all right for me to go from the National into the American league, especially since I was going to play at home. I never thought I would have to get a written release. It now looks like I'm stuck, but I certainly hope to get reinstated."

It never happened. Instead, Jones eventually ended up as a long-time assistant coach for Bud Wilkinson at the University of Oklahoma, and after Wilkinson retired in 1964, Jones took over. He went 9-11-1 in two seasons, and he resigned afterward (though he stayed on as athletic director). Padlow joined the Cincinnati Bengals of the AFL, but after the season, the league disbanded and Padlow's career ended.

Gillman, meanwhile, returned to Granville and his assistant job at Denison. He turned on the film projector and never looked back again. He was not a player anymore. He was only a coach.

—⚭—

Sid and Esther were settling into his new job quite nicely in the small town of Granville that featured the picturesque college of Denison. To the Gillmans, it was a beautiful place—aesthetically and professionally. Though the Gillmans were Jewish and Denison, at the time, had a Baptist affiliation, religion was never an issue.

"They asked if we wanted to go to church; they learned and we learned," Esther said. "There was no disapproval. It made us all better. This is how you learn about each other."

While Gillman was beginning his coaching career, Esther's thoughts kept returning to *her* dream job: becoming the mother to a trove of children. She, largely through the anti-Semitism in her home town, wasn't a schoolteacher. She never earned her college degree. Watching film at home with Sid was fine, but it didn't fulfill her in the same way raising children could. A white sheet tacked to the wall couldn't compare to a blanket wrapped around a baby. "At the time," Esther said, "I never thought of anything else."

On Septemberr 25, 1936, she got her wish, giving birth to her daughter, Lyle. A year and a half later, on January 23, 1938, Barbara—who would become known as Bobbe—arrived to give Sid a trio of women in his household to whom he must attend. The adjustment, as was to be expected, was immediate. Esther spent much of her time soaking the cloth diapers in the bathtub. When Sid arrived home from football practice, he'd take out the washboard and scrub the diapers clean. They'd rinse and rinse and rinse some more before boiling the diapers on the stove to sterilize them for the next day's use. By the time the diapers were ready to be hung dry, it was 2 a.m. Neighbors marveled that the Gillmans' laundry was on the drying line so early in the morning; it was Esther's secret that she performed the chore in the middle of the night.

Denison had mixed results from 1934 to 1936. The team went 13-10-2 in those three seasons, but in 1937, the program had a breakthrough, going 6-1-1. Rogers was making a name for himself and his coaching staff—his career winning percentage of 66.7 is second in school history only to Woody Hayes—but even in the program's down times, Sid always found comfort in his family. If football was his No. 1 priority, his family, at this time in his life, was No. 1-A. When Sid knocked off work in the evenings, he'd pick up the bassinet containing Lyle and set it next to him. If he switched rooms, Lyle and her bassinet came with him. He needed those kids on top of him at all times, so Gillman physically carried them wherever he roamed inside his house.

Likewise, when Lyle went to sleep, she needed her father nearby as she dropped into unconsciousness. So, Sid would place her in the crib, and he'd slowly back away. He'd get to the top of the stairs, and he'd wait. Then, he'd slip down one step. Then another. Then another. When he reached the bottom, Lyle, more than likely, was sleeping, and Gillman could resume his night. He had no other choice. Lyle demanded it. "She was a tough little girl," Sid said. "She had to have her own way." If that meant Sid had to wait on her like a butler while she fell asleep, so be it.

As Bobbe grew into adolescence, her mother could sense the maternal instincts in her blood. If Esther needed a minor chore performed or if Lyle needed to be calmed down, Esther could rely on Bobbe to make sure it was done. You can still see that today. Lyle readily admits that Bobbe is the den mother who makes sure the remaining family sticks together like glue. If plans need to be made, there's a good chance Bobbe is the one making them.

Gillman wasn't destined to keep his family for long at Denison. Even after taking the job under Tom Rogers, he still worked with Schmidt part time, and Gillman's astonishment continued to grow as he watched Schmidt operate. They spent hours together at Ohio State drawing up plays and strategizing about the best times to run Schmidt's eclectic schemes. Schmidt worked hard, and one reason the childless Schmidt saw Gillman as a son was because Gillman worked just as hard and with just as much passion. Schmidt was a pass-oriented coach, and Gillman became fascinated with the art. It was elementary thinking perhaps (though most of the rest of football's coaches hadn't learned the lesson), but Gillman reasoned that since you can score quicker and more efficiently if you pass the ball, it made sense to incorporate the forward pass into your offense. That might have been the most important thing Schmidt ever taught him.

Not only that, but in 1938, Schmidt gave him one of the best gifts he could have received: a job at one of the top collegiate programs in the country. Gillman was on his way back to Columbus as a full-time Buckeyes assistant.

—◊—

Schmidt liked his stand-in son so much that the 26-year-old Gillman was the only assistant coach Schmidt ever hired at Ohio State (athletic director Lynn St. John usually did the deed). Schmidt wasn't concerned that Gillman was Jewish, although this already was becoming a problem for Gillman, considering he couldn't land another job in the Big Ten because of his religious background. Instead, Schmidt gave him $2,500 a year to coach the team's ends.

It was not the nirvana Gillman might have envisioned.

Schmidt was always seen as bizarre. He was confident and sarcastic. He forgot players' names, and if he happened to remember, he frequently mispronounced them. He was also mean. Once, a player named Johnny Vaught—who went on to great success as Ole Miss's coach—made a mistake at practice and asked, "Coach, where do you want me to go on this play?" Replied Schmidt, then the Texas Christian coach: "You can go straight to hell as far as I'm concerned—you're not doing me a bit of good." In that day and age, it was rare for a coach to say something like that to one of his players, and it didn't help Schmidt's relationship with them.

When Gillman joined the coaching staff before the 1938 season, Schmidt's paranoia was impinging on his team's growth. Most of his assistant coaches were rendered irrelevant, because Schmidt ran every part of practice himself. He trusted hardly anybody else, so the assistants chased errant footballs and ran errands for the head coach. Schmidt did everything else. Making matters worse, most of them didn't have full access to Schmidt's playbook. He kept those encyclopedia-thick treasures locked away—literally. Gillman was close enough to Schmidt to have earned access to the entire Schmidt catalog, but he was forbidden from parceling out the knowledge that came with it.

In fact, Schmidt began handing out assignments to his players that featured only the job that particular player was supposed to accomplish on that certain play. In other words, instead of giving an actor the full script of the movie, Schmidt, the director, produced only the lines that actor was supposed to recite. The actor would have no idea of the plot or what else his character was supposed to experience. In effect, he couldn't do his job effectively, because his lines had no context. It was the same thing with an offensive tackle. If he didn't know what the assignment was for the guard next to him—or for that matter, the quarterback and running back—how could he understand the totality of the play itself? Schmidt's paranoia forced him to this measure because he was scared of the consequences if his playbooks fell into the wrong hands. But clearly, it wasn't an efficient way to run a football team.

Schmidt's offensive innovations were beginning to lose their effectiveness, the losses began to pile up, and though the Ohio State students enjoyed his zaniness, his act was wearing thin. A couple of three-loss seasons were followed by 1940's 4-4 debacle, and players began to grumble about him, saying they were poorly conditioned and that they spent too much time on offense and not enough time hitting on defense. They began holding players-only meetings on a weekly basis, and some started skipping practice. Then, Michigan dominated Ohio State 40–0, the Buckeyes worst loss in 35 years, and it was clear that Schmidt was on his way out the door—of his job and, maybe, of his sanity.

At the team banquet, Jim Langhurst, a departing captain, presented Schmidt with a gold trophy, and Schmidt, touched, broke down in tears, saying, "This gets my goat. It sure means a lot to me." The gold trophy, however, simply added to the weight already on his shoulders.

After the banquet, Schmidt, with his job almost surely at an end, traveled to Los Angeles to scout the December 7 contest between Notre Dame and Southern California—which was to meet Ohio State in the second game of the 1941 season. When Schmidt returned, he was told that his five assistant coaches, including Gillman, had turned in their res-ignation letters. Nine days after the USC-Notre Dame game, Buckeyes athletic director Lynn St. John met with Schmidt to discuss the state of the program, and later that day, Schmidt, who finished his term with a 39-16-1 record, was forced to resign. He held out hope that the athletic board would reject his letter of resignation. But that night, during a secret 2-hour, 40-minute meeting at the Faculty Club, the athletic board unani-mously accepted it. Ohio State was moving on.

Schmidt would coach one more season, going 3-7 in 1942 at the University of Idaho, and after the school ended the program, he died Sep-tember 19, 1944, as an insurance salesman.

"When he came to Ohio State, Big Ten coaches were on a fairly well-established pattern," Gillman said after learning of Schmidt's death. "Francis turned things upside down, gambled with a wide-open, lateral-passing game, and began winning games for Ohio State. Rival coaches couldn't keep up with him. Some of his own players couldn't keep up with him either. That was his one fault. He tried to teach too much offense. There were always a few players who couldn't get it all. Those few always kept him from reaching perfection.

"If Francis had any real fault it was his neglect of fundamentals in favor of developing his offensive tactics. His players spent so much of their time learning their assignments on the dozens of different plays he gave them that they had little chance to practice other phases of the game."

Gillman surely is correct, but he fails to mention what might have been Schmidt's biggest lesson to Gillman. His inability to stay organized eventually doomed Schmidt, and it was never more clearly on display than when Joe Williams, the sports editor of the *Syracuse Herald-Journal*, stopped off to visit Schmidt while on his way home from the World Series in Cincinnati. Williams entered the Buckeyes' locker room, and he was struck dumb by the hundreds upon hundreds of Schmidt's plays (highlighted in yellows, reds, and purples) hanging on the wall. These obviously weren't important enough for Schmidt to keep locked away out of sight. Wrote Williams: "The effect, if baffling to the mind, is soothing to the eyes. You find yourself thinking of a sunset in the Swiss Alps." Williams asked local reporter Lew Byrer about it, saying it was a little strange that anybody could walk into the locker room and study Schmidt's playbook. Said Byrer: "Nobody knows what they mean anyway, and I doubt if even Schmidt does."

Gillman realized that in order to surpass Schmidt's level of success, he needed a system that was impeccable in its organization. Any other way would distract him from the task at hand. Any other way could possibly kill his coaching career.

—ᴖᴖ—

Without a job, Gillman returned to Denison to coach, once again, for Tom Rogers. Paul Brown had been hired at Ohio State to replace Schmidt, and though at least one news report 15 years later claimed that Gillman had become friendly with Brown at the time—which is, frankly, hard to fathom—Gillman never approached Brown for a job to stay on as an Ohio State assistant. And Brown never asked Gillman.

So, the Gillmans returned to that small town with that picturesque college, and Gillman helped Rogers lead the team to a 7-1 mark during the 1941 season, the program's best finish in 27 years.

But December 7, 1941, changed the American landscape, sending coaches and potential players into military service as the country declared war on Japan for the Pearl Harbor attack and, later, on Germany.

Gillman didn't have to worry about getting drafted into the military—"I had so many children at the time, I had every (deferment) classification that the good Lord created," he said. But he wanted to make some sort of sacrifice for his country. He was set to join the V-5 program, a naval aviation cadet program, with Tom Rogers, but officers told Gillman he was too overweight. An angry Gillman told them to forget it.

When he accepted his next job at Miami University, Gillman took a night shift at a factory where he was supposed to make metal caps for the bombs the military would drop on its enemies. Gillman would end football practice, and then he'd work from 6 p.m. until midnight, doing service for his country.

His kids, though, remember the ashtrays.

"Daddy used to smoke a pipe," Lyle said. "He made these ashtrays and only daddy could lift them because they were made out of steel. He made these with scalloped edges and a cup where he could lay his pipe."

Said Bobbe: "Yeah, he wasn't very good with his hands. That's all he knew how to make."

"I didn't try to avoid the service, but that's exactly the way it came out," Gillman said. "I eventually got a 1-A card which said I was ready for the service. But the war was just about over by then."

By 1942, with the U.S. entrenched in war in two different theatres, Gillman continued his life the only way he knew how: by coaching and studying football. He was also ready to move on to his next destination. Francis Schmidt had showed Gillman the possibilities of how to expand a great offensive mind, and Gillman, showing his appreciation, wore bow ties in homage for the rest of his life. Tom Rogers showed Gillman it was possible to gain respect and maintain discipline from players without having to yell and embarrass them in front of others, and Gillman, show-ing his appreciation, would name his first and only son after Rogers in homage.

But Gillman was ready to trade one picturesque campus for another, trading Granville for Oxford. He was willing to do it for the chance to run his own team.

five MIAMI (OHIO)

Miami University should be a fantastic football school. The campus looks like the college you've dreamed of attending, and on Saturday mornings, it should be littered with gas grills and RV campers that feature school flags flapping in the wind. Yager Stadium is small by big-time collegiate standards, but fill it with enough people, and the pastoral setting would be one satisfying place to watch a game.

Especially on a day like October 23, 2010, a day that was screaming for somebody to please care about football. Oftentimes in October and November, southwest Ohio resembles the northeast at its worst during its long winter slumber. Cold and gloom underneath skies that are cloudy and gray. But on that day, the sun was shining, and it was just as cold and crisp as you'd want it to be. Cold enough to wrap yourself in a blanket as you watch Miami play, and crisp enough to make you thank the heavens for cool fall days.

It was football weather, and the campus should have been well-stocked with pretty co-eds, hungover frat boys, and nostalgic alumni on their way to the big game. Miami will never be Ohio State, with its six-figure crowds and undying fan support from all over the region. But it should have been better, especially on a day like this when the past reintroduces itself to the present, when the heroes of the mid-20th century get set in bronze and placed permanently in front of the program they helped build.

It's a campus that makes you believe Rockwell—but not Rockne—completed his undergrad work here. But the fact is, the alumni don't turn out and the frat boys stay in bed and the pretty co-eds find other ways to spend their time. Football is an afterthought, and for those who remember the past—who watched when Miami football really mattered—it's a shame.

It didn't used to be this way. Not when men like Sid Gillman, Woody Hayes, and Ara Parseghian coached the team. Not when men like John Pont, Carmen Cozza, and Paul Dietzel played college football. Not when Miami football had tradition.

On that chilled October day, three of Miami's most beloved were honored. Bronze statues in their likeness were placed on the south side of the stadium and were about to be unveiled for all those who remembered the best times of Miami football. The first one was Dietzel who, as head coach, led LSU to the 1958 national title. The next one was Weeb Ewbank, a Pro Football Hall of Famer who coached the Jets and quarterback Joe Namath to Super Bowl III glory. The final one was for Carmen Cozza, who won 10 Ivy League titles in his more than 30 seasons as head coach at Yale and is a College Football Hall of Fame member. All played at Miami. All excelled at Miami. All made Miami proud.

As Miami alum Terence Moore wrote that day, "The statues are bigger than life. Then again, so were the men they depict." And the statues *are* fantastic, detailed and lifelike, and Lucy Ewbank—at that time, the 104-year-old widow of Weeb—giggled when she saw her husband and exclaimed, "You can even see the dimples on Weeb's face." Dietzel, Ewbank, and Cozza were only the first step as Miami honored its history. The school also had planned at a later date to unveil sculptures of Parseghian, Pont, Red Blaik, and Bo Schembechler. All excelled at Miami. All made Miami proud.

But what about Sid Gillman? While all seven honorees—current and future—had wonderful coaching careers, none could claim as much impact on the game as Gillman. Sure, they won championships that Gillman never won. Some of them made more money than Gillman. Some—maybe all—are more beloved than Gillman. But none were the innovative coach that Gillman proved himself to be. None of the seven were geniuses in the way that Gillman was. None atom-bombed bridges like Gillman either, which is why he won't be receiving a bronze statue in front of Yager Stadium anytime soon.

"You can have him," Lucy Ewbank said, casting a temporary cloud over that fine day. "He owed everybody in Oxford when he left."

Perhaps, but at least Gillman made fans care about Miami football. At least, when Gillman was coaching, he made fans look at the present and wonder excitedly about the future instead of today, where some of the season's biggest highlights involve unveiling bronze statues of the stars from yesterday.

—m—

Stuart Holcomb, a 1931 Ohio State captain, was hired by Miami on March 10, 1942, after spending a year at Washington & Jefferson as its football and track coach. A few hours later, Holcomb had hired Gillman. The decision to move from Denison to Miami was not a difficult one for him. For one, he was getting a raise to $3,000 a year, and since he had already volunteered to take some time off from his Denison job to help the Redskins during spring practice, he was familiar with his new squad. Despite the fact that former Miami coach Frank Wilton's teams had won just three times in their previous 26 attempts, Gillman saw his new job as an opportunity to move up in the world of college football. As it does today in comparison to Denison, Miami meant better players to coach, more interest from alumni and local fans, and better exposure for a coach looking to expand his horizons.

The problem, though, was the timing. The Redskins were not playing with a full slate of collegiate players. Really, nobody was. World War II had grabbed many of the nation's best young athletes, and as a result, some universities temporarily had to shut down their football programs. Not Miami, though. Even if the quality of play would suffer by using 17-year-olds who weren't old enough for the military or those players whose physical maladies didn't allow them entry into the service, Redskins football would continue.

"We have one civilian letterman back," Holcomb said before the 1943 season. "We are a Navy V-12 school and we have six of our old boys back with that program. But these Navy boys are on strict schedules, and if they don't keep up with their work, they just can't play. In other words, it's going to be a nervewracking season."

Holcomb wouldn't be around to lead the team for very long anyway. A few months after Holcomb helped the team to a 7-1-1 record in 1943, the program's best season in seven years and the beginning of a 32-year span where Miami did not have a losing record, Holcomb was called into service by the Zanesville, Ohio, draft board. He was appointed to serve his country by coaching the ends at West Point and by becoming the U.S. Military Academy's head basketball coach. But most importantly to Gillman, Holcomb—who would go on to coach at Purdue after the war and then, two decades later, serve as the general manager of the Chicago White Sox—had left the Miami program in his capable hands.

For the first time, Gillman was going to be his own boss, run his own program, and be the head coach to whom everybody answered.

Gillman still had to deal with Holcomb's problems, though. Namely, working around the school's V-12 program in order to find enough capable players to field a team. In the late summer of 1944, only 10 of the 42 players practicing were civilians, and in August, practice had to be suspended for a week because the service boys were due their furlough. Gillman, worried about his players' conditioning, didn't like the vacation so soon before the team's nine-game schedule was to begin. But since it was the service boys' first furlough since June and because it would be their last for the foreseeable future, Gillman didn't have the heart to ask them to stay in Oxford to practice.

Not to worry. Under Gillman's leadership, the Redskins went 8-1 that season, 7-2 in 1945, and 7-3 in 1946. His players could sense something special. Not just in the success the program was experiencing, but in the way their coach interacted with them. The way he taught them. The way he made them believe football was what they were born to do.

"He was so into it; I don't know of anyone who was so passionate about the game," said Ara Parseghian. "He rubbed off on us, because of his enthusiasm for the game itself."

Gillman was beginning to forge his identity as an offensive mastermind, probably because he spent so much time at it. Even though the players he convinced to play at Miami weren't the most talented—one reporter wrote that the players "were just average for teams in the secondary college class"—Gillman made those boys play better than they thought they could. He kept his players interested in football year-round (whether it was legal to do so or not), and they rewarded him with good, solid performances.

When Gillman got working on offense, nobody had the defense to thwart him. The problem with that: Gillman spent virtually no time on defense, figuring he could simply outscore the other team at will. Virtually ignoring a major portion of football was a risky maneuver, but more often than not, Gillman was right. His team *could* outscore just about anybody.

"We would work all week on offense, and about Thursday night, he'd say, 'OK, we'll go work on defense now,'" Paul Dietzel said. "He'd take us, show us where to line up on defense. Then, he'd say, 'OK, back to offense.'"

Thursday? In Parseghian's recollection, waiting until Thursday to talk about defense was premature for Gillman.

"I remember on a *Friday*, we would go out for a light practice," Parseghian said. "He sat down the team and told us what we were going to do on defense tomorrow. Well, tomorrow was the game, and that was the first we heard about the defense that week."

Gillman's approach to the game worked, as his 22-6 record during his first three years at Miami indicated. But the previous three seasons only served as the appetizer for the 1947 squad, poised to become the most successful Redskins team in the program's 60-year history. Fully stocked with talented players after the war and with Gillman still trying to find his identity on offense, Miami embarked on a season in which the winning never ended. It was a season that also would test Gillman's morality meter.

—⁓—

Some of the best players ever to put on the Miami uniform starred for the Redskins in 1947. A few of the guys who were—or will be—

immortalized in bronze in front of Yager Stadium, guys like Dietzel and Parseghian, were the ones who brought Miami into the national spotlight. Much later in his career, Gillman was tapped as the father of the modern passing offense, but in 1947, Miami didn't throw the ball much. In seven of nine regular-season games, the Redskins rushed for at least 175 yards. They passed for more than 200 yards only twice. Yet, when taken against the team's opponents, Miami was a passing machine, finishing with 1,339 passing yards on the season compared to its opponents' collective total of 505.

Gillman was getting good at learning how to be an effective head coach—on the field, in the locker room, and outside the scope of the NCAA. Gillman already had proven he wasn't averse to bending whatever rules his employers or college football's law enforcement put in front of him. He was holding practices throughout the year, an NCAA violation. In his athletic department biography, it actually read that Gillman "lives football year round and takes it for granted all his players will," and there were whispers that some Redskins who performed impressively were making a little extra money on the side. When it came to the non-football tasks of his job, Gillman raised the ire of at least one school administrator by completely shirking his academic responsibility.

In a letter dated March 1, 1946, an unnamed school vice-president wrote Gillman a memo:

Dear Mr. Gillman:

I am aware of the fact that on Tuesday, February 19, you missed most of your physical education classes without having made arrangements for anyone else to handle them.

As you will recall, this is a matter we specifically went over in our conference. I stated and you agreed that whenever you are not there you must assume the responsibility for having someone take charge of your classes. This should not be recurring at all. It does not seem to be fair to other members of the staff and it is bad on the morale; on the whole it creates a very unfavorable situation. A mutual understanding exists that a part of your work is to be with physical education classes and I see no other alternative than to insist that these responsibilities be carried out.

While his insubordination clearly upset whichever administrator wrote the letter, as long as Gillman kept the Redskins flush in victories, his truancy in academia wasn't going to make much difference. And win was what Miami did that year. The Redskins opened the season with a 16-point victory against Murray State; they trounced Kent State 35–7, shut out Dayton 12–0, and dominated Cincinnati 38–7 in the season finale. With the exception of a 6–6 tie vs. Xavier in the fourth game of the season, Miami was perfect, tallying an 8-0-1 record.

The season before, the program had turned down the chance to participate in its first bowl game against Pepperdine in the Will Rogers Bowl, but Miami wouldn't blow off another postseason opportunity when the Sun Bowl offered the school a spot to play Texas Tech on Jan. 1, 1948. Only one problem, though. The Sun Bowl, located in El Paso, Texas, didn't allow black players entry into the game. This had created a firestorm of controversy the year before at the University of Cincinnati when the team had voted to attend the Sun Bowl despite the fact one of the team's stars, Willard Stargel, couldn't make the trip. It was an insult Stargel and some of his teammates never forgot.

With a black player named Bill Harris on the 1947 Redskins team, Miami would have to make a similar decision on its own. Harris, unlike Stargel, wasn't a star. In fact, he didn't have much impact on game day at all. But it didn't make that choice any easier.

The decision on whether to accept the bowl bid and the Sun Bowl's racist provisions seemingly shouldn't have even been in the athletic department's hands anyway. On May 13, 1947, the school's Ad Interim Committee had seconded the University Senate's action that "intercollegiate athletic contests may be scheduled with any school which does not object to colored players on the Miami team, regardless of their policy with respect to the personnel of their own team. This applies whether the game is to be played in Oxford or elsewhere." The motion carried, and 12 days later, the Senate passed a policy that stated that any player that might represent Miami in any intercollegiate athletic contest should be allowed to compete, regardless of race.

Still, the decision to play in the Sun Bowl was left up to the athletic department, and Gillman struggled with his choices. Despite growing up in divisive times in anti-Semitic Minneapolis and knowing a little something about how it felt to be discriminated against, Gillman already showed he would do whatever it took to win. That clashed with his sensibility of always doing what he felt was right. Gillman wasn't sure which way to turn, so he asked Bill Harris for advice. Harris gave his permission for Miami to go to El Paso without him. So, the Redskins did, and when they returned triumphant, they presented Harris with the game ball—one of the highest honors a player or coach can receive from his teammates.

But the decision seemed to bother Gillman many decades later. Yes, the trip was wonderful. The players saw a bullfight in Juarez, Mexico, as part of the pregame festivities, and the athletic department netted a profit of $2,260.28. Miami's 13–12 victory against Texas Tech prompted coach Dell Morgan to exclaim, "They simply had too much hustle and were too fast for us," but the team hadn't done right by one of its own members. Despite his future innovations in how football coaches dealt with race relations, the decision to leave Harris behind couldn't have settled well on Gillman's conscience.

In a videotaped 1996 interview that remains in the family's hands to this day, the interviewer asked Gillman about that Sun Bowl and the decision to play without Harris. Said Gillman: "It wasn't a difficult problem at all. This young man was a splendid guy, but he didn't contribute very much to our football team. He wasn't a star. He wasn't on the traveling squad, so it didn't make much of a difference." The interviewer then asked if anybody had asked Miami not to bring the black player to El Paso, and Gillman said no. Esther Gillman glanced at him and audibly whispered to her husband, "Yes, they did," but out of the side of his mouth, he shushed her before she could complete her sentence. The topic was dropped, and the interview continued in a different direction.

Gillman might have felt guilty, even if he did the right thing for his team and for his program (after all, Miami took a big step forward by playing in and winning a bowl game). But he also caved in to racism. It's unfair to put the sole burden on Gillman, because most other coaches at the time would have made the exact same decision. To a 36-year-old Gillman, football and winning football games were some of the most important values in his life, and you have to wonder if Gillman, with many decades of life to draw upon after that moment and with a microphone hanging off his jacket during that legacy interview, thought that his moral compass might have been off-kilter in 1947.

Maybe, Gillman reasoned, he should have made another decision. Harris didn't get to go to the ballgame, but Gillman was the one who had to live with it.

—⁓—

The film went forward, and suddenly it went backward only to stop and begin again at regular speed. Then, a stop, a start, a flick of a pencil in a notebook, a puff on the pipe, a rewind, a stop, a play, an exhale of smoke. Gillman, with his hand on the remote and his eyes trained on the screen, was fascinated by the moving pictures in front of him. Always had been, always would be.

Game film didn't lie. A player couldn't argue or make excuses against what the film showed he did wrong. A camera was Gillman's eye in the sky, and in a darkened room midway through another week of game preparation, Gillman was the omnipresence who observed it all. Miss a block? Gillman could see it. Turn two yards early on your route? It was there for Gillman's eye. Tackle with perfect form? Gillman made note of that too. He ran the plays back and forth, back and forth, searching for whatever he knew could make a difference on the following Sunday.

It was getting late one night in the late 1960s and the room was dark and Bum Phillips—his defensive coordinator with the San Diego

Chargers and then the Houston Oilers—had done this with Gillman for too many nights in a row, too many weeks in a row. He was tired, and he was fighting to stay awake. Gillman, in a cloud of pipe smoke, barely blinked. He rewound the film, fast-forwarded it, paused it, and watched it all again. It was enough to make a normal man nauseous.

With Phillips's eyelids fluttering in a state of exhaustion, Gillman suddenly exclaimed with excitement in his voice, "Hey Bum, this is better than making love."

Phillips, in his Texas drawl, didn't miss a beat. "Sid, either I don't know how to watch film, or you don't know how to make love."

Thing is, Gillman *did* get excited to watch film. Hell, he watched it into his 90s, probably until the day he died. He couldn't stop learning about the game. He didn't want to stop. When he was coaching, it was one of his major advantages. Gillman could out-coach just about anybody in the game on any given day, but he also could out-work anybody and, most importantly, he could out-prepare anybody.

That wasn't what Gillman had in mind in the summer of 1935 when the former Ohio State star returned home to Minneapolis, looking to make a few extra bucks as a ticket-taker and an usher in one of the family-owned movie theaters. He had his assistant coaching job at Denison, but his uncle, Harry Dickerman, and his cousin, Don Guttman, offered him money for three months of work. They also changed his life.

"He was supposed to take tickets, but he would stand around and bullshit," said Bud Guttman, Don's younger brother. "He was a big man. Everybody knew Sid Gillman. He got $1,995 for working those three months in the theater. He was just a good-willing bastard. People loved him."

They also wanted to help, which was why, one day, Don Guttman ordered the projectionists to cut out all the Fox movie reels that featured football highlights and to save those trimmings in tin cans for Gillman. It was a highly illegal process, but Guttman didn't care. He was helping his cousin, and when Gillman arrived in Minneapolis, Guttman had a gift waiting for him—all the football film he could digest.

"There were all these cans of film, and Sid didn't know what the hell they were," Budd Guttman said. "My brother told him it was a present and that he had to get to work. He was so elated. You couldn't even talk to him, because he would be running the plays back and forth and back and forth."

After Don Guttman showed Gillman how to operate the projectors, Gillman spent much of his summer slogging his way through the film, splicing it together and making notes on 3-by-5 index cards. When the union representing the projectionists found out about the scheme, officials complained and tried to stop Gillman from using the machines.

"It was a big deal," Budd Guttman said. "The unions controlled the booth. The union was tight. If you didn't have a union operator, you were shut down. You wouldn't get deliveries, you wouldn't get film, you wouldn't get anything."

Somehow, Guttman and Gillman got around it. Gillman would start his day of film study at 11 a.m., and he'd go until 5 p.m., breaking only for lunch at Nick's Café where Gillman was in love with the toasted egg-salad sandwiches.

"In the newsreels, invariably, they had a football game, the outstanding game of the weekend," Gillman said. "The Army-Navy game, a Notre Dame game. Since I had started to coach, I'd clip those shots out and study them. I had a strip-slide machine that permitted me to bring the frames down one at a time. That really got me going on film. We were probably the forerunners of film observation in college and pro football."

Remarked Esther, sitting right next to him: "*You* were."

Said Sid: "Well, whatever."

Replied Esther: "You were, dear."

While Gillman wasn't necessarily the first to watch game film, he certainly became an innovator in how to take that film, how to make his own team better, and how to use it to beat his next opponent. That is, if Gillman could remember not to throw the match he used to light his pipe into the pile of highly flammable film in the corner of the projection booth.

"One time, I forgot," Gillman said, "and God almighty, what an explosion."

Gillman started utilizing the film when he took over the Miami job. Each week, he'd drive to the Talawanda Theater in Oxford, procure the RKO newsreels, cut the football highlights, head over to the campus handball court and break down the film. "Sid was a great copier," Dietzel said. "He would copy every play of every team that he could see. There was Michigan, Ohio State, Southern Cal. Fritz Crisler was the coach at Michigan, and he came out with his speed sweep. They did it so well, and the next week, Miami had it in our arsenal. Any time he saw a good play, it was in our arsenal the next week."

It wasn't only studying film on upcoming opponents, though. No, to Gillman, studying one's self was just as important. Which is why he went over film with each of his players, grading them on how well that individual learned what he had been taught and how well he had executed it. Some coaches might have given a check mark if you did your job. Not Gillman. He used a points system (technique and execution were worth one point apiece until Gillman changed it to one point for technique and two points for execution) that determined which players would start the next week.

He continued to use film in that same way at the University of Cincinnati, and he was so entrenched in and obsessed with his movie habit that by the time he arrived in Los Angeles to take the NFL Rams job in 1955, at least one reporter referred to him as Cecil B. DeGillman.

By then, he knew exactly what he wanted to gain from his film study. Gillman knew that watching a game from start to finish led to much confusion because the plays were randomly scattered all around. If a coach watched film in that way, there was no chance he could concentrate on one particular phase of the game. Instead, Gillman took each play that was called throughout the season and transferred it to its own reel.

"For instance, we have a play called Trap 16 and another called Trap 17," Gillman said. "It's the same play, except the first goes to the right and the other to the left. Now, here is a full reel of nothing but Trap 16 plays.

We have other reels containing each play we have used all year long. The same holds true on defense. We have one reel showing every pass we've made into a certain area; we also have a punting reel, a punt return, kickoff return, kickoff reel, a field goal reel, a pass defense reel."

This was how Gillman's assistants spent their summer vacations, taking two months to edit all the reels and then spending the next four months studying them. That's how the coaching staff determined whether the offensive plays were designed properly. "We can knock off the rough edges, get the bugs out, or abandon the play entirely," Gillman said.

He continued using that method when he coached the San Diego Chargers in the 1960s. If you looked at the side of his film canisters, you were likely to see labels that read "quick screen" and "flare screen" and "super screen" and "speed screen" and "slip screen" and "late screen." But the film-watching business could be dangerous. Physically, as Gillman learned with the careless flick of a lit match, and emotionally, as his Chargers coaching staff learned after the unauthorized use of a trash can. One day, after spending hours cutting and splicing and winding film, the coaches took all the film sections and deposited them into waste baskets, which were tagged and separated by position. After the coaches went home, the cleaning crew saw a cluster of full garbage cans and went to work. The next day, the now-empty trash cans had been replaced by brown paper bags. All were very clearly marked.

Do Not Throw Away.

—⚞—

Ninety minutes before the unveiling of the bronze statues on that crisp autumn day in Oxford, the sculptures were covered by red vinyl tarps. Nearby, there were 50 fold-up chairs set up beneath a red tarp underneath an enormous banner that listed every member of the Cradle of Coaches: Earl Blaik, Weeb Ewbank, Paul Brown, Ara Parseghian, Paul Dietzel, Bo Schembechler, John Pont, and Carmen Cozza.

While Miami football has fallen on hard times since current Steelers quarterback Ben Roethlisberger left for the NFL in 2005, the Cradle of

Coaches still envelops the program like a comfortable blanket. "Everywhere you go, you see Cradle of Coaches, Cradle of Coaches," Roethlisberger said. "Every day, you see the list of all the coaches that have been there, and it's awesome." Miami is known as the place where coaching careers are born, and looking at the banner stretched across the back of the Yager Stadium scoreboard, you can see why. Each member of the Cradle of Coaches went on to a top-notch coaching career.

In order to be a member of the Cradle of the Coaches, you had to have graduated from Miami. Considering Woody Hayes isn't on that enormous banner either, that explanation makes some sense. But it's also difficult to process why Gillman—who truly was the first coach to make himself comfortable in the cradle—isn't included.

"Gillman is the guy who deserves most of the credit at Miami," said Jack Faulkner, who played for Gillman at Miami and coached with him for many years. "It started with Sid. He pounded football into us, not only on the field but in the classroom. All of Sid's players were required to take his courses in football theory. We were never far from football."

Either way, Gillman was not involved in this ceremony, except when Lucy Ewbank invoked her 60-plus-year grudge against him. But Dietzel is one of the day's stars, and the reason Dietzel is even here today is Gillman. Dietzel grew up poor—the main dish at most of his childhood meals was bread and butter, with sugar and coffee poured on top—and he knew the only way to get to college was to earn a football scholarship. He did that when he enrolled at Duke in September 1942. His high school sweetheart, Anne, had won a spot on the cheerleading squad at Miami, but that separation was nothing compared to what came next for Dietzel.

With the U.S. in the middle of World War II, Dietzel received his notice that he was soon to be drafted, and instead of waiting, he went home to Ohio and enlisted in the Army air corps. Soon after, the 20-year-old was sent to the Pacific theatre where he piloted a B-29 Superfortress into missions over Japan that led Dietzel to write in his autobiography, "It was just like we all imagined Hell to be."

While he dodged antiaircraft fire from the Japanese and went on bombing runs that destroyed whatever was in its blast zone, Dietzel kept receiving postcards from Oxford, Ohio. Not only from Anne, but from Gillman as well. The sly Gillman figured Dietzel, with a little prodding, would play football at Miami just to be near his girlfriend. Gillman figured right.

"There wasn't any doubt about it," Dietzel said. "When I got out of the service, I was going to Miami." Laughed Anne, sitting next to her husband at the statute dedication: "Let's face it: I was the cause of the whole thing."

At the statue ceremony, the tarps were lifted to showcase the intricate works of art. Despite the football game about to be played, the real stars of the day were the statues. And the cradle from whence they came.

Bob Kurz was the one who came up with the Cradle of Coaches moniker in 1959, and it occurred because he was desperate one week for a news story. The former Marine had taken a job as Miami's publicity man, and every week, he was expected to write a news release that would preview the upcoming game. Kurz was a little burned out on the season— everything he wrote seemed to convey the exact same thought—and he desperately needed a new angle.

"I searched and searched and searched," Kurz said. "And all of a sudden, it hit me."

Cradle of Coaches: With Earl Blaik a legend at the U.S. Military Academy, with Weeb Ewbank winning an NFL championship with the Baltimore Colts, and with Paul Dietzel and Ara Parseghian leading the top two teams in the country at LSU and Northwestern, respectively, the moniker fit. Miami was where coaches came to be born, and therefore, Oxford had become the cradle to some of the best football minds around. The name stuck.

But Gillman was the first coach to take Miami to a bowl game, and he was the one who built the bassinet that eventually housed many of those who now reside in that Cradle of Coaches club. Before Stu Holcomb and Gillman took over the football program, the fan base had grown apathetic. As Gillman said much later, "You could shoot a cannon into the stands and not hit anybody." When reporters drove into Oxford to cover a game in those days, students would be hitchhiking out of town. That's what Miami football meant to them.

One of the new staff's decisions was to dismiss the entire senior class, which had suffered through three straight losing seasons. Even before Holcomb resigned to go into the Army, Gillman established himself as so assertive that many thought he was the man in charge anyway. Said former player Doc Urich: "Sid would rub a lot of people the wrong way, because he was so intense."

Yet, Gillman lost only six times in four years, and coaches around the county noticed. When his senior season was finished, Mel Olix, Gillman's splendid quarterback in the newly installed T-formation offense, was selected to participate in the Blue-Grey all-star game. Soon after, Olix learned why. Every day after his team practiced, Rip Engle—who was about to hire Joe Paterno as his assistant coach at Penn State—and Ray Eliot, a two-time Rose Bowl winner as Illinois's coach, met with Olix and asked him to relay Gillman's offense so they could copy it.

"That was the only reason I was invited," Olix said. "That's all they wanted from me."

It's hard to blame Eliot and Engle. They just wanted a taste of what Miami students, who no longer were thumbing rides out of town during football games, got to see every week. Under Gillman's tutelage, Miami football began to matter. He's not officially a Cradle of Coach contributor. But he knows better.

"Talk about a Cradle of Coaches," Gillman said. "It wasn't any kind of cradle when I got there."

—⚋—

Every summer for the first 13 years of her life, Lyle Gillman—Sid and Esther's first child—traveled with her parents to Minneapolis to visit relatives and relive the memories of Sid and Esther's childhood and courtship. When the family of four, including second daughter Bobbe, moved to Oxford, the journey to Minnesota never went smoothly.

The Gillmans would drive from Oxford to Cincinnati to board a train that would take them to Chicago. Then, they would transfer trains and hop on a train headed to Minneapolis. It never quite went according to plan, and it was always an adventure when an adventure was the last thing the family wanted.

"We thought this was the routine," Bobbe said. "You get on the train in Cincinnati even though you lived in Oxford. You get off the train in Chicago, and then you run, run, run, run. And then, you wave goodbye to the caboose of another train. Us kids thought that was part of the routine, because every summer we missed the connection."

For a coach obsessed with organization, Gillman's continued tardiness on his train schedule must have been frustrating. But to his kids, it was an opportunity to stay a night with their Aunt Lillian, who lived in Chicago. In the middle of the hot Midwestern summer. In a home without air-conditioning.

"We," Lyle said, "hated staying at Aunt Lil's."

Soon enough, the Gillmans wouldn't have fit inside Aunt Lil's place anyway. On Jan. 6, 1944, Esther gave birth to Terry, her third daughter, and on June 13, 1946, Sid finally got a son when Esther delivered Tom.

Living in Oxford, a small college town that was bigger than Granville but a small college town nonetheless, gave Esther an opportunity to introduce her family to the arts at an early age. Lyle and Bobbe already were in school, and when Esther brought them to watch performances by Isaac Stern or Nathan Milstein—violin virtuosos of the day—she could take them all for the bargain price of $6.

"We were coming out of the Depression, people were settling down, but it was more important to be academic," Esther said. "You were always learning, you were always going to the arts."

Even though their dad was always working at his office on Miami's campus, it was also important for the older girls to spend time with their father. On Friday nights, if Lyle and Bobbe had been obedient and hadn't caused Esther many problems during the week, Sid rewarded them by taking them to the campus gym. While he worked in his office, the two girls showered in the luxury—and the wide-open spaces—they didn't have at home. Literally, they took showers inside the gym's locker room, and even more than 65 years later, they marvel at the memory.

"That was a treat—showering in these huge showers and we lived in this little tiny house?" Lyle said. "Oh yeah. That was the treat of the week."

The Gillmans hadn't struck it rich, even if their dad was one of the most famous men in town. The fact that they drove a 10-year-old Ford with doors that were jammed, meaning they couldn't be opened from the inside, was proof of this. But the family had a solution when the ignition was cut and the family had to pile out of the car. Since Bobbe was the smallest, she'd have to crawl through an open window in order to yank open the driver's side door and let the family escape. Even the Dangerous Dan McGrew, Gillman's clunker in college, never had problems like this.

"Bobbe was the designated in-and-outer," Lyle said.

All of which led Gillman to this insistence: the next time the family had to break down and purchase a new car, he would buy a convertible. That, he figured, would make escaping the car a little easier.

At the end of the 1947 season, the family was on the move again, leaving Oxford behind in the rearview mirror of its decade-old Ford. Though Gillman was a head coach running his own football program at Miami, his apprenticeship in college football was not yet complete. He still had much to learn, and he needed to do it under a new mentor. And when an old Miami alumnus came calling, Gillman went running. The war was over, but Gillman was set to join the Army anyway.

—〜—

Earl Blaik, the head coach at the U.S. Military Academy, had been keeping an eye on Gillman. Blaik, who played at Miami from 1915 to 1917 and later worked as an assistant coach there, was already a legend in the coaching business, winning two national titles at Army and putting together a 32-game winning streak. But his line coach had just left for the

Yale head coaching job, and Blaik needed a replacement. When he saw Gillman's variation of Fritz Crisler's speed sweep—the one that Gillman saw on an RKO highlight film and tweaked it so he could run it out of the T-formation—Blaik was convinced that Gillman was his man.

Though Gillman was perfectly satisfied with his current job at Miami and there was no financial gain going from a head coaching position to that of an assistant coach, he needed more seasoning if he was going to step into a major college or professional job. And to do it with Blaik, who Gillman always regarded as one of the best teachers in football, was an added bonus.

Army, at the time, was a plum program. Leaving Miami, not a well-known team outside the Midwest, for the banks of the Hudson River was not an unusual move. Demoting himself from head coach to assistant wasn't really a demotion in Gillman's eyes. Gillman saw Army as a trampoline that would propel him to his next job. He actually hoped it would propel him to become Blaik's replacement.

"He was promised Earl's job," Lyle said. "That's the only reason they considered it. He was so successful at Miami, but it was an obvious step up. My father never changed jobs unless it was a huge step up the ladder. It wasn't weird, not to go from Miami to Army. He wouldn't have considered leaving Miami for even Purdue. But Army was a big deal."

Gillman immediately went to work learning under Blaik, who began using a two-man platoon that season. One set of 11 players for offense and one set for defense. The idea behind Blaik's transition—and he was one of the first well-regarded coaches to implement this maneuver once it became NCAA-legal—was to leave behind the days of iron man football. The goal was to keep players fresher for longer, to cut down on injuries, and to give more players a chance to participate. This was a controversial issue of the day, and there was a movement to abolish unlimited substitutions and return to the good old days when the 11 men who started the game were the 11 men who finished it. Or, as legendary Tennessee coach General Robert Neyland, chair of the NCAA rules committee, put it: get rid of "chickenshit football."

While Gillman learned the importance of Blaik's substitution theories, he was in the middle of transforming Army's undersized line into a technically precise unit that helped lead the program to an 8-0-1 record and a No. 6 ranking in the final Associated Press poll of 1948. Not only were Gillman's men technically near perfect, they were versatile as well. The offensive linemen could be effective in the speedy T-formation offense or they could be powerful in a single-wing formation. They could block moving forward or sideways, and they were quick and strong enough to plow over a defense's secondary in order to provide room for the running back.

Every once in a while, an assistant coach at Fordham University would drive north to West Point to meet with Gillman. They'd sit and chat for hours, talking about football and about their futures. One day, that assistant coach would learn Gillman's option-blocking schemes and add it to the offense that he ran in pro ball. They called it "run to daylight." Though the offensive philosophies between Gillman and the young coach were vastly different (the Fordham assistant would rely on running the football instead of passing it), the two meshed together well. So well that, when Gillman accepted his next job as the head coach at the University of Cincinnati, he had no hesitation recommending to Blaik that 35-year-old Vince Lombardi replace him on the Army staff. Blaik did so immediately.

Gillman, though, wasn't done helping Lombardi advance his career. During the NFL draft meeting in 1958 when Gillman coached the Los Angeles Rams, he went to the men's room during a break and ran into an old college buddy named Jerry Atkinson. Gillman asked what was happening in his life.

"I have my own department store in Green Bay," Atkinson said. "I'm on the Packers board, Sid, and we're here looking for a coach. Do you know a good one?"

"I think the guy you want is right here at the draft meeting, Jerry. Wait, I'll go in ask him."

Back inside the meeting room, Gillman found Lombardi, then the offensive coordinator of the New York Giants. Lombardi told Gillman that he'd be delighted to talk to the Packers. A few days later, Green Bay had its new head coach.

That was 10 years after Gillman had decided to move on from Army and Earl Blaik. Gillman had been led to believe that one day he would take over for Blaik as the head man at Army, but after spending just one season with him, Gillman recognized that Blaik wouldn't retire anytime soon (in fact, Blaik coached the Cadets for another decade).

"I knew it wasn't a place for us and the four children, being civilians," Esther Gillman said. "When the calls came in to come to Cincinnati, we knew that was a good move."

The Gillmans were returning to southwest Ohio. Gillman wanted to be a head coach once more, and this time, he was headed to his former employer's biggest rival. That's where he'd find even more success as the head coach at the University of Cincinnati. It's the same place he'd find many more enemies as well.

six   CINCINNATI

The University of Cincinnati, for most of its history, was stuck with a rather mediocre football program, but when Ray Nolting—part of the famed Monsters of the Midway with the Chicago Bears—arrived in 1945 to coach at his alma mater, he began to change the perception. After the school restarted the program following World War II, he led the Bearcats to a 9-2 record and the school's first-ever postgame appearance in the 1946 Sun Bowl. While Sid Gillman was working wonders in Oxford, Nolting was making a big difference in the Bearcats program.

Until the politically unpopular Nolting went 3-6-1 in 1948, and Cincinnati's Board of Directors began targeting Earl Blaik's understudy at West Point. Even if Cincinnati hiring Gillman was bound to spread another coat of napalm on the Cincinnati-Miami rivalry, that hardly mattered. The Board declined to renew Nolting's contract and then went after Gillman.

On December 19, 1948, a cold, rainy Sunday evening, *Cincinnati Enquirer* reporter Dick Forbes received a telephone call at his home. Forbes picked up, and a voice on the other end said simply, "If you get over to the airport, you might see some interesting people meeting a flight. You might get a story out of it." Forbes pulled on his raincoat and rushed to the airport. Once at the terminal, Forbes spotted Dr. Reed Shank, a member of the Cincinnati Board. The doctor tried to hide from Forbes's sight, but the reporter saw Gillman emerge off an American Airlines plane that had brought him to Cincinnati from Cleveland and then get into a car with Shank. Forbes followed Gillman and Shank downtown to the Central Trust garage where he got his story and his scoop.

Gillman, though, wasn't immediately ready to admit that he was taking the Bearcats job. Earlier that Sunday, he told *Cincinnati Post* sports editor Joe Aston that he would remain at the U.S. Military Academy to coach for Blaik. "I," Gillman told Aston, "cannot leave West Point." Two days later, Gillman proved Forbes right, accepting the $10,000-a-year offer from Cincinnati.

Almost immediately, the 37-year-old Gillman set out to change the culture at Cincinnati, which had grown stale in Nolting's final season. First order of business: make sure the players *look* good. Gillman called each player to the team's locker room, where they met a tailor ready to take down their measurements. During Nolting's tenure, the Bearcats played with hand-me-down equipment, but under Gillman, the brand-new, form-fitting uniforms made the players feel like new men. Gillman also wanted them looking good off the field, and he ordered a big box of black and red silk ties. Before each player got on the bus for the team's first road trip, Gillman handed over the neckwear. "Wear this goddamn tie," Gillman growled, "so you don't look like a goddamn bum."

Gillman was just as tough on the field. After the Bearcats' first workout with Gillman in charge, he looked at his players and said, "This is the worst-conditioned team I've ever seen." That's when the team knew it was in real trouble, and from January to April—eight weeks indoors and six weeks outdoors—the team conditioned, learned Gillman's new system, and sweated until Gillman was satisfied. Players had liked Nolting and many were sorry to see him go. Gillman was completely different in tone, in preparation, and in general football knowledge. If Nolting ran his team like an amateur program, Gillman ran his like a sophisticated organization—methodical, analytical, and professional.

"When Sid came in," said Ray Penno, who played at Cincinnati from 1946 to 1949, "it was like night and day."

Nick Shundich, who would co-captain Gillman's 1951 team, remembered the wholesale change the team undertook. "He made you over from A to Z," Shundich said. Gillman taught different techniques, and he didn't baby anyone. If you couldn't figure out his system, you simply weren't going to play, and he didn't care what your role in the last coaching regime had been. Naturally—and this was becoming a theme in Gillman's coaching career—he upset some of his players along the way.

"Some of the guys didn't really like Sid, some of the really good ball-players," Shundich said. "I replaced a three-year letterman who weighed about 240 pounds. I weighed 200 pounds, and I replaced him because he wouldn't learn Sid's techniques. He resented that Sid was teaching things that were different. As a result, he ended up sitting on the bench, and that's how I made the team."

Some of Gillman's players weren't the only ones who were unhappy with him. Miami University officials also were upset. It wasn't just because Gillman had left Miami of his own accord, and a year later, reappeared 30 miles to the southwest to work for the Redskins' enemy, although that clearly was a source of contention. No, the real problem for Miami people was who Gillman took with him to his new job. Namely, just about anybody of importance in the Redskins program.

George Blackburn, who had replaced Gillman as the Redskins' head coach? Gone to Cincinnati. Joe Madro, Gillman's right-hand man for most of his coaching career? Gone to Cincinnati. Jack Faulkner, who had played at Miami before coaching there? Gone to Cincinnati. Mel Olix, who had been Miami's standout quarterback? Gone to Cincinnati as a student assistant coach. Jim Driscoll, Dan McKeever, and Gene Rossi, all of whom were rising sophomores set to play at Miami in 1949? Gone to Cincinnati.

And former Miami All-American Paul Dietzel, who actually had followed Gillman to West Point? Gone to Cincinnati. Dietzel didn't only spurn Miami. He also rejected Blaik. Following Gillman's announcement as the new Cincinnati coach, Blaik offered to make Dietzel a defensive assistant at Army. "Well Paul, you don't need to go to Cincinnati with Sid," Blaik told him. "You're much better off right here. Why don't you stay here? I'd sure like to have you stay." Responded Dietzel: "Coach Blaik, I have so much I need to learn from Sid." It was only in retrospect that Dietzel realized how insulting that might have been to the legendary Blaik.

The Miami athletic department and its fans took great offense at Gillman's pilfering. The acrimony continues into today. When Miami publicity man Mike Harris announced he was leaving to take a similar position at Cincinnati in 2007, his Miami colleagues jokingly referred to him around the office as Sid Gillman. Miami old-timers today also decline to talk about Gillman, because of a grudge that hasn't worn off in 60 years. Perhaps it's because those who were around Miami at the time knew what was coming. After Cincinnati hired Gillman, Jim Gordon, Miami's manager of athletics, was asked if Miami would have an easier time with a Sid Gillman team because the program would be familiar with his style of play. Said Gordon: "It isn't what Sid's teams do. It's the way they do it."

—⁂—

The Bearcats' first game with Gillman in charge was with the University of Nevada, and in order to gain an advantage, he sent assistant coach Jack Faulkner to Reno so that Faulkner, disguised as a student, could try out for the team. Faulkner was welcomed to the Wolf Pack squad and soon after, he began practicing and learning Nevada's system. He sent reports back to Gillman after every practice, and then, when it came time to enroll for classes, Faulkner somehow disappeared into the wind with his notebook of enemy information. Faulkner would have gotten away with it too, if local Cincinnati store owners hadn't plastered posters of the Bearcats coaching staff around the city and a member of the Nevada traveling party hadn't recognized Faulkner. As a result, Faulkner had to spend the entire game safe in the press box.

Gillman sending Faulkner on the road in disguise wasn't the only deceit he managed at the beginning of his reign as the Bearcats' head coach. Gillman continued his film work and analysis, and he'd call in every player individually and grade him on his technique and execution. Perform well enough on tape, and you might get a nice little handout.

"If you had the right technique, you got $5," Ray Penno said. "If you knocked the guy down but didn't do it right, you only got half the money. Some guys were really good. Thurman Owens was the guy ahead of me, and he'd come out of there with $50." Years later, in fact, Gillman returned to Cincinnati for a golf outing, and during the course of a banquet, Owens—who later became a Bronze Star winner and a brigadier general in the Marines—took the microphone. Said Owens over peals of laughter, "You still owe me $50, Coach."

An extra benefit every once in a while didn't hurt Gillman's feelings when he was at Miami either. Since the Redskins were so ingrained in the fabric of the city of Oxford, local merchants had a knack for providing complimentary items for Miami players. For blocking a punt, a player could expect a free shirt. For each touchdown scored in a game, one merchant offered a weatherproof jacket. If one of his players made a jarring tackle in practice, Gillman might congratulate him by sending him into town for a steak at a local restaurant. Nothing else needed to be said. Gillman took it for granted that if he sent a boy in for steak, the restaurant would feed him for free.

Gillman, if nothing else, was still an innovator.

"But those were innovations that were not part of the rules," said Ara Parseghian, who played at Miami for Gillman and then went up against him as the Redskins head coach. "If he felt it was a stupid rule, he would try to get around it. If he could figure out a way to motivate you a little extra, he would pay you. If the NCAA said you couldn't do something, he would give them more. I was at Miami and recruiting the same guys he was, and we couldn't do any of that. When you're recruiting the same kid, it's not fair competition. That was something I was always P.O.'d about."

Sometimes, though, the deceit didn't pay off. Even with Jack Faulkner's cloak-and-dagger work in Nevada, the Wolf Pack smashed the Bearcats 41–21 in Gillman's Cincinnati debut. But the loss got people's attention in a positive way. Paul Dietzel, who was in Stockton, California, scouting upcoming opponent Pacific, said observers were amazed that the Bearcats had enough firepower to score three touchdowns against Nevada. Soon enough, Cincinnati scored some wins of its own—including, most notably, beating a Mississippi State squad 19–0 that had been favored by 13 points against the Bearcats. The Bearcats even had an impressive performance against mighty Kentucky, which was favored by 33 points, before falling 14–7. The next week, during a booster meeting downtown in the Netherland Plaza hotel, the 300 Bearcats fans in attendance gave Gillman a standing ovation.

Still, the season was up and down as Cincinnati lost badly to Pacific and lost to in-city rival Xavier, but the Bearcats still had a chance to win the Mid-American Conference championship. That's when Gillman really got to rub his departure in Miami's face, dominating the Redskins 27--6 as the Bearcats carried Gillman off the field on their shoulders in triumph in front of a sold-out crowd of 27,000. The Redskins looked disgustedly upon the scene, and it was a moment not soon forgotten by those who watched their old coach celebrate with his new team.

—∞—

Carmen Cozza wanted to play football at Ohio's most popular institution. One of his former teammates from Parma (Ohio) High School had won a scholarship to Ohio State, and since that moment, Cozza set his sights on following him to Columbus. Though the Buckeyes had shown interest in Cozza, he underwent a knee operation in the midst of their recruiting pitch. He took his recruiting trip to Columbus while walking with crutches, and Cozza figures today that his extra baggage couldn't have impressed the Ohio State coaches, who never offered him a scholarship. Instead, Cozza turned his attention to Miami and Gillman in 1947, and with George Blackburn serving as the lead recruiter, Cozza, who was mulling over an offer to play baseball in the Cleveland Indians organization, gave his word to Miami that he would join the Redskins program and Gillman.

Just in time, it turns out, for Gillman to leave for Army and then Cincinnati, throwing the program into disarray. "He took some of the top players, but he didn't know me, because I was on crutches," Cozza said. "He didn't know if I could play a lick." Cozza didn't play his freshman season in 1948 because of his knee, but after Blackburn left for Cincinnati and Woody Hayes came in as the new Redskins head coach, Cozza was converted from a tailback into a safety. And with the Cincinnati game on the schedule set for November 25, 1950, he desperately wanted to beat the team that had embarrassed the Redskins the year before. "We knew we had a good football team," Cozza said. "We wanted to prove it to ourselves and everybody else that we could beat them."

Making matters more frustrating for Miami entering that game was the fact that the Sun Bowl had already made an offer for the Bearcats to travel to El Paso. The bowl committee had sent out a feeler to undefeated Miami as well but ultimately chose 8-2 Cincinnati instead. The Bearcats were favored by nearly two touchdowns in the post-Thanksgiving matchup, but that was before a massive snowstorm hit southwest Ohio, nearly shutting down the entire city. But that didn't stop Miami, looking to avenge 1949's embarrassment, and Cincinnati from taking the field on a layer of ice.

For Woody Hayes, the snowstorm was manna from heaven. With a wet, cold football, Gillman's passing attack would be blunted, and with Hayes's power-running offense, there was little doubt which team could better handle the deplorable conditions. Before his team took the field, Hayes gave a simple instruction: "Take small steps."

They took small steps but produced a giant score. Behind the play of running backs John Pont and Jim "Boxcar" Bailey, the Redskins snow-skied their way to a 28–0 victory by playing solid, fundamental football with no risks and a strong ground game. There would be nobody carrying Gillman off the field on this day. For Pont, the final result was vindication. The first time Gillman met Pont was in 1945 at Miami when Gillman suggested to the skinny Pont that he eat more steak and play football somewhere else. After Gillman turned him away, Pont enlisted in the military, and while stationed in San Diego, he learned how to play halfback. Thanks to the GI Bill, he returned to Miami after the war and had to wait tables in a women's dorm three times a day in order to pay his tuition. By the time of that 1950 Cincinnati-Miami game, Pont scared Gillman. He was a three-time all-conference player, and his No. 42 jersey was the first to be retired in Miami history. Pont didn't have to eat steak after that snowy performance. He already had Gillman's heart on a platter.

"That became a game where it was one of those Michigan–Ohio State rivalry things," legendary coach Ara Parseghian said. "We waited for that one game for the whole year. I was amazed at what Miami was able to do under the conditions that existed on the field. It seemed like Cincinnati couldn't get traction, and we could."

It was the worst that one of Gillman's Cincinnati teams had ever looked, and that night, *Cincinnati Post* sports editor Joe Aston wrote that the Bearcats wouldn't have "beat a Class B high school team." As humiliating as the loss was for Gillman, the win was just as heartwarming for Hayes, who earlier in the year had complained that he didn't have many juniors on his squad. "Most of them," he said, "are playing as sophomores at Cincinnati."

Hayes ended up laughing the last laugh, though. Not just with the four-touchdown win against his arch-rival. But with a job that would change his life while detouring the trajectory of Gillman's career.

—⁓—

While Cincinnati and Miami were battling for supremacy in their little corner of Ohio, the state's most popular football team was tanking yet again. After a 6-3 record and a 9–3 loss to Michigan during homecoming, coach Wes Fesler, who was a hero when he preceded Gillman as Ohio State's All-American end, resigned his position, forcing the school to look for its sixth coach in 12 years. If Miami was transforming itself into the "Cradle of Coaches," Ohio State had earned a reputation for itself as the "Casket of Coaches."

Fesler's decision stunned Ohio State officials. Fesler had received an offer to work for a local real estate company, and he decided the tension of coaching at Ohio State was simply too much. He was also worried about his health. Even after winning the 1950 Rose Bowl, Fesler had suffered numerous nervous breakdowns and felt intense headaches throughout his tenure. He was not the first to feel such pressure in Columbus. After Paul Brown left Ohio State to join the Navy in 1944, the administration hired Carroll Widdoes, who led the team to an undefeated season and a Big Ten championship. The next year, he resigned because of the pressure. The next coach, Paul Bixler, lasted only one season, and because of the stress, he took a job at Colgate at the first opportunity.

Although he had a nasty exit the first time he held the job, Brown—the head coach and general manager of the Cleveland Browns who had coached the 1942 Ohio State team to the national title—was one favorite to reclaim the spot vacated by Fesler. But after a quick flirtation, his candidacy was dismissed. Ohio State athletic director Dick Larkins had built a six-man search committee that selected and interviewed a trove of coaches, including Gillman, for the job.

Now, here's where history gets murky more than 60 years later.

According to his children and his wife, Gillman was offered the Ohio State job, and he accepted it. Then, it was taken away before it was ever announced. Therefore, he never was officially named the coach. Unofficially, he was.

"They called him back and said, 'I'm sorry, Sid. The board met. We cannot hire a Jew,'" Bobbe Korbin, his second daughter, said. "And Dad said, 'That's OK. If you can't hire me, I know of a good guy at Oxford right now who would love to have the job.' That was Woody Hayes. He got Woody Hayes his job."

When Gillman was interviewed about his life in 1996, he was asked about his most difficult times as a coach. Said Gillman: "I really never had any difficult times coaching. I was a very ambitious guy, and I enjoyed Miami of Ohio but I thought I could possibly go on from there into a bigger job. That's the only time I ever had any refusals where Purdue opens up but can't get it. Ohio State opens up, but can't get it. There were two or three big-time universities where I might have had a chance. I just had a sneaking suspicion that religion might have entered into it."

Esther, sitting next to Gillman at the time of the interview, said she even had a letter of apology from the Ohio State Board of Regents. Larkins, she said, badly wanted to hire Gillman, but the Board of Regents' response was, what will the alumni say about hiring a Jew?

It's an interesting detour, and it might very well be true. Imagine the possibilities of Gillman taking over the Ohio State squad. What could have happened? How would history have been changed? "Instead of 'Three Yards and a Cloud of Dust,'" said Patriots coach Bill Belichick, "it could have been 'The Ohio State Express.'"

There are two issues with the scenario offered by Gillman's family.

1) Historical records don't verify that Gillman was anything more than an outside candidate.

According to the *Official Ohio State Football Encyclopedia,* Missouri coach Don Faurot was the committee's top choice, and on February 10, 1951, he accepted the job. But two days later, Faurot called Larkins just as the Ohio State publicity department was planning his welcoming press conference and said he had changed his mind. A week later, Larkins offered the job to Hayes, who took it and kept it.

The Columbus newspapers of the time wrote that Gillman had been interviewed, but there was never an indication that he was one of the top choices. Cincinnati scribe Earl Lawson, five years after the fact, wrote that Gillman never expected to get the job and had "confided to close friends that he knew he wasn't under serious consideration. He was called in for a 'screening' interview, but only at the very end of the selection board's deliberations, and then only as a gesture to appease a certain Columbus faction."

2) It seems unfathomable, considering the friction, bitterness, and animosity between the two for most of their coaching careers, that Gillman would have recommended Hayes for a janitorial position at Ohio State, let alone one of the most powerful head coaching positions in the country. Gillman recommending Vince Lombardi for the Packers job? Yes, that's easy to see. Gillman recommending his biggest rival for a job that Gillman wanted? No.

Yet, Andrew O'Toole—who penned a 2008 Paul Brown biography— writes that Brown actually was in the hiring mix more than previously thought. In fact, the hiring committee apparently was split between Brown and Hayes, and the tiebreaking vote belonged to John Bricker, a U.S. senator and former Ohio governor. It also should be noted that, according to Gillman's kids, Bricker was the one who forbid a Jew to be hired, and in their conversation, Gillman, knowing the final two candidates, gave his recommendation about Hayes simply to spite Brown. At the very least, it's a possibility.

So, what's the answer to this question? Did Gillman accept the Ohio State job only to have it anti-Semitically ripped away soon after? There's little reason to believe that Gillman lied to his adult children about this nugget of information, and it's clear that Esther Gillman, who lived through it with him, was quick to back up his assertions. And just because the newspapers didn't write about it at the time doesn't mean it didn't actually happen. Reporters could have been protecting the school—or Gillman, for that matter—or there's a good chance they weren't aware of that piece of news in the first place. So, should the job have gone to Gillman and not Hayes? Probably.

Either way, we know two things for sure: Gillman didn't ultimately get the Ohio State job, and Hayes did.

—⁂—

Gillman had come a long way from sitting in his Granville, Ohio, home with a white sheet tacked to the wall and a projector by his side. At Cincinnati, he had gotten sophisticated enough to have a shooter film the first quarter of games so the images could be processed and rushed to the locker room at halftime, still dripping wet. The coaches could then make adjustments during intermission and show their players exactly what they wanted.

In-game film-watching was eventually outlawed by the NCAA. Even though Gillman couldn't use film during games anymore, he continued summoning players into his office each week and grading them on their performance from the week before. Money or no money, these meetings determined your life for the next week.

"You were evaluated and graded," said Jim Kelly. "You got two grades on display—technique and execution. That's it. Only two tackles played, and you'd better be rated in the top two."

More than the filmwork, though, Gillman continued trying to determine the best way to build an explosive offense. He still hadn't mastered the idea of exactly what he was trying to do—maybe he didn't *know* exactly what he was trying to do—but a modern-day observer could find elements of what he would unveil in the future.

Early in Gillman's tenure at Cincinnati, he ran plenty of his offensive plays out of a T-formation, with a quarterback taking the snap from the center and three running backs stationed in a line behind him. The Bearcats used plenty of misdirection after the snap, oftentimes setting up the pass. Quarterback Gene Rossi could fake a pitch to the back on the right, fake a dive to the back on the left, fake another pitch to the back in the middle, and then throw a touchdown pass to Jim Kelly on an inside route. Three fakes and a pass downfield on the same play is, to say the least, exceptionally tough to defend.

Gillman and his staff also played with the idea of stretching the field horizontally, placing receivers far off the line of scrimmage, and forcing the defense to cover wider swaths of the field. In 1950, Cincinnati beat Xavier 33–20 to end the Musketeers' 10-game unbeaten streak, and during the game, George Blackburn and line coach Joe Madro were surprised at how well their passing attack had worked. "When they tried to cover our halfbacks, we shot it to our ends," Madro said. "When they ganged up on the ends by staying wide, we pitched it to the back. I believe we could have kept it up all afternoon."

Gillman was making a believer out of his team, and he was making a believer out of his colleagues as well. When he held coaching clinics at the Armory Field House on the Cincinnati campus, Bud Wilkinson and Bear Bryant oftentimes would find themselves in attendance. Bryant, then coaching at the University of Kentucky who never lost to Gillman in three meetings, called him "the best football mind I ever met."

Gillman obviously was not destined to stay in Cincinnati for long.

He had transformed the Bearcats from a mediocre program into a top-notch team. Yes, they struggled when facing the elite programs. But from 1951 to 1954, Gillman led his squads to a combined record of 35-5-1, and during the first four years of his tenure, Cincinnati won the MAC title each season. In 1954, the team started 8-0, the best mark of Gillman's tenure, and Gillman looked to the Gator Bowl for a possible berth, but Wichita rushed for 259 yards against Cincinnati and shut out the Bearcats 13–0. The next week, Gillman's old enemy and employer, Miami, came to town, and with

Ara Parseghian in charge of the program, the Redskins pulled out a 21–9 win. As tradition dictated, his players threw Parseghian into the shower fully clothed and drenched their 28-year-old coach in a baptism of celebration. Gillman had been part of that merriment before, but on this late November night, he sat in his office as dry as the unlit pipe stuck in his mouth.

He stared at the ceiling and pondered his future.

—∞—

More than 2,000 miles away, the Los Angeles Rams job had opened, and team officials were looking for candidates to fill the job. Hardly anybody on the West Coast thought anything about Sid Gillman. Most people had no idea who he was. At the NCAA convention in New York in January 1955, local Cincinnatians were unanimous in their belief that the Rams would hire Navy coach Eddie Erdelatz, but Gillman also had talked to Dan Reeves, one of the Rams' owners. Gillman told reporters he wasn't interested in coaching in the pro ranks, and he might have really meant it. But he had made a good impression on Reeves, and the Rams owner sent his publicity director, a man named Pete Rozelle, to check out Gillman in Cincinnati.

In mid-January, Gillman—who was in talks with the Rams after Erdelatz signed a new contract with Navy—wired Reeves a message that read "I am not to be considered a candidate for the job." That seemed like the end of his West Coast flirtation. "I hope this makes it clear to people in Cincinnati that my whole future is wrapped up with the Bearcats," Gillman said. "I still have a job to do here and I want to get on with it."

Los Angeles Examiner writer Bob Oates knew better. He had heard from his sources that Gillman was just the kind of coach the owners had in mind and that the Rams weren't going away so easily. A rejection wire wasn't going to end their pursuit, especially when they could more than double Gillman's income.

Ten days after Gillman sent that definitive wire to Los Angeles, Edwin Pauley, and Fred Levy, part owners of the Rams, asked Gillman to meet with them in Chicago. The wire asking that Gillman be removed from consideration for the job had no bearing on their decision to interview him. Gillman had what amounted to a lifetime job in Cincinnati, and local businessmen had planned to set him up in a partnership that would have taken little of his time and added significantly to his $12,000-a-year income. Gillman hadn't wanted to apply for the Rams job, only to have to fight off five or six other finalists in order to win the position. But Dan Reeves *kept* calling, and the Rams ownership *kept* wanting to meet with him. Finally, Gillman consented.

"I was interested in pro football. Most college coaches aren't interested. They are two entirely different games," Gillman said. "But while I was interested in the game, I was more interested in California. When I flew into Chicago, there was a hell of a snowstorm and that kind of renewed my California dream."

The Rams offered $25,000 a year and the promise of sunshine year-round. How could Gillman turn that down? When Esther heard the offer, she exclaimed, "$25,000! What are we going to do with all that money?" And so, they went.

Gillman, though, couldn't help but burn some of the bridges he had built so sturdily in Cincinnati. The same way he denied he was leaving West Point for the Bearcats until he actually got on the plane, Gillman said he would not leave Cincinnati. And the story goes that in one of the final days of his tenure, Gillman was meeting with boosters when he was called away to the phone. When he returned, he said, "Gentlemen, I'm here to stay. I'll continue at UC indefinitely and put this program where I want it." Thirty minutes later, he received another phone call. After that one, he returned to the group and said, "Gentlemen, I've just accepted a job as head coach of the Rams."

Before he could officially accept the job, though, Gillman needed to ask one final question. He had to make one last thing perfectly clear to his new bosses, something that had gnawed at him since his days of growing up in Minneapolis. When Reeves called to offer him the job, Gillman said, "I have to tell you something. I'm Jewish."

Reeves, without missing a beat, replied, "Maybe that will help."

seven   ENEMIES

Sid Gillman's religion wasn't his only problem. That alone didn't cause administrators, players, or fellow coaches to dislike him or to deny him access to the avenues he wanted to take. Instead, it was some of Gillman's tactics and his attitude that continued to frustrate those who knew him.

For all the good Gillman did for the football programs he coached and the players he taught and the students he molded, Gillman had given birth to an impressive list of enemies who wanted to blame him for their money, coaching, and personality-conflict problems. Were they right to blame Gillman? In some ways, yes. In some ways, not really.

But this statement was unmistakable: if Gillman's talent and his coaching style could be called a force of nature, oftentimes the tornado of his personality left plenty of wreckage behind.

When he originally denied that he was leaving Cincinnati for Los Angeles in 1955, the Bearcats' boosters were not surprised. They knew all along that he was turning Cincinnati into a national power and that he had no interest in the pro game. One Gillman supporter, after learning of Gillman's wire of disinterest to the Rams, rushed up to athletic director Chic Mileham and requested that he make an announcement over the PA system during a Cincinnati basketball game that Gillman would return. Mileham declined, perhaps remembering Gillman's flip-flop when he left Army.

When Gillman did leave, though, those boosters were not pleased. Particularly when they thought back to the $50-a-plate dinners that were staged for Gillman that added $15,000 to the coaching kitty, the TV set the boosters provided the Gillman family, the courtesy car they gave Sid, and the money they spent upgrading the program. Many opined that he had used Cincinnati to increase his worth to his Los Angeles suitors, and some claimed that Gillman was actually playing hard to get when he sent the wire to Dan Reeves asking to be dropped from consideration and that he did, in fact, want the job the entire time.

As Earl Lawson wrote in a 1955 issue of the *Saturday Evening Post*— an article that daughter Lyle Gillman reviles to this day—"throughout Ohio football circles, people are either all-out admirers of Gillman or thorough-going critics." That included people at his former place of employment who were annoyed at his tactless statements and, as Lawson penned, "his extravagant demands on the athletic budget."

But that 50-50 split of Gillman support drastically fell when the NCAA handed down a one-year probation sentence to Cincinnati. After Gillman left for Los Angeles, the school was charged with giving more than the allowable amount of financial aid to its players and for paying the expenses of recruits for campus visits between the years of 1951 and 1953. When the *Cincinnati Enquirer*'s Dick Forbes reached Gillman at the Rams' offices and asked for a comment, Gillman said in a quote that bounced around the *Enquirer*'s offices for the next few decades, "I'm thunderstruck. Absolutely thunderstruck."

Later, Gillman denied the charges and said he thought he was abiding by the NCAA rules. The punishment stated that the Bearcats couldn't compete in any NCAA-affiliated events for one year, and school president Raymond Walters placed all the blame on Gillman. Gillman said he was not part of any wrongdoing. In regard to the charge that coaches helped arrange off-campus, no-work jobs, he said: "Certainly we helped boys find jobs. . . . The on-campus jobs were closely supervised. It is impossible for any coach to control off-campus jobs. However, every off-campus job was registered in the university employment office, and in most cases, salaries were listed."

Gillman, even more than the $12,000 per year he earned and the other perks the Cincinnati boosters provided, was an expensive coach to keep happy, a theme that never faded in his career. With his almost instantaneous success at Cincinnati, Gillman convinced Chic Mileham that the stadium needed to be enlarged to 30,000 seats at an estimated cost of $125,000. Said Gillman: "We can't expect to play big-time teams if we don't have a big-time stadium." Gillman also requested a $6,000 tarp be purchased so the field could be covered during inclement weather, but those funds never emerged. Yet, thanks to the success of the football program, Cincinnati built a new $1.25 million Armory Fieldhouse and new athletic dorms.

But compared to Miami when Gillman left, the Bearcats got off easy.

"Gillman didn't leave us in as bad shape as he did Miami," Mileham said. "We didn't let him go out and buy every new gadget on the market."

For Miami, the money he demanded the school spend on the football program was a problem when he exited for West Point. But more than the money, he insulted Miami by pilfering Redskins coaches and promising athletes and bringing them with him to Cincinnati. He made enemies in Oxford, and those enemies were never, ever going to let him forget it.

—⁂—

There are no statues of Gillman on Miami's campus. No buildings named after him. No streets that bear his name. Not even the most obvious place of all, the football team's film room, pays him any remembrance. His name is a paradox in the mind of the Miami old-timers. Nobody gathers at local Oxford restaurants and regales companions with tales of Gillman lore. He was the first of the Cradle of Coaches, but he's also viewed by many as a traitor.

That said, many of his former players—Paul Dietzel and Ara Parseghian are two well-known examples—loved Gillman and stayed in touch with him for the rest of his life.

The Miami Hall of Fame was established in 1969, and in that first year, Earl Blaik, Paul Brown, Weeb Ewbank, John Pont, and Parseghian were inducted. Carmen Cozza made it the next year, and in 1971, Dietzel and Mel Olix got their phone calls. In 1972, Bo Schembechler was inducted, and three years later, Paul Shoults had his turn. All of these men bumped against Gillman, and most of them were coached by him. Not all of them liked Gillman, but none could have denied the impact he made in Oxford. None could argue that Gillman's accomplishments didn't merit inclusion.

The Hall of Fame list goes on. Bill Arnsparger in 1976, Bill Hoover in 1979, Wayne Gibson in 1981, Ernie Plank in 1984, Bob Kappes in 1985. All played for Gillman. But the doors to the Hall remained closed to the Miami pariah.

That is the consequence for a man who firebombed the bridges on his way out of Oxford. He was eligible for the Hall of Fame, but the bitterness left behind by his departure continued to fester into the decades following his disappearance. Gillman's family members insist it was Paul Brown who kept Gillman out of the Hall of Fame for as long as he did, and that might be true. But if Paul Brown was hell-bent on punishing Gillman for past deeds from long ago, he wasn't alone.

"A lot of people at Miami were upset when I went to UC," Gillman said.

It wasn't only that Gillman had taken away the core of the Redskins football program when he left. It was that he left behind big bills that somebody needed to pay.

"It was a question of doing what you have to do to create a top team," Gillman said. "Equipment must be first class, travel must be first class; it's good for morale, pride. A football operation is expensive."

Said Parseghian: "He left some bills there . . . I remember there was a lot of animosity. Here he was at the rival school, and leaving some of the things he did and the way he left . . . There was some anger that developed for Sid trying to recruit kids to go to Cincinnati. That's a no-no in coaching. That was a huge situation. A lot of words were spilled over that."

In the next breath, though, Parseghian is touting the positive legacy Gillman had left Miami. Yes, some of those still alive haven't forgiven Gillman for how he departed, and they won't even be interviewed about him. But there are some with fond memories and some who credit him for the satisfying paths they walked once they completed their studies under him. Dietzel loves him, thinks of him as a father. John Pont probably never forgot Gillman's slight when the two first met. Parseghian, who went on to great success as the Notre Dame head coach, doesn't tire of talking about the good that Gillman provided. Paul Brown's family won't speak about Gillman, even in private.

The paradox of Gillman lives on.

—⁓—

The Gillman contradiction can be summed up in these next three sentences. **No. 1:** Gillman did everything he could to win a game or a season, and triumphing to Gillman was the top priority in his career and maybe his life. **No. 2:** Gillman spent a lot of his time trying to correct injustices for his players, trying to make them into better men, or simply trying to do the right thing. **No. 3:** When those two ideas clashed—and, at some points in his career, there was no way to avoid a crash at the intersection of those two philosophies—Gillman chose winning.

That, after all, was what he was paid to do. Win ball games. It didn't matter if his team was made up of the sweetest guys in the world; if they were losers on the football field, Gillman knew he would soon be looking for a new job. Winning was more important to Gillman than to those who played for him, and this made sense. His livelihood—hell, his reason for living—depended on those victories.

There were times when his rules made little sense. There were times when players thought he was just being cruel. Sometimes, it hurt him, and sometimes he got away with it. After Cincinnati beat Western Michigan 27–6 in 1950, Gillman let loose at a booster-club meeting where he questioned the recruiting practices of previous coach Ray Nolting. Gillman charged that Nolting must have recruited players based on what the sportswriters in those players' hometowns had told him. In effect, Gillman was saying that his own players were less than mediocre. The statement was uncalled for, and considering that he would have to use many of those players for the next few seasons, it was just a silly thing to say.

Gillman also banned his Bearcats players from getting married. "Any player, whether he's a new one or an old one, who gets married will get a one-way ticket home," Gillman proclaimed. When he made that decree, some of the players already had sent out wedding invitations, including one that had been addressed to Gillman. Those players approached George Blackburn, Gillman's buffer, and asked what to do. "Get married," said Blackburn. They did, and none of them suffered any consequence as a result.

But sometimes, his impractical rules and inflexibility backfired badly.

In Los Angeles, Andy Robustelli was one of the Rams' top players. Though he had to wait until the 19th round before the Rams drafted him in 1951, he helped L.A. win the NFL title in his rookie year. He became an All-Pro, a Pro Football Hall of Famer, and one of the anchors of the team. But his family lived in Stamford, Connecticut, and just before the 1956 season, Robustelli's wife gave birth to the fourth of their nine children. As his wife recovered, Robustelli needed to stay in Connecticut to watch the kids.

He called Gillman to give him the heads-up that he'd be a couple of days late to training camp.

Snapped Gillman: "I've got a team to worry about, not your family."

"Well, I've got some kids to worry about," Robustelli countered, "and I've got to do what's right for me."

"If you are not here on time, then don't bother to come at all."

"Fine, then I'll take the whole season off and stay with my wife and new baby in Connecticut."

Gillman—who questioned whether Robustelli, about to turn 30 on Christmas of that year, could continue his upstanding play at such an advanced age—was annoyed enough to make another phone call. A few days later, the phone rang in Robustelli's home. The caller identified himself as Wellington Mara, the co-owner of the New York Giants.

"I've been talking to the Rams about you, and they're willing to trade you," Mara said. "I know you're 30 years old, but do you think you could play two or three more years?"

Said Robustelli: "I'll try to play as long as I can, but I don't know how long that will be."

"Well, if you tell me that you can play, or at least will try to play for that long, then I think I can make a trade for you."

"Go ahead," Robustelli said, "and make the deal."

Robustelli lasted a few more years all right. He played nine more seasons, making five more Pro Bowls, recording four more All-Pro honors, helping the Giants to six conference titles and, in 1971, earning his Hall of Fame induction.

And Gillman's Rams team in 1956 after Robustelli helped lead them to the NFL title game in 1955? They finished 4-8 and in last place in the Western Division.

Yet, Gillman also could be a sweetheart.

"He had a warmth to him," said Nick Shundich, co-captain of the 1951 Cincinnati squad who counts Gillman as one of the three most important people he's known in his 80-plus years (along with his father and an economics professor at Cincinnati). "Although he loved his boys and his troops—and we knew he did—he could make difficult decisions. He could bench you, he could change your position to one you didn't like but one that you were better suited for. . . . Every Tuesday, Sid would go to the student union, and he would show movies of the previous week's game and have a question-and-answer session for the students."

When his San Diego Chargers won the 1963 AFL title game and the team party began soon after, Gillman walked over to the microphone and said, "Fellas, the party is over." After tracking down the maître'd, Gillman announced, "Give them the check for everything up to now, and give me the check for everything after. From now on, this party's on me."

But the person who really made Gillman's players feel at home, the one who made them feel a part of the family, was Esther. That began when Gillman coached under Francis Schmidt at Ohio State, and he and Esther started inviting the players to their home for dinner. Not just one or two players at a time, but a dozen here and a dozen there. By the time the Gillmans reached Oxford, the family had to set up tables in the basement because that was the biggest room in the house and it was the only place they could fit such a huge squadron of hungriness. The players, their wives or girlfriends, and their tremendous appetites showed up throughout the night, wave after wave. It wasn't just a dinner; it was a party. The food was good, and it certainly was plentiful.

"I never learned to cook well," Esther said. "I learned to cook a lot."

At first, she didn't have the kitchen equipment to undertake such a huge project. Eventually, Esther maintained a nice collection of cooking utensils, but at the time, when money was still relatively tight for the Gillman family, Esther and Sid were forced to come up with clever ideas, forced to audible their original plans. One day, as she prepared for a dinner party, Esther baked a few hams, made salad in a dishpan and cooked spaghetti in another. When the pasta was nice and soft, she realized she had nothing big enough to strain out the water. Gillman looked around the kitchen, spotted their saving grace and asked why they couldn't just use a window screen instead.

"So," Esther said, "we took it out, poured boiling water over it to sterilize it and drained the spaghetti."

Sometimes, it wasn't the sheer size of the clientele waiting to be fed. Sometimes, nature provided a roadblock that forced the Gillmans to seek alternative solutions. One night, while preparing a meal for 60 Denison athletes, Esther baked six pies and set them on the back porch to cool. She went outside later and was horrified to discover that birds had picked away at all the crusts. Gillman, though, came to her rescue. He rushed to the corner drugstore, bought ice cream, smeared it in place of the missing pieces of pie crust and yelled, "Look kids, pie à la mode!"

By the time the Gillmans made it to Cincinnati, Gillman's Bearcats players took to calling her creation "Jewish Spaghetti." The Gillmans would host a dozen athletes at a time, and as Shundich recalled, "It was the hottest stuff in town."

It didn't necessarily have to be. The food could have been only average, and the Gillmans still would have had scores of football players trampling through their home in order to suck down Esther's window screen—strained spaghetti. But Esther's recipes also weren't spontaneous. They couldn't be. Not when she had half of a hungry team to feed.

Her spaghetti sauce didn't only have to taste good when it was dumped on the pasta. There also had to be gallons of it. And how do you make gallons of what Esther called "Big Batch Spaghetti Sauce?" After years of experimenting, here's the recipe Esther developed.

Ingredients: Pour enough olive oil to cover the bottom of a big kettle and heat before adding the following: six onions diced, one whole bud garlic, three large cans tomato juice, nine cans tomato paste, basil, oregano, crushed red pepper, salt, sugar, two pounds of lean ground beef, mushrooms.

Preparation: Sauté the onions and garlic only until they change color. Add ground beef and brown gently. Add the tomato paste, tomato juice, and seasoned mushrooms, and simmer very gently, stirring occasionally, for at least three hours. If desired, add a batch of meatballs to the sauce, one hour before serving on a bed of thin spaghetti topped with Parmesan cheese.

Serves: 25–30 people.

Esther proved to be one of Gillman's biggest allies when it came time to make peace with some of his players. Even when he insulted them at practice, he could always make up for it by inviting them to Jewish Spaghetti the next night. Their feelings might have been hurt, but at least their bellies were full.

—⚏—

Paul Brown, Woody Hayes, and Sid Gillman grew up as coaches together. Brown and Hayes were raised in Ohio, and after Gillman graduated high school, he played and coached in the Buckeye state. Hayes played at Denison while Gillman was an assistant coach there, and Brown could have offered Gillman a job when he took over for Francis Schmidt as the Ohio State head coach (he, of course, did not). Brown was a Miami alumnus, and he disapproved of how Gillman left his job. Hayes took over for Gillman at Miami, and he disapproved of *what* Gillman left him.

They were interconnected, but they were anything but friendly.

From the 1930s until their head coaching careers were over by 1978, they twisted together in football's DNA. By the end, there was talk that the game had evolved too much, that their coaching methods were no longer useful, that it was time for them to abandon their posts. Some believed their coaching methods were outdated, that they were relics from a different time and place, that the game had left them behind.

But their innovations and their success could not be questioned. Brown and Gillman are two of the most important coaches in NFL history, and very few collegiate coaches can match Hayes's accomplishments.

Gillman and Brown did not get along, and the families today either choose to make nasty accusations or, in the case of Mike Brown, the son of Paul and the current Bengals owner, decline to talk on the record about Gillman and say almost nothing about him privately. Gillman and Hayes did not get along either, though they eventually found common ground and made amends. But all three were so impactful on the game that no matter their feelings toward each other, they learned from one another and used many of the same methods to build coaching records that continue to inspire into the 21st century.

For as much as the three clashed against one another, their relationship roots formed long before they were important, well-known coaches. Though Gillman's kids knew that their father and Hayes lived together for a time and Brown's offspring heard the story of Brown and Hayes sharing a residence, Hayes biographer John Lombardo writes that all three coaches lived together in the summer of 1936.

Brown had already established himself as a successful high school head coach in Massillon by that time, Gillman had embarked on his coaching career at Denison, and Hayes had enrolled at the graduate school of education in order to become a principal or school superintendent (it didn't take Hayes long to change his mind).

As they studied their respective crafts, all three were housed temporarily in the Sigma Chi fraternity house on the Ohio State campus, and soon enough, they began to impact one another.

Gillman and Brown spent their summer vacations learning from Buckeyes coach Francis Schmidt and Hayes took classes, but in the evenings, the three came together to talk football. As Lombardo noted, the trio "would argue and steal each other's ideas, to be used when they went back to their respective coaching jobs in the fall. It was for Woody the equivalent of a football laboratory, as so much of his coaching philosophy can be traced to those skull sessions at the Sigma Chi house."

Together, in the frat house during that summer their descendants never knew about, the three laid a tiny bit of the foundation that would help build their coaching careers into some of the most impressive résumés of all time.

—⚇—

For all of Gillman's innovations—the film-watching, the offensive passing schemes, how he dealt with race relations on his team—Paul Brown was just as inventive. Brown is credited as the first head coach to employ year-round assistant coaches, the first to fashion a facemask for his players' helmets, the first to administer intelligence tests to potential players, and the first to use 40-yard-dash times for evaluation.

The prevailing thought about Brown's absolute disdain of Gillman was that he didn't approve of Gillman's methods of winning. It had nothing to do with his on-field demeanor and play-calling. Brown disapproved of the way Gillman demanded his bosses spend money they didn't have to bolster whichever program Gillman was leading (this included Brown's beloved Miami). He sneered at how Gillman, in nearly every coaching stop he ever made, bent the rules and, in a few cases, clearly broke them. He disagreed with Gillman that winning was more important than anything else.

Brown, older than Gillman and Hayes, was the first to make his mark. He won a national title at Ohio State in 1942, and when he joined the Cleveland Browns in the All-American Football Conference after World War II, he led the team to 11 league title games, winning seven of them, in a 17-year span.

From afar, Gillman learned from Brown. When Brown wanted to impart wisdom on players, he approached it like a schoolroom teacher. He lectured like a professor, and he expected them to respond like students. "First, they write it—they see it," Brown said. "Second, they listen to me talk about it—they hear it. Third, they work it out on the football field—they do it."

This mirrored rather closely Gillman's philosophy: "Write it. Learn it. See it. Do it."

When it came to offensive philosophies, Woody Hayes and Gillman couldn't have been more different. Gillman was about the vertical stretch passing game. Hayes popularized the "three yards and a cloud of dust" scheme that emphasized power rushing. Gillman was precise route running; Hayes was smashmouth football. Gillman was innovative; Hayes was old school. Or as Hayes biographer John Lombardo put it, "Woody's football field was a battleground; Sid's was a laboratory."

Hayes's system, though, worked at Ohio State, and it landed him three national titles and 13 Big Ten championships during his 28-year tenure. Hayes *was* Ohio State football for nearly three decades and it's why every coach that follows will always be compared to him.

Hayes was also a man of paradox. He was verbally and physically abusive with his players, but if you were a member of the Buckeyes football program, you were forevermore a member of Hayes's family. He was oftentimes cruel, and most of the players hated him for long stretches of their college careers. In fact, his career ended the day he punched a Clemson player named Charlie Bauman during the 1978 Gator Bowl.

But Hayes was charitable with his time, and if there was a member of the coaching fraternity who needed cheering up, Hayes was up to the task. Lee Tressel, the longtime coach at Baldwin-Wallace who won a Division III national title in 1978, was a big Hayes fan, and when Tressel taught his football classes, Hayes's book *Hotline to Victory* was treated as the gospel. When Tressel started his coaching career, one of the first moves he made was to travel from Berea, Ohio, to Columbus to study with Hayes's staff.

This was the impact Hayes made across the state. Ohio State and its football program belong to the entire state, if not the entire Midwest south of the Michigan border, and Hayes was more like the governor of Ohio than a football coach.

"The one thing that came across to anyone who was paying attention was that Woody Hayes was a lot more than a football coach," said Lee's son, Jim Tressel, who happened to win the 2002 BCS title as the Buckeyes coach and knew all about those kind of demands.

In 1981, Lee Tressel was dying from lung cancer, and while at a luncheon, one of Tressel's former Baldwin-Wallace players bumped into Hayes and mentioned that he had played for Tressel. Hayes asked about Tressel's health.

"He's not doing very well," the former player said.

Hayes said, "Let's go see him," and immediately dropped in on his old colleague so they could chit-chat for a few hours. Jim Tressel never forgot the touching gesture, and from the time he took over the Ohio State job until he was fired following the 2010 season, Jim Tressel tried his best to emulate Hayes's demeanor off the field when a person in need could be positively affected by the highest-paid state employee.

"To me," Jim Tressel said, "that's what Ohio State and the state of Ohio deserve."

—⁕—

The trio of Gillman, Brown, and Hayes were some of the top coaches of their era and some of the most important in the sport's history, but all three could be tone-deaf to the way society expected professionals to act. True, football coaches are a different animal. Attend most football practices today, at just about any level, and the coaches most likely would shock average fans with the abuse they heap on their players. In that way, Gillman, Brown, and Hayes weren't unique. But the sheer contrast of opinions in the way those coaches made others feel is rare. Some hated the three of them as individuals. Some loved them separately. They hated each other until they didn't. They're intertwined like the DNA of football, but somewhere embedded deep in that code were self-destructive tendencies that still managed to bring them success.

"They all have strong suits," said Ara Parseghian, who played for Gillman at Miami, played for Brown at Great Lakes Naval Training Center during World War II, and then with the Cleveland Browns, and coached with Hayes at Miami (Ohio) in 1950. "Paul Brown was a constant organizer with a terrific ability to place the personnel, motivate the personnel, and innovate. Sid was so passionate about the game, and he was still an innovative guy. And Woody Hayes was a people person. He was a great recruiter and he could talk about the football stuff with anybody. I wouldn't rate him up with Brown and Sid, but he got things done with his ability to deal with people.

"I was the beneficiary of playing or coaching with all three of them. You talk about doing post-graduate doctoral work."

While it's unclear when exactly and what exactly caused the dissension between Brown and Gillman, Hayes had good reason to be annoyed by Gillman. After Gillman took the Cincinnati job—and in the process, stole away Miami coach George Blackburn and a number of Redskins players—Hayes was hired to regenerate the program. He saw Gillman's success with the Bearcats, and he simmered. Though the Redskins had gone 8-1 in 1948, when Blackburn succeeded the West Point–bound Gillman, at least six of those starters had transferred to Cincinnati.

Hayes, though, could recruit. He had originally caught Gillman's attention when Hayes, then at Denison and looking to nail down his first big-name recruit, wooed a high school player named Bill Fleitz who already had committed to Gillman at Miami. Hayes convinced him to change his mind and play at Denison.

Once Hayes established himself at Miami and Gillman at Cincinnati, the two battled through hellacious fights to entice recruits to their respective programs. After Hayes took the Ohio State job—the position Gillman apparently recommended for Hayes after an anti-Semitic establishment wouldn't give it to Gillman—their hatred expanded. If Hayes lost a recruit to Gillman, he thought it was because Gillman was cheating, and if Hayes won out, Gillman's family thought it was because Hayes was crossing an ethical boundary. "Woody would say, 'Sid Gillman sends his daughter here. Why wouldn't you come?'" said Lyle Gillman, Sid's oldest daughter, who has a diploma from Ohio State.

The two wouldn't appear on the same radio or television shows when Hayes was still at Miami, and if the two found themselves at the same event, one or the other left the scene. Which made it strange to hear that Hayes endorsed Gillman when he interviewed for the Los Angeles Rams job.

"Hayes is no dummy," one football insider told Earl Lawson of the *Cincinnati Post* after Gillman moved west. "He wants Gillman out of college coaching. Big Ten schools never touch pro coaches. Now Hayes knows that if he should lose his job at Ohio State someday, Gillman won't replace him. That would kill Woody."

Though Gillman had to be content that he and Hayes split the only two games they coached against each other, he could enjoy it when another Bearcat gave Hayes a beating in the most literal sense. During the 1949 season, as the Miami freshmen faced the Cincinnati rookie squad, Hayes, wearing a loud sports coat, watched from the Nippert Stadium stands as his future star running back Jim "Boxcar" Bailey dominated. Some Bearcats supporters in the crowd began yelling racial epithets at Bailey, and one of the ringleaders was a Cincinnati basketball player named Joe Luchi.

When the insults were too much to bear, Hayes stood up and yelled, "Don't make fun of him." Luchi stood up to challenge Hayes, who walked down two steps to meet Luchi. "You little son of a bitch," Hayes said, and began to pull off his jacket. But Luchi took advantage with Hayes in the middle of disrobing and bloodied his nose. Ray Penno, a Bearcats football player who sat a few rows away, immediately ran for Gillman's office underneath the stadium.

"Coach," Penno said when he found Gillman, "there's a free-for-all going on out there with Big Woody Hayes."

Gillman chuckled and said, "Couldn't happen to a nicer guy."

Chances are, Gillman wouldn't have minded seeing Brown catch a beating either. Instead, Brown was usually the one smacking around Gillman's teams.

Brown won their first three meetings, including the 1955 NFL title game when the Cleveland Browns beat Gillman's L.A. Rams. But when Brown took over the expansion Bengals as owners and coach and faced the Chargers in Cincinnati's first game at the beginning of the 1968 season, Gillman finally beat his biggest foil, 29–13. Brown, however, beat him in 1969 and 1971, and after Gillman took over for Houston's Bill Peterson in 1973, the Bengals ended the Oilers' season with a 27–24 win.

That's why it was nearly automatic for Gillman to praise Brown whenever anybody asked about him. "I can understand Paul. No other person in the world can build a football team better than he can," Gillman said in 1968. "As far as I'm concerned, he's the guy that made pro football what it is today. There are football coaches more knowledgeable from a football standpoint but he's got the organization, the system."

It was clear that Gillman, who attended some of Brown's football camps earlier in their careers and admitted that he took some of his ideas from Brown and expanded on them, respected Brown. But it was also clear that he didn't like Paul Brown the man. Perhaps that was because of the long-held Gillman family belief that Brown did all he could to exclude Gillman from the Miami Hall of Fame, or because it was in response to Brown's loathing of Gillman.

Gillman's disdain for Brown wasn't usually reserved for the public space, but Gillman's players knew how he felt. While game-planning for a Brown-led team, one player remembered Gillman going into a rant as he stood at the chalkboard, writing so much and so hard that he might as well have whittled the chalk into a nub. As chalk dust settled all around the room, Gillman, with his gruff voice, shouted, "We're going to fuck Paul Brown, and we're going to fuck the Bengals."

In 1974, the Bengals started the season 4-1, but they lost two of their next four, including a 34–21 defeat to the Oilers. When Cincinnati prepared to travel to Houston for a rematch, Gillman took his shot. After Brown refused to exchange game film with Gillman, the Oilers coach went on a rant while talking to Ed Menaker of the *Cincinnati Post.* In the middle of his outburst, Gillman called Brown "senile."

Asked Menaker: "You want to go on record as saying Brown is senile?" Responded Gillman: "Write it. The old man is senile. He needs to quit football. You write it."

Menaker did, and when Brown read it, he couldn't believe it. Especially when the Astrodome crowd of 44,000, watching the Oilers dominate the Bengals 20–3, began chanting "Brown is senile" over and over. Brown was humiliated, and he had Gillman to blame.

Gillman and Brown vehemently disliked each other until the days they died, but Gillman and Hayes reconciled and grew to maintain a relationship in their later years. Tom Gillman remembered seeing Christmas cards from the Hayes family, and when Hayes was in poor health in the years before he died, Gillman called to send his well-wishes. Hayes wept in appreciation.

Many years after their initial wars, Gillman and Hayes happened to bump into each other one morning in the coffee shop of a Chicago hotel. They exchanged a quick greeting, but then Hayes, in an awkward moment, offered an olive branch. He asked Gillman if they could spend time together so Gillman could explain his passing offense. Eight hours later, the two finally broke for dinner, new pals with new respect for each other. Later, Hayes said, "You know, I still don't know what the hell he was talking about."

—⁂—

Gillman, especially in the earlier days of his career, never escaped his Judaism. He wasn't an especially religious Jew, but that hardly mattered to those who hated him for it anyway. By the time he was finished with coaching football, the Jews who had looked up to him wanted to claim him as their own. That's why the wall in his second-floor study in San Diego was littered with plaques from Jewish groups that honored him with some kind of recognition. If anybody asked Gillman what religion he practiced, all he had to do was point to the wall of his office.

Or show the induction letters from the National Jewish Sports Hall of Fame, the International Jewish Sports Hall of Fame, or the Southern California Jewish Sports Hall of Fame—all of which claimed Gillman as a member.

"Yeah, there are three of those," Gillman said. "I hope that ends it right there."

"Why?" Esther asked.

"When you're in three Jewish Halls of Fame, that's enough."

Just before he was inducted into the Pro Football Hall of Fame, the Canton (Ohio) Jewish Community Center threw him a banquet in celebration, and during his speech, Gillman said, "I've been blessed. . . . The man upstairs decided he was going to give a person 50 years of one thing they love more than anything—coaching. I've enjoyed it so much I could sing a Jewish song."

The truth is, though, that if Gillman knew many Jewish songs, he almost certainly didn't know what they meant. Gillman simply wasn't a man who put much stock in his faith. But Esther was raised in a religious home, and her side of the family stayed that way for years. Lyle, their first daughter, remembers an incident when her kosher-keeping maternal grandparents were shocked when she accidently placed the dishes reserved for meat in the same vicinity as the dishes reserved for milk. Citing Jewish tradition, they immediately buried the contaminated plates in the backyard. But that orthodoxy hardly rubbed off on Gillman.

Instead, Gillman was a Jew who didn't call attention to himself or his beliefs. When one of his grandsons was bar mitzvahed, he had to excuse himself from his current coaching duties, telling his boss that he had a communion to attend. "How did he even know the word 'communion?'" Lyle asked. While his parents expected him to attend Hebrew school while growing up in Minneapolis, he rarely went to class. His family acknowledged the holiest of the Jewish holidays, but other than that, they rarely attended temple.

Gillman loved the music, the ancient chants that have been repeated in synagogues throughout the world for thousands of years. He just didn't delve into the prayers and what they represented. If there had been a blessing for winning football games, he might have gone to temple more often. But there isn't, so he didn't.

When Gillman entered into his coaching career, his religion held him back for jobs he probably could have attained otherwise. The Ohio State job that ultimately went to Woody Hayes, the University of Illinois job, the Minnesota job, the Purdue job. It was clear to Gillman that the athletic directors at some schools wanted him to lead their football programs— some went so far as to tell him that they were going to hire him—but Gillman ultimately got none of them. Gillman was visibly uncomfortable when talking about this topic late in his life, but his family is adamant that his Judaism prevented him from securing any of those positions.

"We had great college teams, and I was an ambitious sucker," Gillman said. "Every time a job would open up in the Big Ten, I would (make a) play for it. But as soon as they found out I was a Jew, that was the end of it."

This occurred at Indiana University. A secretary who took dictation at a Board of Trustees meeting remembers the scene quite well, and she repeated the story for Sid's daughter, Bobbe Korbin, nearly six decades later. In the secretary's recollection, Indiana needed a new coach, and one of the trustees mentioned Gillman as a candidate, saying, "Sid Gillman is a great coach." Another trustee, though, reminded the room, "He's Jewish, you know." Because the secretary also happens to be Jewish, she cringed during that moment as silence descended over the room. Then, neither a word for Gillman nor against him was raised, and the meeting moved on to the candidate. What was left unsaid was that Gillman had been dropped from consideration. Because he was Jewish, and, at that point in history, completely unhirable.

In Granville, Ohio, the Gillmans sent Lyle to a Catholic school, but Esther made sure to celebrate the Jewish holidays with her children as they grew. They did not attend school on the first day of Rosh Hashanah or on Yom Kippur, and while at Miami, Esther had to drive her kids to Hamilton, about 15 miles away, for Sunday school at the town's small Jewish community center.

A couple of times, Yom Kippur—the Day of Atonement where Jews forgo eating and drinking to cleanse themselves for the sins they committed in the previous year—fell on game day, and though Esther would attend the contest, she'd honor her heritage anyway and continue her fast. Someone invariably would offer her food and drink, and Esther would say, "No, today is my holiday. I'm sitting here, but I also have the holiday in my heart."

While his religion wasn't necessarily in his heart or on his mind, Gillman inspired those who didn't realize that they belonged, too. To Ron Mix, a Hall of Fame offensive tackle during Gillman's decade as the San Diego Chargers' coach, Gillman was a revelation. Mix grew up in Boyle Heights, a neighborhood in East Los Angeles that at the time was a Russian Jewish ghetto. But during high school, there was a shortage of Jews around him, and it was an uncomfortable experience. In fact the only other Jewish person he knew at school was his brother. So, Mix heard the misconceptions and the stereotypes every day. When Mix—who described himself as short a father figure and short on identity—learned about Gillman, who was then coaching the Los Angeles Rams, he realized something important: Jews *could* succeed in sports.

"Jews were All-American football players and leaders of the Los Angeles Rams," Mix said. "My world had begun an expansion that continues to this day."

In 1983, it was clear to Jews around the world that Gillman had helped break the stereotypes that allowed those who followed him to succeed, and Ben-Gurion University in the Negev honored him by establishing a chair in Gillman's name as part of the Academic Department of Physical Education and Sports. It was the first program of its kind at an Israeli university, and it was a four-year course of study where students would learn the theories, science, and psychology of physical education.

"A nation that yearns for permanent peace must have sound minds and bodies as part of its overall growth," Gillman said. "The physical education and well being of all Israeli citizens represent an essential effort in the building of the nation."

Yet, the appreciation showed to him by Jews around the world wasn't necessarily reflected by the players he coached. Some loved him, some hated him, some just tried to survive. But none ever forgot him.

"He was tough," said Bobbe Korbin. "But he never expected them to do anything that he wouldn't do double."

But it was those three ideas that summed up the Gillman contradiction—winning is No. 1, always try to do the right thing, and winning always triumphs over doing the right thing—that followed him from job to job, from the college game to the professional ranks. Not just in the way Gillman thought about his career and his life. But in the way others see him.

Which is why, after Gillman left Cincinnati for the NFL, the following two contradictions could be written about him in the span of only nine months.

"This fellow is so well liked," Bud Furillo of the *Los Angeles Herald and Express* penned in January 1955, "you would think he goes around paying off mortgages instead of beating the stuffing out of everybody with his solid coaching."

And . . .

"If, as some people suppose," wrote Earl Lawson for the *Saturday Evening Post* in October 1955, "professional football is just a cold-blooded business in which personal relationships are no factor, then Sid Gillman now is completely at home."

eight   LOS ANGELES

The Los Angeles Rams had been searching for a new coach for what felt like forever. It had been six weeks—which, in football coaching search standards, is an eternity—and the team's owners were getting nervous.

Thanks to a contractual arrangement with his colleagues, Dan Reeves, the team president and one of the owners of the franchise, was the only one who could hire a new coach. The other owners wanted to procure recently fired San Francisco 49ers coach Buck Shaw, but Reeves had so much power that he vetoed their request. Reeves had discussed the opening with the University of Kentucky's Blanton Collier, Georgia Tech's Bobby Dodd, and Navy's Eddie Erdelatz, but for one reason or another, they had not been interested or had been discarded. It appeared to the outside observer that perhaps Reeves didn't know what he was doing, and it seemed like the team was rowing in circles with no idea how to get out of their maelstrom.

Truth be told, it might be possible the Rams *didn't* know what they were doing. They certainly fired coaches enough times—coaches, mind you, that were successful—to make it seem like the human resources department simply enjoyed the thrill of processing tax forms for new hires.

In his second year as coach in 1949, Clark Shaughnessy led the Rams to an 8-2-2 record and was fired after the season. Joe Stydahar was hired, and in three years, he went 17-7, helping L.A. win the NFL title in 1951. But after losing the first regular-season game of the very next year, Stydahar resigned, saying the dissension between him and assistant coach Hampton Pool was too great. Pool performed well as the Rams' head coach, but not surprisingly, after going 23-10-2 in three seasons but in trouble because of a possible player and assistant coach revolt, he also found himself without a job. As the story goes, Reeves and Fred Levy, two of the team's owners, invited him to dinner one night at a fancy restaurant on the Sunset Strip, and before Pool knew it, he had been fired between the herring and soup courses.

"The Rams were firing guys left and right," said Melvin Durslag, a longtime columnist who spent most of his career at the *Los Angeles Examiner*. "It was a drunken operation over there."

Reeves and Levy were owners when the Rams were in Cleveland—this was the NFL reincarnation of the team Gillman played for in 1936 when it was in a different league—and after winning the NFL title in 1945 but losing $50,000 in the process, Reeves moved the team to Los Angeles. Reeves and Levy sold part ownership of the team to Ed Pauley, Harold Pauley, and Hal Seeley for $1 apiece to help share in the losses. And the financial losses were plentiful. In 1947, the first year of the new partnership, the organization lost $253,300. In 1953, Harold Pauley died, and Bob Hope bought his ownership shares. So, technically, the Rams were an organization of pure comedy.

"The team drew very well, but they still lost money," Durslag said. "Pro football, in those days, you were a success if you could break even. These were so-called sportsmen in those days. They did it because they were rich guys.

"It was kind of a turbulent team, a turbulent existence. It was a very tough place to coach. These guys were a goofy bunch."

A strong coaching record? An innovator like Shaughnessy? An NFL title for Stydahar? A deep thinker like Pool who won 67 percent of his games?

"That didn't seem to matter around there," Durslag said. "It was rollicking days when the wine flowed freely."

Though it took 39 days between the time Pool choked on his soup and Gillman said yes to Reeves's job offer, Reeves was ecstatic in his choice. He was certain Gillman was the man for the job, and even though he knew a lack of pro experience could hinder his new coach, he would allow him grace time to adapt. Gillman was 43 years old, and Reeves had wanted a younger man who could lead the team for many years. That, in fact, was one reason he didn't want Buck Shaw, the former 49ers coach who had been the choice of the owners and the fans. Shaw was 13 years older than Gillman, and for Reeves, that was too ancient.

Even though he knew the lessons that Shaughnessy, Stydahar, and Pool had been unfortunate enough to learn, Gillman ignored them anyway, saying he wasn't frightened by the high mortality rate of Rams coaches. He wanted to test himself in the pro game and he was thrilled he didn't have to recruit high school players anymore.

"With the Rams," Gillman said, "it was nothing but football."

As soon as he accepted the job, Gillman flew to New York to join Reeves for the NFL draft, and he then returned to Cincinnati for most of the next month to hire a staff and start breaking down film on his new team and his new league. After all, Gillman had seen the Rams play on TV exactly two times in his life.

While he, Esther, and his two youngest kids, Terry and Tom, prepared to depart Cincinnati and move to the West Coast, his oldest daughter, Lyle, had no idea of their new adventure. She studied at Ohio State and majored in languages, and in the middle of her sophomore year, she traveled to Mexico City with a roommate named Jeri Lippey to live as a foreign exchange student. Her roommate's parents happened to be visiting in mid-January, and as Lyle and Jeri walked to Sanborn's restaurant to meet her family for lunch, they passed a newsstand that showcased newspapers from around the world.

Lyle looked at the cover of the *Los Angeles Times* and saw a cartoon of her father walking past a graveyard filled with the headstones of all the former Rams coaches. That's how she discovered her dad had a new job. "I looked at everybody and said, 'I think my dad is the new Rams coach,'" Lyle said. "And I thought, 'How do I call him?' I'm in Mexico City, and I had no idea. None."

Gillman didn't arrive in L.A. until mid-February, 23 days after he took the job, when he hopped on a TWA flight that took him to his new home. Almost immediately, he met with the press, wearing a well-cut charcoal gray suit, and he appeared enthusiastic about getting along with the men who would chronicle his team in a way like nothing he had ever experienced.

Those good feelings didn't last long.

As the team entered its first training camp under Gillman in mid-July 1955, the preseason workouts in Redlands were more relaxed for the Rams than they had been in ages. Team morale had been terrible the year before, leading to a revolt against Pool, but under Gillman, one rookie said, "I'd give anything to make this ball club, but if I don't, it still will have been worth the time and effort just to work under the best coach I've ever known."

But Gillman was already developing a problem with the press. He had told his players not to discuss him or his assistant coaches with the media, and when practice began, he announced that the press couldn't talk to anybody unless the head coach sat in on the interview. Considering the number of newspapers that covered the Rams at the time, this was a rather unusual (and quite insulting) demand, and it did not go over well with the team's beat writers. To Gillman, it made sense because Pool had been undone by the backbiting of his players and the players were less likely to insult their coach if he sat right next to them, but logistically, it was impossible. The writers liked Gillman because he was a great character and because he talked their language, but this decision was a no-go for them.

It led *Los Angeles Herald & Examiner* columnist Bob Hunter to write an open letter to the new Rams coach in which he penned, "What I want to ask you, Sid, is this: Who do you think will win (in the battle between coach and press)? You're darn right. So I'm sending you this friendly warning to (reconsider) . . . Sid, it happens that the reporters assigned to cover your ball club are major leaguers. You're a bush leaguer. You're moving into the fastest football league in the world, coming up from university competition—second-rate university competition at that."

Hunter then advised Gillman to extend an olive branch to the writers and to tell them he was wrong and that he was sorry. "If you don't,"

Hunter threatened, "just wait until you lose two ball games and they'll run you out of town—I'll have to help them . . . Prove you're only a bush-leaguer in the same sense a rookie is coming into the majors for the first time . . ."

Naturally, that kind of response didn't convince Gillman to cooperate.

"I'll never read a sports page as long as I live," Gillman informed Durslag soon after Hunter's column appeared.

"Sid," Durslag asked, "what are you going to do at breakfast, then?"

"I'm going to eat my eggs and look out the goddamn window."

But as was sometimes the case—remember Gillman's threat to kick any player off the Cincinnati team who dared get married?—Gillman didn't follow through. After an exhibition loss to the Redskins, nobody was censored from answering questions about any subject. In fact, when he needed to make a point in his postgame interview session, Gillman picked up the chalk and gave the scribes a brief football lesson on his office blackboard.

—⚏—

Even with the coaching upheavals, the Rams drew crowds of immense proportions at Los Angeles Memorial Coliseum. The Rams could play the 49ers and draw 102,000 people. They'd face the Bears, and Gillman could look into 100,000 faces in the crowd. For a coach like Gillman, who was lucky to draw 15,000 at Cincinnati, this was an unfamiliar experience. It took him a couple games to relax in such an environment, but soon enough, he began to learn how to handle the immense crowds and the colossal expectations each fan brought to the stadium.

What made the transition easier for Sid and Esther was that they were surrounded by family for the first time in their married lives. After Sid's mother died, Gillman's father remarried and moved to L.A., and a number of Esther's family already lived there as well, including her mother. That cocoon of familiarity surely made life easier for Sid and Esther as they adjusted to the L.A. lifestyle.

Plus, the Rams immediately started winning, and that always made for pleasant days.

As he studied film in Cincinnati before making the trek to L.A., Gillman determined that the problem with the Rams organization was that there was *too much* offense and not enough defense. Quarterback Norm Van Brocklin threw the ball *too much* with too many interceptions. When the Rams scored, they scored *too fast*, leaving the defense not enough time to rest in between series. *Sports Illustrated* explained it this way: in years past, the Rams were a slugger, not a boxer. The sluggers were oftentimes more exciting to watch, but the problem was that a good defensive fighter could use his tricks and figure out ways to counterpunch without getting hit himself. Gillman turned his team into a boxer with a good defense, and in 1955, that was the difference for L.A.

In the Rams' opening three games, Van Brocklin's 66 passes attempted were 15 less than the season before, and behind a new game-planning approach, L.A. won those three matchups with the help of a sturdy defense. As opposed to 23.8 points per game allowed the year before, the Rams defense, thanks to 11 interceptions in the first three games, allowed only 16.7 early in 1955.

"With a good defense," Gillman said, "you'll have a chance in every ball game. You can't depend on matching the other guys touchdown for touchdown." Considering the gains Gillman eventually made in offensive innovation and considering his thought process at Miami and Cincinnati when defensive preparation often waited until the day before the game, that statement is deliciously ironic.

But for the 8-3-1 Rams, it worked, and when they beat the Packers 31–17 on December 11 to edge out the 8-4 Chicago Bears to win the Western Division, his team carried him off the field on its shoulders in front of 90,000 fans.

A picture of that moment hung in Gillman's office for the rest of his life, and after the game, it was no stretch when he told his squad, "You not only are the greatest players I've ever been with, but as a group, you're the greatest bunch of men." Then, Gillman stuck his hand into his pocket and brought out a cuff link that he said a friend had sent to him from Chicago. On the gold link, shining in the light of the locker room, Gillman read the inscription: "Chicago Bears, 1955 football champions." Then, pausing a moment, Gillman delivered the punch line: "Someone back there jumped the gun."

Less than a year after Reeves had hired little-known Gillman to lead his squad, Gillman had the Rams in the NFL title game. Looking back at him from the opposite sideline was a coach he knew very well: his old nemesis Paul Brown. The Cleveland Browns were the New York Yankees of the NFL, and after Brown had taken that team to four straight All-American Football Conference championships from 1946 to 1949, he had resumed his success when owners allowed Cleveland into the NFL. From there, the Browns won five straight division titles and went 2-3 in NFL title games from 1950 to 1954. Gillman, in his first year in pro football, had made the NFL title game. But this was where Brown lived.

Earlier in the season, the Rams had beaten the Browns 38–21 in an exhibition game, but as Brown and Gillman knew, the result didn't mean anything in the grand scheme of a season. As L.A's players walked by Brown in the tunnel after the game and jeered him and his team, Brown countered, "OK, OK, but what about December?"

By December, the Rams had no answer for the Browns in the most important game of the season. Before the contest, Gillman had called Brown "a genius," and he made sure to point out that he wasn't being facetious. But in this game, it was all about protection. Van Brocklin, who threw six interceptions, got little of it from his offensive line. Meanwhile, 34-year-old Cleveland quarterback Otto Graham, in the final game of his career, threw for two touchdowns and ran for two more, and got so much help from his linemen that a reporter joked that he could have written a letter to Cleveland before he threw.

Afterward, Gillman wasn't devastated. He knew the Browns were a better team. He knew his squad would improve once he had more time to work his magic. He would look at the film from 1955 and apply it to 1956 and make his team into a title-winner instead of only a title-contender.

Yet, after the game, Tex Schramm, the Rams' general manager, had some sage words of advice. "Just remember," Schramm told Gillman, "it isn't always going to be this easy."

The reality was that it would never again be that simple for Gillman in L.A.

—⁓—

One of the biggest problems Gillman encountered during his first three years in Los Angeles was a 6-foot-1, 190-pound veteran quarterback from Eagle Butte, South Dakota. He had a temper and a knack for winning, and he was known as the Dutchman. Norm Van Brocklin was an outstanding signal-caller, a first-rate punter, a two-time NFL title winner and a 1971 Pro Football Hall of Fame inductee. He was also a gigantic pain in the ass.

"I wish I could start to describe him. He was a redneck without really being a redneck," longtime Los Angeles sports writer Melvin Durslag said. "When he was with the other players, he referred to Sid as The Rabbi. He was one of those crazy guys who talked a lot. But there was a side to him that wasn't too bad. And Esther loved him. They knew about The Rabbi and so forth, but they never took his anti-Semitism seriously. Sid was willing to overlook his personality, probably because he could throw the ball straight."

He threw it awfully straight in the 1955 season, helping the Rams to the NFL title game. He was a Pro Bowler that year, but he also threw nearly twice as many interceptions as touchdown passes. Early in 1956, after a 27–7 season-opening victory against the Eagles, Gillman declared that the Rams no longer had a starting quarterback. Not coincidentally, Van Brocklin had turned 30 that March, and thinking that 30 was the gateway to football decline, Gillman yanked Van Brocklin after an early interception, inserted Billy Wade, and watched as the third-year quarterback pushed the Rams to the easy win. In February 1955, just after Gillman took the job, he had declared that he didn't think there was a better quarterback in the NFL than Van Brocklin. Just 20 months later, Gillman was an even bigger fan of Van Brocklin . . . as the team's punter.

"I felt that Van just might not have it after he threw that first pass that was intercepted," Gillman said after beating the Eagles. "In this league, we can't wait to see if one of our quarterbacks is right or not. By waiting too long, we could lose a ball game."

But by making the switch too soon, the team lost eight of its next nine games. Gillman, for the rest of the season, used a combination of Van Brocklin, Wade, and Rudy Bukich, and the result was a disastrous 4-8 mark. It wasn't simply a matter of Gillman liking the younger Wade better than Van Brocklin or that Van Brocklin was upset with Gillman's decision. No, a big reason for this dispute was a power struggle between the coach and his Pro Bowl quarterback.

Gillman wanted control from the sidelines. He wanted to call all the offensive plays, and he didn't want his quarterback to change anything from the time he huddled up the offense to the time he took the snap from the center. Gillman was the man in charge, and anything less was unacceptable. Van Brocklin, meanwhile, wanted to call his own plays. He had played in the NFL for seven seasons, and he knew what he was doing. He wanted the coach's input to rot in the back of his throat, and to be left alone to do his job.

During this era, it was common for quarterbacks to call their own plays, a practice that many quarterbacks continued into the 1970s. But in the 1980s, when TV began having an increasing influence in the game, coaching egos expanded and a team that allowed its quarterback to call his own plays quickly went extinct.

The issue of who called plays for the Rams in 1956, though, provided a distraction all season. Not only with Gillman, Van Brocklin, and Wade. But also with the newspapermen and the fans who watched this soap opera disaster slowly unfold before them.

After the third loss of the year, while Gillman attended a Rams Club's ladies day luncheon at the Biltmore, one matronly looking woman bluntly asked Gillman, "Why do you call the plays?" Gillman replied that it was easier to inform the four coaches in the press box what play had been called so they could more accurately determine what the opponent was doing in response. If a quarterback called the plays in the huddle, those in the press box would have been less effective at their jobs.

The questions, though, wouldn't stop.

A week later, Gillman said that plays would continue to be—and always be—called from the sidelines. "No one will ever make us believe it isn't the best thing," he said. "We think the quarterback should have a system of audibles. Sometimes he can see a situation in the line we can't. Occasionally, a quarterback can rub the play off. Occasionally, too, the quarterback can put in a play of his own. Occasionally. If a quarterback is given too much leeway, he can stand out there on the field and thumb his nose at you.

"We believe that, and we'll live and die with it. If it doesn't work, I imagine there'll be some other person who would be delighted to come in and take over and let the quarterbacks call 'em."

The questioning, though, continued. At a Rams Fan Club meeting, one booster challenged Gillman by asking him what he thought about the fact that the last-place teams in the Western and Eastern divisions had plays called in from the sideline. Gillman remarked that he didn't see the significance of it. Somebody else commented, "When you call signals for Van Brocklin, you're jeopardizing his job." Replied Gillman in an icy tone: "Lady, if he calls the signals, he's jeopardizing mine."

When Van Brocklin was asked about the brewing controversy, he kept clear of any fireworks. "I like to call my own plays," he said. "But Sid calling them is perfectly OK with me."

The next weekend, Gillman relented and decided to let Van Brocklin start and call his own game. That approach didn't work either, as the Rams lost their fifth consecutive game. Afterward, a reporter asked Gillman how many plays had been called from the sideline, and a testy Gillman responded, "I don't know how many plays I called. Why don't you ask Van Brocklin?" He also said he didn't know who would call plays the rest of the year. "It seems," Gillman opined, "that the one important thing in the city of Los Angeles, even of more importance than the elections, is who is going to call the Rams signals."

The next week, Gillman had made two decisions. He was going to start Wade the rest of the season, and further piercing Van Brocklin's skin, he said he wasn't sure the Dutchman was going to be the team's backup quarterback. He also had decided to let Wade call the plays. "It's developed into such a tremendous issue," Gillman said. "I was worried about the effect of the arguments on the squad. I didn't want them taking sides."

Maybe so, but Gillman also had displayed a strange sense of weakness. A few days after saying nobody would ever change his mind about the play-calling, he had completely changed his mind. All of his quarterbacks were nervous, because Gillman had proven that at the first sign of trouble, he'd yank them from the game and let somebody else throw passes.

Though Wade's start provided temporary relief when he threw two touchdowns to beat the 49ers 30–6, Gillman turned back to Van Brocklin after another three-game losing streak in order to beat the Colts. But Van Brocklin was obviously unhappy. Well, less happy than normal anyway. During the middle of one game in Baltimore, the Rams were getting blown out, and in the fourth quarter, Gillman found Van Brocklin, a reserve that day, sitting on the bench.

"Dutch," Gillman said, "go ahead and get warmed up."

Replied Van Brocklin: "Fuck you. You got yourself into this mess. Get yourself out."

Gillman didn't want players taking sides over the issue, but that was impossible. Van Brocklin could be grumpy, and since a stubborn college coach like Gillman was intent on calling the plays, it was highly unlikely the two would become fast friends. Some agreed with Van Brocklin. Some thought the team needed him as the starter. Some were afraid of him. Some thought he was simply an arrogant jerk.

"Van Brocklin was such a nasty bastard on the field," said Ron Waller, a halfback who was Van Brocklin's teammate for three years in L.A. "I remember trying to make a block during a game, and a guy stepped on my face. I was bleeding and everything. He said, 'Get the fuck up off the goddamn ground, you son of a bitch.' And he gave me the ball the very next play."

The next season, though, Gillman changed his mind once again. He started Van Brocklin in all 12 games, and though the team went 6-6, leading Rams general manager Pete Rozelle to assure the media that the ownership still had confidence in Gillman, Van Brocklin threw for a club-record 20 touchdowns.

It was clear, however, that Gillman and Van Brocklin were finished with each other.

In early January, Van Brocklin announced his retirement from pro football. Van Brocklin made the dubious claim that he and Gillman had never had a cross word with each other, but that for some reason, Gillman had lost confidence in him. "He never told me why," Van Brocklin said. "He just sat me on the bench."

Almost immediately, Van Brocklin became a hot prospect for other teams, and since the Rams still owned his rights—and since nobody believed Van Brocklin's intentions—the Rams began taking calls from interested suitors. Though Van Brocklin had returned to his off-season job as a salesman for a company that produced pipe-line coating, the Rams quickly traded him to Philadelphia.

But much like Andy Robustelli, who Gillman had dispatched after he turned 30 and who then solidified his Hall of Fame career with the Giants, Van Brocklin wasn't through by the age of 31. Ever since he had been drafted by the Rams, he had to split the quarterbacking duties. At the start of his career, he platooned with future Hall of Famer Bob Waterfield, and by the end of his time in L.A, he was trying to hold off Wade. But when he went to Philadelphia to play for coach Buck Shaw, Van Brocklin finally had control of his offense.

Before the 1960 season, Van Brocklin announced that it would be his final year before retirement, and he had one of the best seasons of his career, earning his first All-Pro honors and bringing Philadelphia an NFL championship. That season, Van Brocklin called his own plays.

For his part, Wade became a solid quarterback, leading the league in passing yards (2,875) and interceptions (22) as Gillman and the Rams rebounded with an 8-4 record in 1958. And though Wade finished as a two-time Pro Bowler, Gillman blamed himself for not feeding Wade's development because of Van Brocklin. Gillman wanted Wade to be more like Y.A. Tittle or Tobin Rote. Instead, he finished his career on the same plane as more modern passers like Neil O'Donnell and Steve DeBerg. Good, but not great. Solid, but forgettable.

Van Brocklin, meanwhile, went on to a 13-year coaching career with the Vikings and Falcons and finished with a 66-100-7 career coaching mark. He never lost his grumpiness. One day after a soccer-style foreign-born kicker beat the Falcons on a last-second field goal, an Atlanta reporter asked him what he thought when the ball sailed through the uprights. "I was thinking," Van Brocklin said, "they ought to tighten the goddamn immigration laws in this country."

Van Brocklin also had a hatred for sportswriters. One night during a Falcons training camp, three writers and Van Brocklin sat in a Greenville, South Carolina, restaurant booth, and just as he was about to dig into his prime rib, Van Brocklin looked at a reporter named Frank Hyland and said, "Hyland, you're a whore writer."

Retorted Hyland: "I may be a whore writer, but you're a loser." Van Brocklin, turning red, declared that to be a falsehood, and Hyland said, "Oh yeah? Check your record." At that point, Van Brocklin leaped over the table to choke him and the two skirmished. After Atlanta opened the 1974 season 2-6, the Falcons fired him, and Van Brocklin returned to his pecan farm in Social Circle, Georgia, about 50 miles east of Atlanta. A reporter called later to check in on him, and Van Brocklin's wife answered the phone. "Can my husband be happy on the farm?" she asked. "Let me put it this way: pecan trees don't drop touchdown passes."

On that point, Van Brocklin and Gillman could agree.

—⚏—

While the rest of the football world had come around to the notion of breaking down game film in order to scout the opponents and improve their own teams, Gillman, when he first took the Rams job, used the film to change his approach on how to coach his wide receivers. Though receiver Tom Fears—who once spent six seconds as a fighter pilot in the 1943 Humphrey Bogart film *Action in the North Atlantic*—was near the end of his Hall of Fame career, Gillman studied how Fears continued to get himself open. He was more a ferocious blocker than a pass-catcher by the 1956 season, his last year in pro football, but Gillman was impressed.

"We were just beginning to understand how moves are made by a receiver," Gillman said. "Fears was one of the greatest 'move' men in the history of the game. He didn't have much speed, but he could turn 'em on their heads. We studied Fears, and we began to coach what he was doing."

Gillman also longed to make it easier to study tape of the Rams' upcoming opponents, and since there wasn't already a system in place, he helped develop the NFL's first film exchange, where coaches sent their opponents their game film the week of their meeting so the two squads could study the other's tendencies. Of course, Gillman didn't always show his opponents everything.

"If you got one of Sid's videos," laughed Nick Shundich, one of his former players at Cincinnati, "you got everything but the touchdowns."

Gillman, though, wasn't alone in leaving extras on the cutting room floor. As Jack Faulkner—who coached under Gillman at Miami, Cincinnati, L.A., and San Diego—took over the Denver Broncos job and prepared to face his old boss, Gillman discovered Faulkner's game film wasn't complete. Gillman called to complain to Faulkner—who, by the weirdest of coincidences, was missing some of San Diego's most recent play-calls as well—and Faulkner replied, "Well, I'm only doing whatever you've taught me."

At least, Gillman and Faulkner had sent each other *some* of the film. The NFL eventually had to implement rules and regulations on film-swapping so that one team couldn't withhold tape from another. The new regulations stated that a team had to send out film within 24 hours of the final snap of its most-recent game. There were no overnight mail-delivery services in those days, but if Gillman's opponent was playing by the rules, he should have received the package by Thursday.

"If we were going to play the Raiders next week, on Sunday night a copy of that game film, usually broken down into offense and defense, had to be sent out," said Bob Hood, who Gillman hired as the San Diego Chargers' full-time photographer in 1965. "Did you get it [by Thursday]? If it was the Oakland Raiders, hell no. They always figured out a way to misroute it."

It was just another example of teams—not just the ones coached by Gillman—looking to gain the tiniest advantage any way possible. They'd leave out the touchdowns on the game film, they'd stash away extra players where hopefully other teams and the league couldn't find them, or they'd send a spy into enemy territory.

Regarding that last point, the issue of spying is why most football coaches today, college and pro, are so paranoid. It's why practices are closed to fans and the media, it's why teams oftentimes lock themselves away in practice bubbles, and it's why teams are so vigilant about making sure other teams aren't peering in on them. Even in today's NFL, there is the threat of spies videotaping their opponent's sidelines or covertly filming their practices. But in Gillman's day, teams blatantly sent spies to their opponents' practice fields to gather information.

Gillman employed spies from time to time, but he wasn't one of the worst offenders. "Sid Gillman at San Diego doesn't do it either," Raiders coach Al Davis once remarked, "but everybody thinks Sid does." Gillman, though, had the trick pulled on him as well.

In 1955, Fido Murphy, a scout for Bears coach George Halas, sent a spy to watch Gillman's zone defense perform. While the Rams practiced at Hollywood Park, the intruder hid under the scoreboard with his lunch and a thermos of coffee. The spy didn't know what time the Rams would begin practice, so he stayed all day while quite possibly setting a world record for the longest game of hide and seek.

"He was so close to the players and coaches that he could hear 'em talking," Murphy said.

But if you wanted impressive spy stories, Al Davis was the person to ask. It's partially because Davis participated in the nefarious practice. Once, when the Chargers prepared for the Bills, Davis posed as a reporter and asked a Buffalo player to diagram a play the Bills had employed to score a touchdown. The player obliged. Later, the Chargers used that exact same play to score their own touchdown. At the expense of Buffalo.

"There have been some funny things happening in our league," Davis said. "One year, Buffalo paid a former Oakland player to scout the Raiders all season. Well, the guy didn't want to rat on his former teammates, but he needed money, see, so he warned his former teammates that he was a spy and everyone just treated him accordingly and he still collected his money from Buffalo.

"Then there was the famous 'paper cup episode' in 1962 . . . San Diego caught some Denver spies watching their practice. They were supposedly drinking Cokes out of paper cups, but when they got caught, the cups were empty and there were plays written all over them."

Almost immediately, Gillman called up his old buddy Faulkner.

"I got him, I caught your man," Gillman bragged.

Responded Faulkner: "I don't know what you're talking about."

Of course, no matter what Davis said, Gillman did get in on the act and the art of spying occasionally. When the Kansas City Chiefs hired Don Klosterman away from the Chargers, Klosterman was stunned to learn that coach Hank Stram's teams practiced out in the open. Klosterman informed Stram that Gillman's men had watched every practice the Chiefs went through whenever they prepared for the Chargers. In response, Stram ordered that a tall fence be placed around the perimeter of the practice facility.

Gillman's retort: he dispatched a Marine officer named Col. Frank Barnes to walk into Chiefs practice while wearing his uniform. Nobody said a word, and Gillman continued receiving his reports. It didn't seem to affect the relationship between Stram and Gillman. Before each game when their teams met, Gillman and Stram, rather than shake hands, bumped bellies. "Let me see that game plan, Dapper," Gillman said to Stram, and Stram handed over his papers. Gillman examined Stram's plans, rolled them up, threw them on the ground and stepped on them. As he walked away, Gillman said, "It'll never work."

Spying or no, Gillman knew winning football games was about who worked hardest and not about who employed the sneakiest coach. Put in the work, create a solid game plan, and Gillman figured he'd be successful. Until, of course, he wasn't.

—⁂—

Sid and Esther's two oldest kids, Lyle and Bobbe, grew up in the late 1940s, and yes, the stereotypes in their cases were true. They could have been typecast as the two children of the Donna Reed family a decade before *The Donna Reed Show* ever existed. If Wally and the Beav had been two Midwestern Jewish girls, they might have been Lyle and Bobbe.

Sid and Esther's two youngest kids, Terry and Tom, spent some of their youth in the 1960s, and yes, the stereotypes in their cases were true as well. They were part of the counterculture, hanging out at Berkley and expanding their minds in whichever way possible. As author Sally Pont puts it, the culture that surrounded Terry, Tom, and many other youths of that era was "a Charybdis of psychedelia."

In a conversation long after they were grown, Esther confided that she saw the two pairs of siblings differently. Lyle and Bobbe had Midwestern values, and after dates and high school parties, they'd return to their parents' bedroom—safely in the house by curfew—and gush about everything that had happened that night. Meanwhile, when describing Terry and Tom, her tone while in conversation with Pont became "amused and somewhat naughty."

"They're the liberal thinkers," Esther said. "Tom and Terry taught me a lot."

By the time the Gillmans moved to Los Angeles from Cincinnati, Lyle was enrolled at Ohio State and Bobbe was a junior in high school. Since Bobbe didn't want to move to L.A. when she was so involved at her own high school and since she had accumulated enough credits to graduate a year early, that's exactly what she did. Two years later, she was at college in California, but Bobbe was miserable. With her father struggling with the Rams, Bobbe heard the whispers that Gillman would lose his job.

"I would cry from Sunday when we would lose until I got it together again by Thursday," Bobbe said. "Only to start all over again Sunday."

Lyle wasn't all that happy at Ohio State either. She didn't get involved in campus activities, and she didn't go to football games.

"I didn't care about it," Lyle said. "I never liked Ohio State, because Woody was coaching there. I wanted to go to Michigan and Dad wouldn't let me, mainly because it was too expensive because we were out of state. I didn't want to go to Cincinnati because of him. He wanted me to go to a place where I could date Jewish boys, because I had never really dated Jewish boys before. I just wanted to get out of college."

Lyle did find a Jewish boy in Columbus. By the time she was a sophomore, a medical student named Jay Malkoff had given her his fraternity pin. They were engaged the next year, and after turning 20, Lyle and Malkoff married at Leo S. Baeck Temple in L.A.

While at Ohio State's medical school, Malkoff knew a student named Bill Korbin, who was two years older. When Malkoff was set to graduate and looking for internships, he visited California and called Korbin to ask him if he could give a tour of the hospital where Korbin was completing his residency. Or better yet, a shared meal.

Said Malkoff to Korbin: "Why don't you come out to the Gillmans' for dinner?"

That's where Korbin met Bobbe. More than 50 years later, the two are still together.

"We had to elope in 1960, because we never could get Sid to commit to a date," Bill Korbin said. "We couldn't even get together with him to tell him we were married. We were going out to dinner with him to tell him, and at the last minute, he said, 'You don't mind if a couple football players go to dinner with us, do you?' What are you going to say to that?"

Gillman's hectic work schedule wasn't only limited to his two oldest children. It also severely limited the time he could spend with the two children who still lived in his house. This was another way the college and professional games for Gillman were different—the way it affected his family. When he coached at Miami and Cincinnati, Gillman was nearly always busy. But Esther was around most of the time, making Jewish Spaghetti and listening to the Cleaveresque tales of Lyle and Bobbe. But in Los Angeles, Gillman was a ghost and Esther, much of the time, was with him.

"I know Terry and Tom suffered from his absence and resented it," Bobbe said. "When he was in college ball, he was gone a lot, because they did their own recruiting. They had to travel a lot, but we never felt it. He was never home, but when he was home, it was quality time."

When Gillman was home from Rams practice in L.A., though, he spent much of his time in the garage, which had been transformed into his own movie theater. He couldn't help the kids with their homework, because he had reels of homework to finish himself.

"After dinner, he would go watch film. There was no post-dinner chatting. And this was in the off-season," Terry said. "I'm shocked he ever sat down with us at all . . . I don't remember him being gone all that much, but he was always absorbed in football. We never had a dad who was looking for things to do around the house."

Tom learned at an early age how to take care of himself, how to be responsible, how to be left alone.

"Mom and Dad were seriously busier when we were growing up than they were with Lyle and Bobbe," Tom said. "They were further in their career. The whole thing was about his job.

"I always knew my parents loved me. I always knew there was a home. I never felt a want of anything except for time with my dad alone. That is what a father has to give a kid, no matter what. I didn't get it, and that's OK. I get plenty of everything else and then some. . . . Everything I learned from my dad—and I learned a lot—was by osmosis. I can't remember one thing that he said, 'You do it this way and you do it that way.' It was seeing him working hard and doing this and that, and that's how you do it."

Terry and Tom quickly learned the secret to spending time with their dad, even when he was knee-deep in the middle of football film. They'd sneak out to the garage, and, much like their mother did in 1934 when all the two could do was tack a white sheet to the wall, they'd watch film and listen to their father's explanations. He would patiently describe off-tackle plays to Terry, and Tom would walk in on a Saturday and go through an entire game with Sid as he cut and spliced the film.

The entire family knew football. It's mostly what Gillman thought about, and since his wife and kids all took turns in the film room with him, they were some of the most knowledgeable fans in the stadium when one of Gillman's teams played. They were also some of the rowdiest.

The family would walk through Tunnel 7 in the old L.A. Memorial Coliseum configuration, and from there, they'd find their seats on the 50-yard line, 25 rows up. The people around them—hell, the people halfway around the stadium—knew exactly where they were.

"Esther is the worst person in the world to sit next to at a football game," Gillman said. "She's on her feet, yelling and jumping around, and the people next to her take an awful beating. They become pretty angry, but then they find out she's the coach's wife, then they feel sorry for her."

"The people who sat in front of the Gillman kids," Bobbe said, "would turn around to my mother and ask, 'What do you feed your kids? Raw meat?'"

Today, Tom says he was close to his mother—maybe more than the other kids because he was the youngest and because he was her only son—but he actually might have been around his father more than his sisters. In Cincinnati, Tom would stay in the Bearcats' dressing room after the game until the last reporter had departed from Gillman's office. But because Tom also had an innate ability to earn the trust of Gillman's players, he actually spent more time with them than with Gillman.

"I was probably the only white boy in the world who knew about these high-low poker games and Jackie Wilson songs," Tom said. "These were my best buddies."

When Gillman took over in L.A., Tom backed off. He knew there was a place for him, and it wasn't to get close to anybody. But sometimes he got to travel with Gillman's squads. Once in the early 1960s, when the Chargers were in Arkansas for a preseason game, Tom went out drinking and carousing the night before the team was scheduled to leave. Hung over and late, the Chargers had to hold the plane on the tarmac until Tom arrived. His father was steamed.

"The look he gave me said it all," Tom said, many years later chuckling at the memory. "He didn't say a word. He didn't have to."

—⁓—

Two years into his Rams tenure, Gillman was completely bamboozled. The team had gone 4-8 in 1956, and he wasn't sure what to make of it. He knew at that point that the bright California sun he had dreamed hadn't prevented a thunderstorm from drenching his coaching career. He admitted that this was the toughest job he had ever encountered and that he was befuddled.

"I've been mixed up all my life for 45 years," Gillman said. "But never like this."

After breaking even with a 6-6 record in 1957, which pleased the owners enough to grant him a four-year contract extension, the Rams roared back with an 8-4 mark in 1958. But by 1959, it wasn't only that the wheels were coming off. The engine was beginning to smoke, and the chassis was beginning to crack.

For the first time in his career, for the first time in his football life, Gillman wasn't successful. Before the 1956 season, the last time the Rams organization recorded a losing record was in 1944. The franchise had been through five coaches who, for one reason or another, had left their post or been fired. None of them had lost more games than they'd won. But in 1959, L.A. was en route to a 2-10 season. It was a colossal failure, and for Gillman to be associated with that idea was unprecedented.

Gillman, nearly four decades later, couldn't believe how naive he'd been before accepting the Rams job.

"Can you imagine going from Cincinnati to Los Angeles?" Gillman said. "If somebody had said after the first few months that I could forget it and go back to Cincinnati, I'd have been tempted."

After the 1956 season was mercifully finished, Esther had seen a stronger version of her husband emerge. That year, Gillman had talked to his wife about football more than ever before, and Esther marveled at her husband's ability to take the punches landed by the fans and by the Van Brocklin debacle and maintain a pleasant home life. Esther, the eternal optimist, probably had something to do with keeping his spirits up during those sleepless nights when Gillman tossed and turned, the fast-forwarding and rewinding of his game films unable to soothe his mind to sleep.

"Maybe the law of averages caught up with us," Esther told a reporter after the 1956 season. "Losing is something new. It's not pleasant."

With that statement, Esther rose from her seat and went to her bay window to look at the gorgeous mountain vista view below. "Every morning we wake up to the sound of bulldozers carving new lots out of mountains," Esther said. "It's sounds of progress. I say to Sid, 'Everything is all right as long as those bulldozers keep moving.'"

And if that message didn't work, Gillman could always retreat into his love of jazz music. As one astute writer put it, "To Sid, jazz is the elixir, the cure-all, the youth machine, even in defeat a precious ennobling balm to the spirit."

After a tough loss in New York, Esther and Sid could seek out Dizzy Gillespie playing his trumpet at a Manhattan jazz club, and by the time Gillespie's cheeks began to puff outward, Gillman could smile again. He could drop the needle of his turntable onto a record by his high school idol Art Tatum, the nearly blind piano virtuoso, and listen to him improvise like he was Johnny Unitas, Bart Starr, and Van Brocklin rolled into one specimen. Or Gillman could sneak out with Esther after curfew to listen to Louis Armstrong at a local club and then bask in the afterglow when Armstrong, knowing how much the coach liked jazz, came off the stage and threw his arms around Gillman.

But those musicians couldn't help on the field or in the film room. They couldn't soothe the wounds left by the fans who carried signs into the stadium that read "Put the lid on Sid." It couldn't take the edge off his frustration with his team and his bosses.

"The Rams were owned by five guys. Dan Reeves was the principal owner, but they did a lot by committee," Tom Gillman said. "I think my dad was frustrated in having to placate five individuals, four of whom didn't know their rear end from a hole in the ground about football. Another frustration was having a general manager, and a lot of the decision making was in somebody's else's hands. He and [Pete] Rozelle had a terrific relationship, but there were all these sources of conflict."

And as the losses piled up like the dirt around new construction, it was clear Gillman's job prospects were in deep trouble. For Gillman, construction was about to end. The sounds of progress were about to be halted. The bulldozers were about to stop moving. They were, in fact, about to slide completely off the cliff.

—⁂—

To hear his kids tell it, Gillman wanted to trade for Cardinals standout running back Ollie Matson soon after he arrived in L.A. The owners weren't interested, not at the price the Cardinals wanted for a man who would become a six-time Pro Bowler and an eventual Hall of Famer. Only two years later, though, the opposite was true. In 1959, Rams general manager Pete Rozelle wanted Matson on his team, and Gillman, knowing Matson would turn 30 years old after the 1959 season, wasn't interested. Especially at the price the Cardinals still wanted.

Gillman was overruled, and in February 1959, the Rams sent the Cardinals nine players for Matson's services. At one point in his career, Matson probably would have been worth it. He was a 6-foot-2, 220-pound speedster who had won a gold medal in the 1952 Olympics in the 1,600-meter relay and had struck bronze in the 400. When he turned pro, he was considered the most versatile running back in the league. But in his 14 seasons, he played on only two winning teams, and that certainly did not include the 1959 Rams.

Instead, that L.A. squad was decimated of talent by its pursuit of Matson. Nine players for a 29-year-old Matson? That was insanity, and ultimately, it cost Gillman dearly. The team also was hit hard by injuries, and after losing to the Lions, despite the fact the Rams were a two-touchdown favorite entering the game, Gillman sat in his office dejected and confused. Quarterback Billy Wade, on his way to the shower, stuck his head inside and said, "Sorry, Coach. My fault." Gillman told him to forget it, but slowly, Gillman's optimism was going down the drain.

That 17–7 loss to Detroit was important for another reason. That's when Rams ownership began to envision a future without Gillman in charge of the team. Two games later, following an eight-point loss to the 49ers, Rams assistants Joe Madro and Jack Faulkner told Bob Kelley of the *Long Beach Press-Telegram* that all hope had been lost by the current staff that they would have jobs after the season. Faulkner, in fact, asked Kelley for job suggestions. But the Rams weren't set to fire Gillman quite yet, in part because they wanted to give him a chance to miraculously save the season.

On the Friday before the second Lions game of the year, the Rams' plane took off from the runway, and somewhere over Denver, the No. 3 engine went out. As gasoline poured from the plane, Esther leaned over to a reporter and whispered, "This is a good omen. We've had all the bad luck we can have now. Things must get better." Though the plane delivered the team to Detroit in one piece, which was largely considered a positive sign, life on the ground did not get better. It only got worse.

In a press conference five days before the Baltimore Colts game, reporters asked Gillman about his job status. He told them to ask the owners. Five days later, though, Gillman had news to tell. A few minutes before the Colts game, Gillman gathered his team and told them he would not return for the 1960 season. Not because he had resigned. He was adamant about that while talking to the press later. He did not quit. He had been fired.

The media was informed that Gillman was finished before the Rams-Colts game began. After making his own statement to the media, Gillman went to the back of the press box and sat down. Alone and defeated for the first time in his life, Gillman, though he shared in much of the blame for L.A's downfall, had been the victim of a terrible trade, feuding owners, and a team that had begun to turn its back on him.

Former Rams halfback Tom Harmon had called the 1959 team "gutless." And after the Colts scored three touchdowns in the final 15 minutes of the Rams' season to earn the come-from-behind win, Baltimore quarterback Johnny Unitas proclaimed, "There isn't anything wrong with the Rams except they lack guts."

The strange thing was that not many people really seemed to believe the blame lay at Gillman's feet. Yes, the team had gotten away from him—the whispers of Van Brocklin hadn't been completely erased by his old friends who remained on the team—and yes, his overall record of 28-31-1 was less than sterling, but the Rams' ownership continued its dysfunction. The trade of Ollie Matson was a disaster (he was quite good in 1959, but he was largely irrelevant in his final three years with the club), and the Rams organization was in such disarray that they wouldn't return to the playoffs for another eight years, three coaches later.

"It was one of the most unhappy decisions that I personally ever had to make," Reeves said the last day of Gillman's tenure. "I have made mistakes this year, and they have been rather selfish mistakes. Some of the players made mistakes—some of them on the selfish side. But I don't think any of Sid's mistakes were selfish."

It didn't matter. For the first time in his career as a head coach, Gillman had been fired. He had failed in his quest. He was out of a job, and maybe out of coaching for good.

—⚇—

When the Rams fired Gillman in December 1959, he thought about taking his talents into another discipline. Maybe he'd leave behind coaching—and dealing with meddling owners who didn't know football—and

move on to a profession where he wouldn't be hamstrung by factors beyond his control.

Maybe show business was the way to go, especially when he was offered a part in the TV show *The Rifleman*, which featured Chuck Connors
and ran for 168 episodes. He played a character named Ben Tooker, and
yes, Gillman wore a bow tie with the rest of his Western garb.

"I can't ride. I can't shoot. I can't act, and I'm not very pretty," Gillman quipped. "The script-writer really faces a problem when it comes to
figuring out my role."

But when he wasn't on the studio lot filming, the phone in his house
kept ringing and ringing. The degree of loyalty and the amount of heartwarming wishes that came gushing from the other end of the phone line
from friends and colleagues stunned the Gillmans. If football is a heartless
game where winning is all that matters—and to Gillman, that's exactly
what it was—there's also a close-knit brotherhood that embraces the coach
or players who have fallen on hard times. It helped Gillman's mind-set and
the ability for others to hire him that he wasn't, in large part, blamed for
the Rams mess. Esther especially was touched by the outpouring of love
and support the family received as it headed into an unprecedented, unemployed reality.

"It was a very trying time for him," Gillman's son-in-law, Bill Korbin, said. "He was unemployed, and when they came to him with the offer
to coach the new team, he was on the fence. He was reluctant. He didn't
know whether to take it or not, because he didn't know where it would
take him. It was an unknown quantity."

Gillman's nature was not to gamble. Not with his money and not
with his investments.

Fortunately for Gillman, Lamar Hunt and Bud Adams *were* men
who gambled and were men who came from money—money that dripped
heavy with oil. Hunt's father, H.L. Hunt, was the founder of Hunt Oil,
and at one point in his life, the poker player-*cum*-oil baron was one of
the richest men in America. Adams's dad, K.S. "Boots" Adams, built his
fortune by starting as a warehouse clerk in Phillips Petroleum before even-

tually, at the age of 38, becoming the president of Phillips 66, which he then turned into a $1.8 billion empire.

Lamar Hunt and Bud Adams, aside from rich fathers and fat bank accounts, had something else in common. They each wanted to own an NFL team, and when that venture failed because the NFL had no use for them, they decided to establish their own league to compete against the establishment. They called it the American Football League, and they planned to place teams in cities including Dallas, New York, and Houston. And, luckily for Gillman, Los Angeles.

When the AFL opened for business before the 1960 season, there was little reason for the NFL to take its counterpart seriously. When the news broke that the AFL owners were starting their league, Browns coach Paul Brown—who had dominated the doomed All-America Football Conference that collapsed in 1949—stood up in his locker room and said, "A new league is starting. Don't pay any attention to it. It's not going to succeed. It's a bunch of sons of rich guys who don't know anything about football."

NFL coaches also were on guard against working for the new league. One of Hunt's first orders of business for the team he owned, the Dallas Texans, was to hire a head coach, and he set his sights on the New York Giants' defensive coordinator, a coach by the name of Tom Landry.

"Mr. Hunt, I'm very thrilled and honored," Landry told him. "I really appreciate it, but I'm not interested in the job."

Asked Hunt: "Why aren't you interested?"

"I don't think your league is going to make it."

That, of course, was the risk—and also perhaps the road to redemption—for Gillman. If he wanted to stay in coaching and stay off the TV studio set, the AFL offered him that chance.

The AFL was going to be a gamble, but it didn't take him long to decide it was a risk worth taking. And it was there, in the American Football League, where Gillman would have the best years of his career and help change the face of the game as we know it.

nine   SAN DIEGO

Less than a month after the Rams discharged him, Gillman sat inside the swanky Beverly Hills Hilton hotel and watched as Los Angeles Chargers owner Barron Hilton announced that Gillman had been hired to coach the new team. Almost immediately, Gillman announced he would hold a five-day tryout for anybody who wanted a shot at playing pro football. The Chargers, after all, needed players. Most of those who showed up had no business attempting to infiltrate the game. "I think every out-of-work truck driver who ever played football showed up," Gillman said.

A desperate Paul Lowe also made an appearance.

Lowe, who had a wife and four kids, had been a three-sport star at Oregon State and had tried out for the NFL's 49ers. He was an undrafted free agent running back when he signed with San Francisco before the 1959 season, meaning he had very little chance to make the team. To make matters worse, he suffered an injury during a preseason game. Though he obviously had talent and athleticism, San Francisco didn't take him seriously and cut him.

Lowe, needing to find a job to support his brood, applied to become a police officer, but instead, officers threw him in jail after their screening process revealed he had an arrest warrant due to an outstanding traffic ticket. Lowe was in the slammer for 18 hours, and while there, he kept his head down to avoid looking at anybody around him. Eventually, his mom arrived and bailed him out. Instead of becoming a man of the law, Lowe took a job in the mailroom at Carte Blanche, the credit card company started by hotel magnate Conrad Hilton and run by his son, Barron Hilton. Instead of faking out defenders, he was shucking the company's mail. His career was on life support. His prospects for pro football had been, ahem, returned to sender.

But he heard about the Chargers tryout, and team general manager Frank Leahy, remembering his talent at Oregon State, invited Lowe to participate. "When they had tryouts, everybody and their grandmother showed up looking for spots," Lowe said. "Plumbers. Carpenters. Shoe-shine boys. You name it." But the mail clerk was extra-special. Lowe survived the tryouts, earned a signing bonus of $800 on his $6,500 salary, and set about trying to make the Chargers' regular-season roster.

He didn't make much of an impact on Gillman at first. During the Chargers' first training camp, Gillman continuously confused Lowe with Luther Carr. Gillman would call Lowe by Carr's name, and Lowe would say, "No Mr. Gillman, I'm Paul." Sid would respond back: "Whatever." After six weeks of two-a-day practices, Gillman told Lowe, "If you don't do something pretty quick, you're gone." This time Gillman wasn't confusing him with anybody else.

For Lowe, that meant back to the mailroom. Out of football. Perhaps, this time, for good.

But in the first preseason game against the Titans, Lowe took the kickoff return, went right, suddenly found himself with a wide-open space and dashed the length of the field for a 105-yard touchdown. "The thing I remember after that," Lowe said, "is the referee running right beside me. That guy was fast." When he returned to the sideline, Lowe tracked down Gillman and asked, "How's that?"

It was plenty good enough for Gillman, and Lowe, during the course of his 10-year career, became one of the AFL's biggest stars, maintaining a rushing average of 4.9 yards—the best mark of any regular running back in league history.

Lowe had something in common with Gillman. Neither was immediately wanted.

Gillman, just like with the Rams five years earlier, was not the Chargers' first choice. General manager Frank Leahy, the former Notre Dame coach who won five national titles for the Fighting Irish, hired his former assistant Bob McBride to coach the team, but 24 hours later, McBride changed his mind. Hilton talked to local sportswriters, and they recommended Gillman as a potentially good hire.

The Chargers were Gillman's second choice as well. Tex Schramm, when he was the general manager for the Rams, had been the beneficiary of Dan Reeves's decision to hire Gillman in 1955, but he left L.A. and went to a job as the assistant director of sports at CBS. In 1959, Schramm, itching to return to pro football, took a job for the NFL expansion Dallas Cowboys.

When he got to Dallas, Schramm called Tom Landry, the Giants defensive coordinator who had already turned down the AFL Dallas Texans job. Landry couldn't resist an NFL head coaching job. He said yes to the job offer. Schramm's second choice after Landry, though, was a certain unemployed NFL head coach he knew from Los Angeles.

"If he would not have hired Landry or if Landry would have not taken the job, then Sid Gillman would have been the head coach of the team," longtime Cowboys personnel man Gil Brandt said.

Like Gillman's inability to wrestle the Ohio State job away from Woody Hayes, one has to wonder what Gillman's career track—and his life track—would have looked like if *he* had been the one to build the Cowboys into America's Team. Maybe he wouldn't have fallen through the cracks of history. Maybe a dozen books would have been written about him by now. Much like Landry and his fedora, maybe Gillman and his bow tie would have been an iconic NFL image. The mind boggles. So close. So very, very close.

"Isn't that," said Lyle Gillman, his oldest daughter, "such a bitch?"

Instead, Gillman stayed in L.A., and Hilton met with him to gauge his interest in the Chargers job. Soon after, Gillman ascertained that Hilton didn't know a thing about football. "That," Gillman said, "is the type of owner you want to have." It meant the two could work up an agreement. Gillman wouldn't tell Hilton how to run the hotel business. Hilton would leave Gillman alone when it came to determining the best way to run a football organization.

While Gillman began to help build a brand-new team from the ground up, he soon received a major promotion. No longer would he be at the mercy of a general manager who wanted to trade half his team for a running back about to turn 30. When Frank Leahy resigned in July 1960 because of health issues, Gillman took over his job and his $50,000-a-year salary. Gillman would receive help from other team executives who could handle the business deals, ticket sales, and travel issues, and Gillman finally could have what he wanted—nearly full autonomy over the personnel direction of the team.

The first thing he needed? Tons of personnel. That's why he tried out 208 potential players (though he signed only eight). That's why the taxi squad, made up of practice players who weren't eligible for games, put together by Gillman was just about the biggest ever assembled. If Hilton was going to pay for it—and the taxi squad was so important that year that the Chargers paid seven of those players full-time salaries—Gillman would exploit it in the name of the team. He had figured one of his biggest mistakes with the Rams was not maintaining a deep taxi squad, especially in 1959 when his team was hit hard by injuries, and he was not going to make the same mistake with the Chargers.

"We had 50 players coming, 50 going, and 50 in mind," Gillman said years later. "Our recruiting system was like a Montgomery Ward's catalog. We went everywhere."

In fact, there was an old joke personnel man Don Klosterman used to tell explaining that when tribal warfare broke out in Africa, only three civilians remained in Katanga Province. Two were missionaries. The other was a Chargers scout.

The Chargers did not have to go far to find one of the most important players who lasted the entire life span of the AFL. Ron Mix was an All-American offensive tackle at Southern California, and after he failed to sign with the NFL's Colts, he accepted the Chargers' offer and almost immediately became an AFL standout.

Today, Mix spends his days in a nondescript building in a nondescript office park in San Diego's Mission Valley. Just enter through the glass doors, step to the left, open another door, and walk inside Mix's law office. It's cool and casual. The pretty secretary is wearing jeans and flip-flops, and when Mix greets a visitor, he's sporting khakis and a button-down. Mix, when he talks, doesn't tell you what you want to hear. He tells you what he thinks, and if he needs to peek at his e-mail, he'll stop the interview for a minute to refresh his inbox. He's checking to see if an opposing attorney will accept his offer to settle a case before it goes to trial, and when he sees the good news, Mix mutters, "How cool is that?"

Pretty cool for the Hall of Famer who went to law school, learned a few things, sparred with Gillman over salary a few times, and then opened his own law firm when he was finished with football. But, growing up in Los Angeles, he watched from afar as Gillman took over the Rams, and he remembers Gillman fondly today. He recognizes Gillman's innovations and the professional way he ran the organization when hardly anybody else with the Chargers and the league seemed to know much else.

"It was up to Sid to set the tone, and he did," Mix said. "Whenever he was around, the intensity of everything picked up dramatically. We could be in an offensive line meeting with our line coach Joe Madro, and Joe, fortunately for all of us, was a funny, interesting guy. Sid would come into the room, and boom, a new atmosphere would suddenly take over. He was very well respected by all of us. He had a great work ethic, and it was contagious. He had that intensity about him. It projected that this is not a game, but that this is a serious business."

Mix and his teammates, though, also realized this. If you did your job well, Gillman could be your best friend. Unlike, say, Miami coach Don Shula, who traded offensive guard Carl Mauck to the Chargers before the 1970 season.

"If you fucked up, Sid was on your ass," Mauck said. "He didn't put up with any shit. Let's put it this way: if you left him alone and played OK, he was fine. If you couldn't, he was on your ass. Shula was on *everybody's* ass."

Mix, though, could respect that demeanor since he played well enough to keep his ass Gillman-free most of the time.

Yet, while growing up and while starring at USC, Mix had no great desire to play football. There wasn't much money in the pro game, and it was far behind baseball in capturing America's attention. Until he was drafted by the Colts and the Chargers, he never even thought about playing football for money. He was more interested in the law.

Mix is an intellectual, but when it came to football, he didn't have the slightest interest in figuring out what Gillman was doing with the Chargers' offense. What Mix cared about was using his speed and size in open space, which allowed him to escort a running back down the field by knocking off the linebackers and defensive backs in his teammate's path.

But he wasn't quick enough to escape the occasional Gillman barb. In 1963, Mix walked across a freshly asphalted parking lot without shoes or socks, and quite obviously, burned the bottom of his feet. Said an exasperated Gillman: "You are the only stupid Jewish lawyer in the world."

What Mix *could* understand, though, is that, after the 1960 season when the Chargers went 10-4 and won the AFL West Division before losing in the league's title game, the organization couldn't afford to remain in Los Angeles. In order to survive, the Chargers had to make a move to the south.

—◊◊◊—

Jack Murphy was a man who wanted an answer. He wanted something better for his city. He wanted Barron Hilton to be the man who provided that answer and to be the man who would provide San Diego one of its most important assets. When it appeared that the Chargers would fail out of L.A., Murphy, the sports editor of the *San Diego Union* and one of the most influential men in the city, drove north with *San Diego Evening Tribune* sports editor Gene Gregston to convince Hilton to abandon L.A. for their fair city.

Murphy was just the man for the job. As one of his staff writers penned many years later, "Murphy had a way with dogs, women readers and communities. He had the ability, possessed by few in his line of work, to shape an area's thinking." Murphy did all the talking that day. He told Hilton what the owner already knew. The Chargers couldn't compete with the NFL's Rams in L.A. Hilton needed to forge his own path in a new city. Hilton needed San Diego.

Hilton, by then, knew that returning to L.A. would be difficult, if not impossible. The final realization might have hit home in mid-November 1960 when the Chargers played host to the Oilers. It was a meeting between the AFL's East and West Division leaders, and the Chargers were riding a three-game winning streak. Many observers believed the Chargers could draw 30,000 fans into the immense L.A. Memorial Coliseum that sat as many as 100,000 for Rams games. Only 21,805 showed up.

It led Hilton to begin thinking seriously about San Diego. Those relocation feelings were exacerbated when L.A. beat Denver for the division title in front of a tiny crowd of less than 10,000. The next day, the Rams, in the middle of a 4-7-1 campaign, drew 77,000 spectators vs. the 49ers. Despite the Chargers' success, Hilton knew the public wasn't buying. A week later, Hilton said his plans were to continue operating in L.A., but he also said he'd be willing to listen to offers from a new city. Already, the Chargers' business manager and PR director had made a trip to San Diego to talk to civic leaders about the possibilities of moving, and the courtship from San Diego officials had already begun in earnest.

A few days after the Chargers lost to the Oilers in the AFL championship game, Hilton visited San Diego, and the enthusiasm displayed by the city—more than 1,000 residents had pledged to buy season tickets and two TV stations had offered to help with promotions—amazed him. He worried about the lackluster Balboa Stadium and he fretted about game parking, but Hilton also was excited about the possibilities San Diego offered. Namely, enthusiasm from a city that did not feature major-league professional sports. L.A. didn't care about the Chargers, but San Diego would roll out the red carpet with open arms.

"It was similar with the L.A. Rams and L.A. Chargers to the Dallas Texans and the Dallas Cowboys," said longtime football executive Carl Peterson, who grew up in Southern California and was an enormous Rams fan. "The Rams were so well-established . . . Lord, they drew some people. They outdrew anybody. When they played those 49ers games, it was 102,000 people. It was pretty hard to break into that with professional football. Barron Hilton recognized that after that first year."

Hilton's bank account recognized the problem as well. He lost close to a million dollars in 1960. Hilton made the call. The team would pack up and go. San Diego was getting a major professional sports team, thanks in large part to Murphy. San Diego was getting the Chargers.

—⁊⁊⁊—

In front of the house in Sherman Oaks, overlooking the San Fernando Valley, a sad sign shimmied in the breeze. "For Sale," it read. To the point, a finality. The Gillmans' time in L.A. had come to a close, and not because of their choosing. But they looked forward to a new start. Esther had once said that as long as the bulldozers kept moving, everything would be OK. For the Gillmans, those bulldozers had begun lifting dirt again.

The Gillmans were sad to leave L.A., their home for the past six years, but San Diego would be a fresh canvas for them. The city committed to spending $500,000 to enlarge Balboa Stadium—and eventually would approve creation of a $27 million stadium that opened in 1967—and 15,000 residents requested season tickets.

Gillman's first trip to Balboa to inspect his team's new home, though, left him unimpressed. The stadium had been built in 1914 for the Panama-California Exposition, and it was used mostly for high school games. As Gillman used to say, if someone spilled a Coke in the top row, it would run all the way to the bottom of the stands. And the restrooms did not feature enclosed toilets—just a row of 20 of them, side by side. When Gillman bent down on the field to pick up a hunk of turf, it dissolved and trickled through his fingers.

"He thought it was a piece of shit, basically," sportswriter Jerry Magee said. "He was picking up turf, and it was crumbling in his fingers. Literally, crumbling. When he discovered that, he knew what the transition was going to be like."

It wasn't as easy as San Diego and its new tenants thought it might be. Games weren't selling out, and Gillman had to participate in silly promotions. He lived in La Mesa, northeast of downtown, and he could look out his window and see a hill with a large cross on it. Sid pointed to it and told a reporter, "See that? It's my inspiration. If we don't win and make money, I'm gonna be the next Jew nailed up there."

Gillman, though, would find temporary salvation in another top-notch All-Pro quarterback. A quarterback Gillman trusted to call his own plays in the huddle. A quarterback whose time with Gillman was all too short.

—◊—

During the 10-year history of the AFL, no quarterback attempted more passes, completed more passes, or compiled more passing yards than Jack Kemp. He was not the top quarterback around, but that wasn't the core component inside Kemp's body anyway. He was a thinker, a do-good-er, a man who spent less time thinking about football and more about how he could make the world a better place. Most of all, when his teammates looked at Kemp they saw a special glow radiating from his inner soul.

"It's hard to describe," Mix said. "But whatever it is, Jack's got it."

Kemp wasn't a jock. Not in the stereotypical sense. He was a cerebral athlete, a philosophical signal-caller, a highbrow quarterback. The kind of man who'd learn a new word every day and then use it in a sentence. "One time he told me, 'You know, Paul, I really like your perspicacity,'" said 11-year veteran Paul Maguire, who played with Kemp in L.A., San Diego, and Buffalo. "I didn't know whether to punch him or thank him." (Maguire should have thanked him. Perspicacity means "to show keen understanding.")

Kemp talked politics so much that teammates began referring to him as The Senator, and the first time Chargers quarterback John Hadl walked into the room he shared with Kemp, he found him lying in bed reading a book about Barry Goldwater. When Bills coach Lou Saban happened by in the locker room, he'd order Kemp to get his mind off politics and get it on the playbook. His mind wasn't just politics, though. Kemp also thought hard about ways to improve life for those less fortunate.

"He really believed in a lot of social issues," said nine-year veteran Booker Edgerson. "He was very concerned about society and where it was going. I always admired him for that."

He was concerned about equality between blacks and whites, and at one team Halloween party, he wore a T-shirt that read, "Burn, Baby, Burn. Stokely Carmichael for President." Stokely Carmichael being a 1960s civil rights activist who coined the term "Black Power." Kemp referred to himself as a bleeding-heart conservative, and quite a few people call him the most admirable man they've ever met.

After retiring from football, Kemp represented western New York in Congress for nearly two decades and eventually served as Bob Dole's vice-presidential running mate in the 1996 presidential election. Gillman loved Kemp and often referred to him as a future president of the United States. Kemp ran as a Republican, but if he were atop the Presidential ticket in 1996 running against Bill Clinton, Gillman—a lifelong Truman Democrat—probably would have voted for his quarterback. As it was, Gillman did *not* vote for Dole ("Oh, hell no," Lyle Gillman said. "No, no, no, no."), but after Dole selected Kemp for his presidential ticket, Gillman and Esther were invited to sit in Kemp's box seat as he gave his acceptance speech at the Republican National Convention. Lyle and Bobbe thought it was an honor, but Terry and Tom refused to let their father go. So, Gillman didn't. And Kemp never got to be vice-president.

Yet, Gillman did give him a major opportunity in 1960.

Kemp started his career in Pittsburgh in 1957 but only got limited playing time. Two years later, knowing he needed extra seasoning, the New York Giants added him to their roster and sent him to the Canadian Football League with the understanding that the Giants would bring him back in 1960 to be their starting quarterback. But Kemp didn't impress the Calgary coaches, who thought he threw the ball too hard, and after playing in only two of the team's first 14 games, he demanded his release.

He soon found himself in the same position as Paul Lowe: trying out with the truck drivers and short-order cooks and hoping to land a spot on the newly formed Chargers roster so he could rejuvenate his career. Gillman, it turned out, didn't mind how hard Kemp threw, and if the Chargers' receivers couldn't handle the force of his passes, Gillman made it clear he would find somebody who could. Gillman liked Kemp so much that he named him the starter in L.A. in 1960 and then let him call 85 percent of the team's plays. Although Kemp's shoulder was chronically dislocated, his arm strength was so superior that he could throw the ball 90 yards with his three-quarter motion (if he threw it overhand, his shoulder would pop out of the socket).

While Gillman obviously loved Kemp as a man and a player, the truth is Kemp slipped in 1961. Under his leadership, the team went 12-2, but Kemp's completion percentage dropped from 52 to 45, his passing yards fell from 3,018 to 2,606, and his touchdown total plunged from 20 to 15. Defense was the team's strength that season, but just like in 1960, the Chargers lost to the Houston Oilers in the AFL title game. Kemp threw four interceptions in the 1961 finale, leaving San Diego a game short of the ultimate goal and Kemp short a championship ring.

He didn't look much better at the beginning of 1962, completing an anemic 28.9 percent of his passes before breaking the middle finger of his throwing hand against an opposing player's helmet in Week 2. Kemp tried to play through the injury, but every time the center snapped the ball against Kemp's hand, excruciating pain ran through his finger. He'd grimace and either hand the ball off or pass for an incompletion, and while in the huddle to call the next play, he'd jerk his finger back in place. But Gillman knew. In Kemp's condition, with his finger flopping back and forth, he was a detriment to the team. With his team splitting the first two games and with running back Paul Lowe out for the season with a broken forearm, Gillman made one of the worst decisions in his coaching career. It might have been a mistake, or Gillman might have been hoping he didn't get caught. But either way, Kemp would haunt Gillman for the rest of the quarterback's playing career.

In those days, the injured reserve list didn't exist. This meant that if a team's player was lost for the season with an injury, his team had to keep him on the roster. Otherwise, that squad would have to place him on the injured-deferred list, leaving him open for any other team in the league to sign him. The caveat to that was that a team could release a player before the weekend and then withdraw him from the waiver wire immediately after the game, but that method could be used only twice in a season. The caveat to that caveat was that in order for Gillman's team to recall Kemp and keep him safe after putting him on waivers, the Chargers couldn't have a full active roster for Week 3 of the season. Gillman forgot about that last part.

It didn't slip past the eyes of Jack Horrigan, who had covered the Bills for the *Buffalo Evening News* and who had been hired as the AFL's PR director. Horrigan told Bills coach Lou Saban that Kemp was available for the minuscule waiver fee. In other words, Buffalo could secure the services of Kemp for a measly $100, and there wasn't a thing Gillman could do about it. Two other teams claimed Kemp as well, but depending on whom you believe, the Bills won him in a coin toss or the league awarded Kemp to Buffalo because the organization needed a quarterback and the AFL wanted more parity in the standings. A dazed Kemp said he wouldn't leave San Diego, but Bills officials threatened to put him on the reserve list and cut off his $1,200 weekly salary. Kemp packed and went, made five more Pro Bowls and won two AFL championships with his new team, beating the Chargers in both title games.

It was only years later that Gillman could laugh at himself for his colossal error.

"You're looking at the only guy who gave away a future President for $100," Gillman said, before looking at the bright side. "But he might someday make me Ambassador to Israel."

—⁓—

The Chargers had been the light of the league in the first two years of the AFL's existence. Gillman, whose squad was fined $4,000 before the 1960 season even *began* because he had started training camp before the July 1 start date, had taught the other franchises how to play pro football. The Oilers were better than the Chargers in the 1960 and 1961 championship games, and after losing Kemp in 1962, San Diego went into a free fall, losing six straight and finishing the season an embarrassing 4-10.

Gillman, though, had set the tone for what he expected from his players and from his owner, and the rest of the league paid attention and tried to follow suit. He had begun to install the kind of offense he had spent his career formulating, figuring that if the field was 100 yards long and 52⅔ yards wide, he needed to find a way to use every inch of it. In effect, he began spreading out the opponent's defense to its breaking point, and because of that new idea, the team believed it was going to win, because as star receiver Lance Alworth said, "We knew we were better coached."

Gillman demanded punctuality of everybody, which is why Ron Mix found himself with his face in the dirt one night during training camp after he and Jacque MacKinnon had sneaked out of the University of San Diego dorm room only to return at 2 a.m. and discover that Gillman was still awake watching film. Just to get in their shared apartment, they had to creep past Gillman's window without being spotted. Both immediately got into the crawling position.

Just before they reached Gillman's window, Mix put his hand on MacKinnon's shoulder and said, "Wait a minute. Don't you feel silly? Here we are, two grown men, college graduates, and we're crawling on our stomachs in the middle of the night so our coach won't see us."

Said MacKinnon: "Yeah, I do feel stupid."

"I was thinking we might stand up and walk like men. What are you going to do about it?"

Responded MacKinnon: "I'm going to keep my head down until we get past Sid's window."

That's the respect Gillman earned, in part because he never stopped working. In the off-season, Gillman would be upstairs late at night sitting in his underwear at the team's Lafayette Hotel headquarters, smoking a pipe and studying film. If he got hungry and went downstairs to the lobby to order a midnight steak, it wasn't uncommon for him to forget that he was wearing only an undershirt and boxer shorts. Gillman's mind, even during the off-season, was on one track, and oftentimes, that track didn't include the idea that it was necessary to wear pants in public.

An obsessive coach, however, didn't necessarily equate to a football team that turned a profit. This was not unusual in the early years of the AFL, but it didn't go unnoticed by Conrad Hilton, who looked at his son one day and said, "I have been looking at the financial results of Carte Blanche and the Chargers. I noticed both of these lost a million dollars. What kind of record are you trying to set?"

Even with the financial losses, Gillman was developing the organization's character. The hard work, he figured, would pay off sometime. It had to. But, like the 1956 and 1959 seasons in L.A., Gillman had to make a major adjustment after the disastrous 1962 season in San Diego. And he needed outside help to do it.

—␣␣—

It was hotter than hell in this godforsaken place. A place that looked like the epicenter of a recently commenced nuclear holocaust, a place where even the weeds died under a white-hot sun. It was at this place where Sid Gillman set up training camp for 1963, in Boulevard, California, about 65 miles east of San Diego and just north of the Mexican border. The Chargers would practice in 90-plus-degree heat on this barren land in the Colorado Desert, where sawdust covered more of the football field than grass, where you could wind up nose to nose with a snake if you were tackled in the wrong spot. The site, appropriately enough, was called Rough Acres, and that was actually a misnomer. It was much worse than that. A more appropriate name would have been "Abandon All Hope Ye Who Enter Here Acres."

On July 18, the day before practice began, Gillman called a team meeting. "Gentlemen," he said, stating what had already become obvious, "a camp is not a country club." That was especially true in 1963, and it was a corrective measure taken because of the previous training camp at the University of San Diego. In 1962, the team trained on the campus overlooking San Diego Bay that featured pristine practice fields in mild temperatures. Gillman thought he ran a lackadaisical training camp, and as a result, the team won four of 14 games and lost too many players to injury. In 1963, he wanted to toughen up the Chargers by having them practice in hell.

Gillman, though, needed more than that. Practicing in unbearable temperatures prescribed by Dante in prisonlike settings wasn't all he wanted to change. So, during that initial team meeting, he laid out the squad's future plans. We must get in top physical condition, Gillman said, and that's why the team would begin weight training and isometrics. In a couple of days, he continued, a man named Alvin Roy would arrive in camp, and he would explain the future strength and conditioning program.

"If you have an appointment, keep it," Gillman told his team. "It'll cost you one dollar a minute if you are late. And if we have reason to believe that you were late intentionally, the fine goes up to $10 a minute. Any excuses better be good ones."

Four days later, a special meeting was held after lunch, and Gillman introduced Roy to the squad. Roy, Gillman said, was the future of pro football preparation. Eventually, every team would hire a strength coach, but for now, there was only one team who employed one and that was the Chargers. Roy got to work immediately, introducing the team to the makeshift weight room he had set up next to the locker room. By the time Roy was finished with his demonstration, it was 2 p.m., only a half-hour before the team had to report to the locker room to begin practice.

"As if our two practices a day isn't enough," said Paul Maguire, who sat around a table with his teammates and drank iced tea before they suited up for the afternoon workout. "As if two meetings a day isn't enough, now this."

"The weights are going to be good for us, Paul," Ron Mix said. "During my senior year at USC, 25 of us lifted, and of that group only one person was injured that year, and he only sprained his ankle."

"Well," Maguire retorted, "when I was at The Citadel, 25 of us drank, and my group had 30 percent fewer cavities."

Roy, a former trainer for the U.S. team in the 1952 Olympics who had learned a few secrets from what he termed the "Ruskies," placed the Chargers on a weight-lifting regimen. But that wasn't the only practice he added. In addition to working out twice a day, Roy told the squad that it needed more protein. He held up a bottle of pink pills.

"This stuff is called Dianabol and it's going to help assimilate protein and you'll be taking it every day,'" Roy said.

"And, sure enough," Mix said, "it showed up on our training tables in cereal bowls."

In those days, there was no such word as steroids. Well, it wasn't a word the layman knew anything about anyway. Dianabol was a steroid, a chemically produced form of testosterone that promoted healing and strength in those who took it. It was legal in those days, simply because it wasn't illegal. It wasn't an issue, because nobody really knew what it was. (Unfortunately for those current-day body-builders who would be so inclined, it's banned in the U.S., though readily available on the black market.) And the Chargers took it, in 5-milligram increments three times a day for at least the first four weeks of training camp. If you didn't take the pill, the team lifted $50 from your paycheck. For those who took it—and some estimated that more than 90 percent of the team did exactly that—they noticed the improvement almost immediately.

At the time, the steroid had only been on the market for five years. Those who took it knew the benefits, but the consequences and side effects were still only being discovered. Yet, the effects were unquestionable. Players saw the immediate benefits. They were most definitely stronger.

But there were still questions that hadn't been answered. About a month into camp, tight end Dave Kocourek visited his personal doctor for help in treating an injury, and when the doctor asked him what medications he was taking, Kocourek made mention of the Dianabol. The doctor was shocked. "They're giving you this stuff?" the doctor asked. "Have you seen the literature that accompanies these pills?" Kocourek had not.

"I still remember what it says," Mix said. "It was in big red letters. It said, 'Dangerous. Not to be taken over extended periods of time, will cause permanent bone damage, liver damage, heart damage, testicle shrinkage.'"

Kocourek went directly to Gillman and showed him his doctor's literature.

"Sid looked at [the literature] for a couple of minutes and he threw it on the ground and said, 'What do these guys know? They don't know anything about football. They're doctors,'" Mix said. "That was it."

Mix, though, wouldn't let the issue die. He and some of his teammates asked for a meeting to discuss the Dianabol, and from then on, the Chargers were not required to take the little pink pills that had been placed in the little brown cereal bowls. Though coaches still apparently encouraged players to take the pills, most of the team stopped the practice. After the 1964 season, the pills were no longer available.

Aside from a 1987 *Los Angeles Times* story that detailed Roy's methods, the story of the Chargers and the Dianabol had been largely lost to history until ESPN.com's T.J. Quinn in 2009 published an investigative piece on that 1963 squad. Considering that team, through Gillman's leadership, was professional sports' first team-wide steroid ring at a time when Dianabol wasn't illegal, Gillman's foresight was impressive. It was, no matter what we think about steroids today, tremendously innovative.

"Sid doesn't leave a stone unturned," said Chargers receiver Keith Lincoln, who also said he and quarterback John Hadl did not take the Dianabol. "Some people came into the league that were on the taxi squad for a year or two. The next year, you'd see them and they'd be 50 pounds heavier. Now how do you do that?"

Gillman first met Roy at a college football coaches' conference where Roy gave a presentation about the benefits of lifting weights, and Gillman traveled to Baton Rouge, Louisiana, to meet with Roy and see his system in person. The two ate at Cajun restaurants, and they talked about strength training and football. Gillman was hooked, because he liked the idea of weight training.

The problem with the program Gillman and Roy implemented is that it was dangerous for the Chargers' health. That leaves questions that are impossible to answer. Did Gillman know the dangers of Dianabol—which, at the time, was available through a doctor's prescription? If so, did he care? Was winning more important in this instance than doing right by his players and their future health? At this intersection of winning and right and wrong, those who knew Gillman well can have their own opinions. But nobody can know for sure.

"I give Sid the benefit of the doubt on that," Mix says today. "There were a few of us on the team—just a few—who lifted weights. We were very strong compared to the other players on our team and the players on other teams, and Sid saw the benefit of this. . . . Who knows what conversation—if any—the trainers had with Coach about it.

"Did he turn a blind eye? Probably. He's so focused on winning and coming up with any edge a team could have. Who knows? I have no idea. . . . There's no question at some point in time that Sid became aware of what it was. There's no question he did not mind if players voluntarily took them, but he stopped making it mandatory. Is it a black mark on him? I don't think so."

Bobbe Korbin, his second-oldest daughter, and Lyle Gillman—his oldest girl—defend him voraciously. As does his only son, Tom.

"I think that if Dad had been told this is harmful for the body, he never would have done it," said Bobbe, who also doesn't buy the story of her father tossing the doctor's literature on the ground and then completely ignoring it.

Said Lyle: "My husband was the doctor, and Buzzie (Malkoff) would yell at Dad and say, 'Stop going to the freaking trainers when something is wrong with you. Go to a real doctor.' He listened to those trainers for everything. He treated those three trainers, including Alvin Roy, like doctors. So, if those guys came up with a program to make them stronger and make them faster and to make them turn green, he would do it."

Astrid Clements, Roy's daughter, also defends her father.

"The U.S. weightlifting team used them. Just like high-protein supplements to make you stronger and healthier," Clements says. "I'm telling you, my father would never have hurt anyone. If there was something that would have hurt someone physically, emotionally, or psychologically, whatever, he would not have used it."

Not all were so eager to acquit Gillman of his knowledge. In his ESPN.com article, while discussing potential long-term damage to players' health, reporter T.J. Quinn quoted offensive guard Pat Shea saying, "It makes me angry. To do something like that . . . People that you trusted—Sid Gillman; Barron Hilton, the owner; the other coaches—no respect for us at all." Mix also told Quinn that Roy's major character flaw was that he wanted results, consequences be damned.

But Tom Gillman thinks that current-day criticisms of actions taken in 1963 when Dianabol was not an illegal substance are unfair, particularly since Roy died in 1979 and Sid is no longer around. Gillman did defend himself in 1973, saying, "It was commonly accepted then. Our doctor prescribed them. Anybody who says I made them take drugs is a big liar. But that's dead and gone . . . I know what I've done. I know what I am." But these days, nobody except the offspring of Gillman and Roy are expected to defend them.

"I thought they were kicking a dead man, because a dead man can't kick back," said Tom Gillman, who's also adamant that his father didn't know the harmful effects of the steroid. "I don't have to revise my memory of it. I heard some of those players; I read what they said. I just couldn't believe it. It could be that something went on that I didn't see. But I was out there off and on. I saw nobody force anything on anybody. I'm not defending my dad. I'm just saying what I saw."

Even after the coaching staff stopped requiring players to take the Dianabol, some Chargers didn't curtail their usage. "It was too attractive not to take them, because they worked," Mix said. According to the ESPN.com story, Chargers team physicians continued to write prescriptions for some players between 1965 and 1970, even though it was done quietly and under the table.

And Houston Ridge continued to use it.

Ridge, a defensive lineman who played four seasons in the AFL, broke his left hip during the 1969 season, an injury that ultimately ended his career and permanently disabled him. But because he was so upset with the way the Chargers' medical staff treated him that he filed a $1.25 million class-action lawsuit in 1970. He alleged that he had taken three amphetamines and three muscle relaxants (and of course, the steroids) before a game against the Dolphins, and after he broke his hip, he said the drugs dulled his awareness of the pain.

"I do know that Houston at San Diego State was a 210-pound linebacker, and then when he came to us, he was 275," Mix said. "I was surprised because I didn't know that (the steroids approach) was still going on."

In answering the complaint, Chargers team doctor Paul Woodward argued "that plaintiff was cognizant of any relevant risks involved in any drugs used by plaintiff."

During the Ridge trial, a lawyer, when questioning Gillman, asked, "Mr. Ridge has testified under oath that while he was on the bench after he came out of the game, and he was limping down the sidelines, that you said to Mr. Ridge: 'Can't you play a damn game without getting hurt?' Do you remember making that statement?"

"I don't remember," Gillman said.

"And he also said he heard you say, just as Miami was on the (Chargers') 20-yard line, 'Where is that damn Houston Ridge? Can he run at all?' Do you remember making that statement?"

"I don't remember."

When he was asked if it was true that he told Ridge to "Throw away those crutches and walk; you can't make this team on crutches," Gillman admitted he might have said that but he might also have been kidding.

Ridge's lawyers didn't find any of it funny and ultimately Ridge and the Chargers settled the case for $295,000 ("It's garbage," Gillman said, "and I don't like to talk about garbage."). But Mix, who has legally represented Ridge in other matters, says today that Ridge wasn't an innocent bystander.

"Oh please, Houston ran into it with his eyes wide open," Mix said. "He took them, and it was his own choice."

Whether Gillman knew the Dianabol was wrong, there's no doubt Gillman, a year after a 4-10 season, was willing to try anything to turn around his team's fortune—be it requiring his team to swallow the little pink pill or putting them through hell at the post-apocalyptic Rough Acres. And that's exactly what happened, as the Chargers swept through the AFL and destroyed the Patriots in the 1963 title game, Gillman's shining moment. But as per often, Gillman's tactics were questioned. Gillman's brilliance, once again, had collided with his moral judgment. Once again, his brilliance triumphed. But at what cost?

—⚹—

Gillman wanted to be in charge. When he wasn't the man making the final decision, that ultimately led to problems and often curtailed Gillman's employment. But when Frank Leahy resigned as Chargers general manager before the 1960 season, Gillman took his chance. The owner, Barron Hilton, stayed hands-off in the day-to-day personnel decisions, and he provided Gillman plenty of money to lubricate the team's engine. Gillman ran the squad, and he operated it the way he saw fit.

Gillman didn't care that his popularity took a large dip with the players because of his dealings as the general manager. He was convinced that it was essential for the coach and the general manager to be of the same mind, share the same blood, and be the same person. The two positions, he said, aren't separate. Instead, he was willing to accept full authority (and all of the blame) in order to hold both positions.

"He wanted that, because he wanted the power," said Tom Bass, Gillman's former assistant in San Diego. "I think it caused a lot of ill feelings between the players and him. He didn't have a lot of tact when it came to dealing with players. He let it get personal."

That would have been fine if Gillman was only the general manager and spent most of his time on the phone in his office. But Gillman wasn't. He was in the locker room, on the practice field, in a player's face offering instruction and criticism. This jerk who wouldn't give you the money you wanted? You had to see him every single day for hours at a time. And since players didn't have agents representing them, they were on their own dealing with a shrewd man who controlled the Chargers' money coffers. Some simply couldn't move past that frustration.

"Sidney is nothing but a Jekyll and Hyde and there's a place for people with split personality," Chargers tight end Jacques MacKinnon said. "He praises you on the field when he's playing fatherly coach. Then he gets you behind a closed door and turns into a monster when you want to talk salary with the general manager. He's a tyrant, despot, and an old meanie."

Sometimes, Gillman so badly outflanked his players in the general manager's office that it smashed their spirits. Once after a tough negotiation when Gillman wouldn't budge off his original offer, four-time All Pro defensive end Earl Faison rose from his chair to leave Gillman's office. Just before he reached the door, Gillman called out to him. Faison, at that moment, thought Gillman would give in to his demands. He turned back to his coach, expectations suddenly high.

Gillman, working on his pipe and with his eyes cast downward, reached for a box on his desk and said, "Take a couple of pieces of candy as you go."

"That," Faison said, "just crushed me."

While dealing with tight end Dave Kocourek, Gillman, the general manager, preached the value and importance of patience.

After his 1961 season, in which Kocourek led the team with 55 catches for 1,055 yards, he asked Gillman for a raise. Gillman said, "Dave, you've got to be in the league four or five years to get more money." A few years later, Kocourek went back and tried again. Said Gillman: "Ah, you're too old to start talking about money."

Soon after, Gillman traded him to Miami. That was a consequence of asking for too much compensation. If Gillman thought a player who was dissatisfied with his contract might become a distraction, he shipped him away, even if it ultimately hurt his team. He did it to defensive tackle Ernie Ladd, who wanted $1 million before the 1965 season. He did it to Earl Faison, who also was proving to be a distraction with his contract demands. Gillman knew he couldn't pay, so he had to watch two of his better defenders walk away.

"I was very unhappy when our team traded them," offensive tackle Ron Mix said. "That presented a gloom to the team, an actual gloom, to see them leave."

"Sid was a tough son of a bitch," said sportswriter Jerry Magee, also a Gillman admirer. "He wouldn't grant them major raises and things like that. He was a tough negotiator, and then he was asking them to play for him. That's a tough thing to do."

And even though Gillman's negotiating tactics cost him with certain players on the field, others understood the distinction between Gillman the coach and Gillman the GM.

"You're a professional, and you're doing your job," running back Keith Lincoln said. "You're not going to get a better paycheck anywhere else. What do you want to do? Quit? You're not going to quit. Some people have to bitch and complain just to be happy. There were some that would grouse, 'He acts like it's his own money.' But he had a job he was doing too. I never begrudged him that."

Said Mix: "It detracted from his success, but the truth is: we don't really know what went on. Was the contract negotiations—and the final say—really in Sid's hands, or was he just the messenger? Looking back on things, we don't really know. Our perception—and the perception Sid wanted to give—was that he was the one calling the shots. It created hard feelings. In some instances, it caused us to release players that were great players because of contract disputes. As I look back now, I don't know who was really calling the shots. Was it Sid or was it ownership? I have no idea."

But as Gillman knew, it didn't matter who the players blamed. He, just like everybody else in the organization, was at the mercy of the owners and a changing AFL landscape in which the rest of the franchises were beginning to creep up on the Chargers.

—m—

Through all the plays that are made in a game and all the games that make up a single season and all the seasons that make up a coaching tenure, it's tough to pinpoint any one moment that changes a franchise's direction. If 1964 was the season in which the Chargers organization began slightly sliding, the 1964 AFL championship was the game in which the decline might have started, and Mike Stratton's hit on Keith Lincoln might have been the moment where everything changed.

As *Sports Illustrated*'s Edwin Shrake once wrote, "If there is such a thing as the perfect back, he might be Keith Lincoln, who runs, blocks, catches passes and throws the option pass and plays with injuries that would keep lesser men in the dispensary." If that wasn't impressive enough, Lincoln was a natural halfback but played fullback in San Diego so that he and Paul Lowe could share the backfield together.

By that 1964 AFL title game, Lincoln was one of the Chargers' most important pieces, but as his teammates tried to win Gillman his second-straight championship, disaster struck. With the Chargers leading 7–0, Tobin Rote threw a screen pass to Lincoln, who had already opened the game with a 38-yard run. But as the ball floated toward him, Bills linebacker Mike Stratton was desperate to make sure Lincoln didn't catch it. Stratton succeeded, lowering his head, colliding with Lincoln's midsection, driving him into the ground and breaking one of Lincoln's ribs. Lincoln, on the turf and in agony, rolled one way. He rolled onto his back. Then he rolled the other way, trying to catch his breath and relieve the pain. He was hurt, and it turned out, he was done for the day. It was termed "The Hit Heard 'Round the World," and it was devastating to San Diego, which was shut out the rest of the day and watched as Buffalo rolled to a 20–7 victory and the league title.

On that franchise-turning play, Stratton was scared that Lincoln was going to make him look silly if he caught the screen pass. It was a play the Bills had seen plenty of times before. Gillman's play call allowed Rote to throw to a receiver on a 10-yard curl route, but if the linebacker—in this case, Stratton—dropped back to cover that receiver, Rote had Lincoln open on the screen pass near the sideline. It was usually a win-win for the offense, but on this day, the only person winning on the play was Stratton.

"I didn't want to be out there in a championship game in the middle of the field with no help trying to tackle Keith Lincoln," Stratton said. "When I got up, I figured Lincoln would get back up, we'd go back to the huddle and we'd start over again on the next play. When he didn't go back to the huddle, truthfully, I was happy. I didn't want to hurt him badly, but good gosh, he'd already wreaked havoc on us before."

As Lincoln rolled around on the turf, the Chargers looked at each other in shock. Without Lincoln, their chances for winning had been blown to bits, particularly when Lowe injured his leg and finished the game at half-strength. When the game was over, the injured Lance Alworth rose from his seat in the press box and declared he still believed the Chargers, who had gone 8-5-1 and had lost to Buffalo twice during the regular season, were the better team.

But the decline, whether anybody knew it, had been set in motion.

San Diego had another opportunity to prove it was better than Buffalo the following season in the 1965 AFL title game, but that day went even worse. Before that season began, Rote retired, leaving John Hadl as the quarterback in charge. Hadl, who had been inconsistent enough to let the middle-aged Rote keep his starting job in 1963 and for some of 1964, played well, helping the Chargers maintain the title of AFL's top offense. The defense wasn't bad either, ranking No. 1 in the league as well. Throw in the fact the Chargers whipped Buffalo 34–3 earlier in the season, and you could see the overconfidence bubbling to the surface.

Not only did the Bills offense dominate the Chargers vaunted defense, but Gillman's offense was made impotent, taking a humiliating 23–0 beating in front of the San Diego crowd. The Chargers never got in the red zone, and on the other side of the ball, Buffalo's offense didn't let San Diego's defense get near Kemp. "Look at me," Kemp said, pointing to his uniform after the game. "I'm still all white."

Never again would Gillman get that close to another AFL title as a head coach. Nor, for that matter, any kind of league championship game.

The 1963 AFL championship would have to do. At the age of 52, Gillman had reached the peak of his head-coaching career. But Gillman had much more to offer. His thoughts and ideas led to Super Bowl titles.

His coaching tree—those coaches who worked under Gillman—is one of the most impressive in history. If you include just the two generations on the tree immediately after him (those who coached for Gillman—like Chuck Noll, Al Davis, and Dick Vermeil—and those who coached for those Gillman directly influenced), Gillman was responsible for 8 Hall of Famers, 12 Super Bowl titles, 1 AFL championship, and 24 AFC/NFC conference titles.

Midway through his San Diego tenure, Gillman's coaching career had already peaked. But the impact of his innovations was just beginning.

Sid as a senior at North High School.

(*Above*) Sid reaches for a pass in a game against Michigan in 1932.
(*Below*) Sid (*2nd from left*) at Ohio State, circa 1933.

(*Above*) Sid talking to a recruit at a booster event at Miami University, 1947.
(*Below*) Sid (*3rd from right*) as an assistant coach at West Point, 1948.

(*Above*) Sid and Esther in 1952, during his time at the University of Cincinnati.
(*Below*) Sid en route to a UC game with unidentified passenger, circa 1950.

(*Above*) Sid carried off by his Los Angeles Rams players after winning
    the NFL Western Division title in 1955.
(*Below*) Sid during his successful years as head coach of the San Diego Chargers.

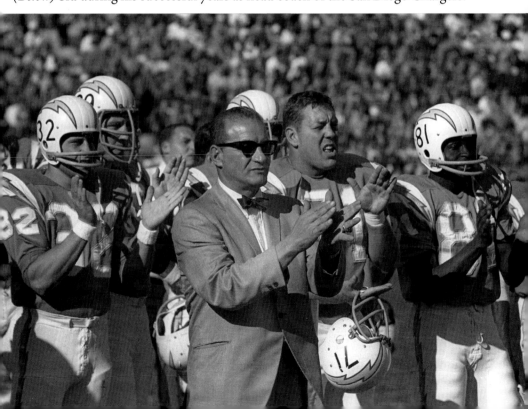

Sid coaching in San Diego.

Sid with Chargers running back Keith Lincoln before an AFL All-Star game.

(Above) Sid and Esther in 1989.

ten INNOVATIONS

When Sid Gillman reached the NFL with the Los Angeles Rams in 1955, he wasn't that much different from other professional coaches of his era. He had absorbed many of Francis Schmidt's zany passing schemes when he was at Ohio State, and while at Miami and Cincinnati, he clearly proved he was ahead of his time by using misdirection plays and stretching the field vertically and horizontally. In the conservative NFL, Gillman's offensive scheme was a bit unusual, but it wasn't as extreme as Schmidt's ideas. Whereas Schmidt visited the ether of football management and play-calling, Gillman stayed in the framework of acceptable offensive football. Years later, Gillman said, "God bless those runners because they give you the first down, give you ball control, and keep your defense off the field, but if you want to ring the cash register, you have to pass." In L.A., though, he ran the ball quite often.

When he got to the AFL in 1960, though, Gillman's mind-set shifted for a couple of reasons. First, since every AFL team was an expansion team with watered-down talent, defense wasn't as well played as in the NFL. It would take time to build up the AFL talent level, and Gillman deduced that he could exploit that deficit through passing. Second, the football used in the AFL was a Spalding J5-V, which happened to be a quarter-inch longer and slimmer than the Wilson football used by the NFL, and that made it easier to toss the ball with accuracy. Third, Gillman had outstanding offensive personnel. Quarterback Jack Kemp threw the ball superhero-like distances, running backs Keith Lincoln and Paul Lowe smoked defenses with their athleticism and speed, receiver Lance Alworth jumped higher than anybody else around him, and the Chargers' offensive linemen utilized their intelligence and quickness.

Since Gillman wanted to use every inch of the football field, he stretched the field vertically by throwing the ball deep and horizontally by placing his receivers far off the offensive line. Very few professional coaches had seen anything like it, and almost nobody could figure out how to stop it.

"He was so far ahead of his time," coaching legend Bill Walsh said, "people couldn't totally understand what he was doing."

In the 1930s, when Gillman played at Ohio State under Sam Willaman and coached at Denison with Tom Rogers, the single-wing offensive formation was in vogue throughout most of college football. It was a scheme built for power running plays to the side of the field where there were more blockers, and teams also used it for short, quick passes. From 1932 to 1939, the average yardage for the top NFL passing team was 1,438 yards, and when compared to 2001–2010, when the league leaders averaged 4,585 yards per season, it's clear how much those earlier squads relied on running the ball.

In the 1940s, though, coaches like the University of Chicago's Clark Shaughnessy and Chicago Bears owner-coach George Halas began to popularize the T-formation. While the single-wing often overloaded nine players to one side of the football, the T-formation featured balance on the offensive line and in the offensive backfield. This made it easier for teams to pass, because receivers raced off the line quicker, the quarterback counted on equal protection from his right and left sides, and the ball stayed behind the line of scrimmage longer, keeping the defense more off-balance.

The T-formation called for the quarterback to line up under center, and directly behind him, parallel to the line of scrimmage, were the fullback and two halfbacks. When coaches began rejuvenating the T (it had been popular even before the single wing but had fallen out of favor in the 1920s), passing increased in the league. The top-rated NFL squads from 1940 to 1949 averaged 2,382 yards per game, nearly 1,000 more than the decade before.

Gillman didn't begin using the T-formation as his offensive scheme of choice until 1946, his third year as Miami's head coach. Gillman had learned from Schmidt about the attributes of the single-wing, double-wing and I-formation offenses, but Gillman was slow to use the T-formation because he knew he needed a top-notch quarterback, a smart and versatile center, and a strong running back. He wanted the ability to use different formations—some on the ground and some in the air—and the T relied on a quick center-to-quarterback exchange, which was not a hallmark of the single-wing or double-wing formations. In 1946, Gillman found the right chemistry with quarterback Mel Olix, center Paul Dietzel, and running back Ara Parseghian. Though he had used a short-punt formation earlier in his Redskins coaching career—the precursor to the current-day shotgun where the ball was snapped to the tailback who then, depending on where the opposing safety was, could pass or punt the ball—Gillman went exclusively to the T-formation.

It was a system built on fluidity and keeping the defense guessing. Already, Gillman put his receivers into pre-snap motion, but with the T, two of the running backs also could go into motion and end up as receivers. In 1947, his last season at Miami, Gillman used 120 variations of the basic T, and if he had remained in Oxford, he had plans to add another 60. The problem for defenses was that even if they could figure out the system—where the play was supposed to go, how the blockers would get there, and which men would be in motion—they still wouldn't know which of the five potential receivers Olix would pass to. Or, because Olix had such a great sleight of hand, if he would pass at all.

Before the Cincinnati game, in which Miami dominated its biggest rival 38–7, Gillman gave each player a mimeographed 200-page book that covered every play the Bearcats had used that year, plus plays from other teams that used a similar system, including the NFL's Bears. Gillman also thought to put in the plays he would have tried if he had implemented the same system the Bearcats used. That's probably why Bearcats coach Ray Nolting, whom Gillman eventually would replace, suddenly began acting friendly toward Gillman. Some thought Nolting was just hoping to get a peek at Gillman's book.

"Those who say the T is doomed must mean a T without any variations," Gillman said in 1948 before exiting Oxford for West Point. "As far as I'm concerned, we're just beginning to explore the possibilities of the T."

While at Cincinnati, Gillman specialized in that field even further. After the Bearcats beat Tulsa 47–35 in 1951, Gillman was so impressed by his opponents' offense that he incorporated the Split-T formation into his scheme. With the Split-T, the quarterback, after taking the snap, slides along the line of scrimmage (where the offensive linemen are spread farther apart than in the traditional T) and either hands off, keeps on the option, or lofts a pass. But Gillman found this too limiting and not conducive to the passing game. When he landed in Los Angeles, he implanted the Spin-T, in which the quarterback spun away from the line—which then allowed him to throw back across the field. With the Rams, he also began placing his receivers—which he referred to as "X, Y, and Z" receivers, lexicon that continues into today—three to six yards outside the offensive tackle rather than the 5 feet away they normally stood.

His opponents in L.A. weren't impressed, because, in some ways, he had installed a college-style offense for a professional team. It wasn't *that* much different than other pro teams of the era, but it was just slightly enough off the norm to be noticeable. At the Pro Bowl in 1955, Gillman coached the West squad, and during the game, Detroit tackle Lou Creekmur asked Rams rookie Ron Waller, "You guys won the damn West championship with this bullshit offense?"

Gillman still hadn't settled on his true offensive philosophy at this point. He knew he wanted to stretch the defense to its breaking point. He just needed the right personnel, and he needed a league in which defenses and field goal kickers weren't the stars. He needed the AFL, and he needed the Chargers.

—⁂—

Gillman, the coach, had evolved in the three decades prior when he had decided that installing a conservative run-based offense wasn't the way his team would play. He had tried the misdirection and option play of the T-formation, he had tried running more than he passed it, and he had tried throwing in the stodgy NFL. Gillman had been successful for most of his career, and with his film work, innovative as well. But unless he took the San Diego job, he would not be remembered as the father of the modern-day offense. For Gillman, it was about finding the right league, the right owner, the right general manager, and the right personnel.

Not to mention a never-ending ability to push the envelope on what was considered the correct professional offense. Players might have thought some of Gillman's ideas were ignorant, but by the time he honed them in San Diego, there wasn't any doubt that his "bullshit offense" was highly effective.

"First, we're going to stretch you horizontally," Gillman explained. "The field is 53⅓ yards wide, and we're going to use all of it, stretching the defensive perimeter. Then, we're going to stretch you vertically. We're not going to throw long promiscuously, but you have to fear our long game. Some coaches feel that if you throw short, you'll open up the long game. I approach it exactly opposite. Once we throw long successfully, then we can throw short."

Gillman also made sure he employed a tight end who could catch four to six passes a game between the hash marks. Since the Chargers would stretch the defense horizontally by lining up receivers outside those hash marks, a linebacker who usually played the run often had to match up one-on-one with the tight end in pass defense—a mismatch in favor of San Diego.

It helped that in the AFL, most teams played a 4-3 defense (four defensive linemen, three linebackers) with man-to-man coverage in the secondary and one defensive back as a safety valve. That meant the speedy Lance Alworth oftentimes was matched against a cornerback without any help from a safety who had to cover the entire deep part of the field. That's when the Chargers could stretch the field vertically, sending Alworth on a deep pattern where either he'd lose the defensive back in the process or out-jump him when the ball fell back to Earth.

Even with an innovative passing attack, Gillman's squads were structured in their running game. They'd run an off-tackle play, but they also taught their linemen three or four different ways to block it. That meant the Chargers could run the same play four consecutive times, and on each snap, the defense would see something different.

Or as current Washington State coach Mike Leach said in 2005: "There's two ways to make it more complex for the defense. One is to have a whole bunch of different plays, but that's not good, because then, the offense experiences as much complexity as the defense. Another is a small number of plays run out of lots of different formations. That way, you don't have to teach a guy a new thing to do. You just have to teach him new places to stand."

Even the Chargers' running backs, Paul Lowe and Keith Lincoln, found new places to stand and lined up as receivers, meaning the defense saw five receivers spread across the width of the field, running routes at various depths. The offense grew complex enough that when Paul Dietzel, Gillman's versatile center at Miami who won a national championship as LSU's coach, visited Gillman and sat in on team meetings, Dietzel didn't have the foggiest idea what Gillman was talking about.

Gillman didn't lack for confidence either. That's what happens when you spend hours a day in a film room, breaking down your opponents' tendencies until you know them as well as you know your own child's favorite food, if not better. Gillman also placed great importance on organization and fundamentals, because he had seen how a lack of either doomed his mentor, Ohio State's Francis Schmidt.

Yet Gillman was not the type of coach who worried about beating the opponent's defense. He wanted the opposing coaches to worry about stopping Gillman's offense.

"Everybody had to work like hell to keep up with him," said Joe Collier, who coached against Gillman in the AFL. "We were forced to be more creative on defense because of Sid."

While his counterparts worked like hell to keep up with Gillman, he never grew tired of searching for more information. It's because he never believed that he truly had all the answers. After scout Al LoCasale returned from a trip, Gillman would begin the interrogation. What did you see? What was new and different? Did you see any new drills? Any new training routines? What about equipment? Tell me, tell me, tell me.

It was that thirst for information, that hunger for knowledge that gave Gillman an unconventional idea in San Diego. He believed football, with its different receiver routes and intricate spacing, was more mathematical than others thought, and he was determined to find a math expert to prove it. So he sent assistant coach Tom Bass on a mission: find somebody who could lay it all out in a mathematical equation. If, as Pythagoras is credited as saying, "Numbers rule the universe," why couldn't math improve Gillman's offense?

—⚬⚬—

Tom Bass was a junior offensive guard and linebacker at San Jose State, but a week before the polio vaccine was made public in late 1955, he contracted the life-altering disease. He would spend the next few years in and out of hospitals, and his playing career abruptly came to an end. Though he barely missed the vaccination window, he gained something valuable in its place: the opportunity to coach.

Bass worked with Dick Vermeil, then a backup quarterback, at San Jose State before Don Coryell hired Bass as an assistant at San Diego State in 1961. Before the 1964 season, Bass received a call from San Jose State asking if he'd be interested in returning to his alma mater to coach, and since San Diego State couldn't give him a raise, Bass planned to accept. But that night, he took a call from Chargers assistant Chuck Noll, saying Gillman wanted to talk to him. Bass spent five hours with Gillman discussing football, took the job, moved into Chargers headquarters at the Lafayette Hotel, and began learning Gillman's offense while watching film 14 hours a day.

Bass would become a defensive coach, and with the Chargers, he analyzed the opponent's defense on game day in the press box and kept his head coach up to date on what was occurring. But what Gillman really wanted Bass to figure out was where a receiver should line up on passing routes so that, no matter how many drop-steps a quarterback took, the length of time the pass was in the air never changed. In an offense that had become so dependent on a quarterback's timing, the number of seconds it took the ball to leave a quarterback's hands before it hit the receiver was of the utmost importance. The solution? Math.

"We thought about it," Bass said, "and if you look at (passing) patterns, they are all geometrically designed."

In the spring of 1964, Gillman sent Bass to meet with a San Diego State mathematics professor, and over coffee at a restaurant near campus, they hashed out the problem. As they talked, the professor drew triangle after triangle until it began to seep into their brains that the basic shape was the solution. The first leg of the triangle represented the route run by the receiver until he cut or broke the route (in other words, when he changed direction), the second leg was the line from where he broke the route to where he caught the pass, and the third leg—the most important leg—was the line from the quarterback to where the receiver caught the ball.

Gillman wanted to keep that third leg as consistent as possible. When the ball was snapped at the left hash mark and the quarterback threw to the right sideline—a long throw, distance-wise and time-wise— the coaches had to determine how to cut down on the seconds the pass was in the air. With the help of the professor—not to mention Euclid— they determined that if the receiver on the right side lined up four yards closer to the offensive line, the flight time of the ball was nearly the same as if the quarterback was throwing to a receiver on the left side.

"What [Gillman] did was take every pattern and actually measure where was the optimum place to throw the ball, how long the ball should be in the air," Bass said. "And by seeing the alignment of the wide receiver, [the quarterback] saw a consistency in the pattern. If he was going to throw an out [route], the ball was only in the air so long no matter where you were on the field. . . . The receivers could line up either inside the numbers, outside the numbers, two yards outside the numbers, two yards inside the numbers. It was a triangle.

"His passing game, because of that, became very precision-like, because you weren't making that long throw across the field. In order to do that, you had to be very constant in your drops, constant in your alignments. When you coached with him, it was very important that all these things were maintained."

Gillman, taking the math a step further, divided the football field into seven passing zones across the width of it. Basically, he was making seven running lanes for his receivers, and though the rules of the game forbid a team from using seven eligible receivers at a time, that wasn't the point. He came up with this "Field Balance Theory" to continue widening the field, balancing the pass attack and stretching the defense, and Gillman figured if he could control more than half of those passing zones, his scheme was going to succeed.

"If there was a Mount Rushmore for pioneering football geniuses, Sid Gillman's likeness would be on it," wrote Ron Jaworski in his book *The Games That Changed the Game.* "For two years, I was the lucky recipient of Sid's incredible knowledge, and I'd equate my experience with him to being the same as a physics student getting daily one-on-one tutoring with Albert Einstein."

Said Dan Dierdorf, a Hall of Fame quarterback who's now an NFL analyst: "Some guys are just smarter than others, and he was one of them."

Bass would say the same about the time he spent with Gillman as the Chargers defensive coordinator in the 1960s. After leaving San Diego, Bass went on to coach with the Bengals and the Buccaneers, but in 1990, he developed a post-polio syndrome, which "destroyed everything I had in my right leg." Bass kept at it. After serving as an ambassador for the NFL in Europe, he became a poet and the author of several books.

Yet, his meeting with that professor at that coffee shop changed the trajectory of Gillman's scheme. In a small way, that coffee date changed the way NFL coaches ran their offenses.

—m—

In order to make his system work, Gillman needed a quarterback who thought just like he did. That's why San Diego signal-caller John

Hadl oftentimes was referred to as "Sid Gillman Jr." The two spent so much time together in meetings, in the film room, and on the practice field that it was like they were joined at the hip and at the brain. Hadl wasn't as pretty as Esther, but Gillman probably spent more time with him during the season. It's no coincidence that, during his 16-year career, Hadl led the league in passing three times, in touchdowns twice, completions twice, and in yards per completion twice while under Gillman's tutelage.

"Everything an offensive coach does is aimed at giving his team an advantage—say, single coverage on a wide receiver downfield—but if the quarterback can't recognize and seize it, it's down the drain," Gillman said. "Given the choice between an arm and a brain, I'll take the brain. There were guys who threw the ball better than John Hadl, but not many who could out-think him."

What Gillman wanted from his quarterbacks, aside from flawless-ness, was a strong enough arm that could make all the necessary passes in Gillman's system. Gillman didn't worry so much if a quarterback wasn't mobile, but intelligence and accuracy were a must.

With the quarterback taking the snap and dropping back into the pocket, his receivers ran their routes based on a precise number of steps in order to keep the timing as in sync as possible. Oftentimes, the quarter-back released the ball before the receiver made his cut or turned around, because the receivers were trained to know where the ball would be at a certain time. If the primary receiver was covered, the quarterback—all while bouncing on his feet and holding the ball high to let the pattern develop—looked for the secondary receiver, who began his route a split second after the primary receiver started his. That was so the quarterback, if the first option was covered, could reset his feet and look for the second receiver before he had made his break.

"Nowadays, this emphasis on timing is so universal—in theory if not entirely in practice—that it's difficult to believe how influential Gillman was in establishing it," wrote Grantland.com's Chris Brown.

If the defense was playing zone—when a defensive back is responsi-ble in defending only a certain space on the field and not a certain receiver, as in man-to-man—Gillman knew the way to win was to outnumber the defenders playing pass defense. That's why the "Field Balance Theory," in which he divided the field into seven passing zones, was so important. If a defense had four players in pass defense, five receivers spread across the field usually won that battle.

But more than that, Gillman tried to instill an attitude in his quarterbacks in which mistakes were not tolerated.

"He wanted perfection. He wanted absolute perfection," said Dan Pastorini, a 12-year pro who spent 1973 and 1974 in Houston with Gillman. "You were not allowed to miss a play, not allowed to miss a read. You don't throw into double coverage. You make a wrong read and you get sucked into throwing into double coverage, it would drive him batshit. There could be no mistakes."

In effect, he wanted a younger version of Sid Gillman as his quarterback. Or at the very least, Gillman's brain inside that quarterback's head. And he couldn't ever be satisfied.

"No, he never will," his longtime assistant Joe Madro said in 1987. "There'll always be new horizons."

—⚋—

The first time Lance Alworth showed up for work at the San Diego Chargers' headquarters in 1962, Al LoCasale's secretary took one look at him and dismissively said, "We're not giving you money, because we're not getting the paper." The 22-year-old had been mistaken for a paperboy. That's how young he looked, and it earned him the least macho of nicknames: Bambi. His youthful demeanor, though, didn't convey the necessity Gillman would have for him in his San Diego scheme. On the field, Alworth was not a scared deer. No, when he ran his routes, Alworth was a shark.

Al Davis, then Gillman's assistant coach who would become one of the most controversial NFL owners in history, recognized Alworth's potential when he watched him as a running back in Arkansas's Wing-T offense. Davis signed him to an expensive two-year, $50,000 deal, but it was money well spent, as Alworth's Hall of Fame career attests (he was the first AFL player to be elected). Because if Gillman's offensive system was a major building block for the AFL's success with its emphasis on passing and long balls, Alworth was a major building block of Gillman's offensive system. As league founder Lamar Hunt once said, Alworth made the AFL look like a wide-open league, because Alworth always found himself so wide open.

"He was the perfect player for our offense," Gillman said. "His speed in the open field, his intelligence in reading defenses—nobody was better suited for our offense. He was just fantastic."

Alworth also provided Gillman the deep passing threat he needed. Alworth was perhaps the fastest runner in the league, and he could jump in the air and hang longer than anybody else. Alworth said he couldn't leap high when he tried, but when he wasn't thinking about it, he wasn't just like Bambi. He was like Shamu.

"In high school as a basketball player I could never cram the ball into the basket," Alworth said. "But I have pictures of myself going up for rebounds with my hands above the rim. If I'm concentrating on the ball, I don't realize how high up I've gone."

His time in San Diego, though, was not destined to end well. In fact, it crash-landed disastrously.

Alworth led the league in receptions in 1966, 1968, and 1969, but in 1970, his production was sliced in half, and many of the passes once earmarked for him were thrown instead to Gary Garrison. Not coincidentally, Alworth had turned 30 that season, and since Gillman always held to the theory that a player began his inevitable decline at that age, Alworth's importance to the franchise decreased.

In 1970, Gillman looked at the franchise's decline and tried to jumpstart the team by trading away the best receiver the AFL ever knew. It seems that the hurt feelings continue into today. Alworth, along with his old teammate John Hadl, did not return multiple messages to offer answers about Gillman, and others, like Earl Faison, politely declined to talk after they'd been reached. Some couldn't let go of grudges, and it appears Alworth was an example.

But that didn't take away the impact Alworth made on Gillman's team, and it didn't take away from the impact Alworth had on Gillman's career as well—or on Gillman's view of the world. Along with Jack Kemp, the Southern-born-and-bred Lance Alworth helped Gillman determine that some of the off-the-field changes he wanted to make to the squad would be accepted by those who played for him.

—⁓—

When Ernie Wright entered professional football as an offensive tackle for the Los Angeles Chargers in 1960, he knew about the NFL's unspoken quota of five black members per team. There were no black players on the bench, none who were developmental players, none who were reserves. If you were black, you were starting. Otherwise, why wouldn't the team just save that reserve spot for a white player?

The NFL's personnel men also made sure there was an even number of black players for each squad. That way the blacks could room with the blacks, the whites could room with the whites, and nobody would have to be uncomfortable.

Not all teams bothered filling the quota, though. For instance, the Redskins didn't integrate their squad until 1962, and it wasn't by owner George Marshall's choice either (the Kennedy administration basically blackmailed Marshall into breaking the color barrier). Gillman thought Marshall's views—and the man himself—were disgusting.

"Marshall refuses to use Negro players. He's dead wrong from both a moral and practical standpoint," Gillman said in 1961. "From a moral standpoint, Marshall's policy is disgraceful. He's living in the Dark Ages. From a practical standpoint, he's ruined his football team. It's impossible to compete in any sport without using Negro athletes."

The AFL had a different attitude toward integration. Knowing that the league couldn't survive without the use of black players, the league heavily recruited the historically black colleges to help fill its team's rosters, and while doing so, the owners found some of the top football players in the country.

The 1961 Chargers squad featured 8 black players out of an active roster of 33, and by 1964, there were 12. Then, 13 in 1966. That's not to say the entire AFL was completely welcoming to black players. The country, after all, was still in the middle of the Civil Rights era when tension between races was still heavily burdened by history. "There were very few members of the American Football League who were also members of the NAACP," said Michael MacCambridge, author of *America's Game.*

Gillman obviously wanted to win, and he knew that using the top athletes, regardless of their skin tone, would lead him to what he so badly desired. But he also remembered growing up in anti-Semitic Minneapolis, and he remembered when he couldn't get a job in the Big Ten because of his religion. He remembered the gut-punch that discrimination landed on him repeatedly in his younger days. And he remembered his lifeguarding job when he was home from college one summer.

Originally that summer, Gillman wanted a job working street construction so he could spend his days outside doing the heavy work. Though his father was connected politically, Gillman had arrived home from Columbus too late for that type of work, and instead, took a position as a lifeguard at a city pool. Considering this was in the middle of the Depression, any way for Gillman to make money would have been welcome. With the sun shining, Gillman's skin began to brown. Gillman, in fact, would get so tan that his friends nicknamed him Schvartz, a racially insensitive Yiddish slang term.

One day, two white men walked by the pool, saw Gillman in his chair, and said loud enough for him to hear, "Look at that nigger. He's got a job and we don't." An enraged Gillman ran after them and proceeded to blast them with his fists. The two men sued, and while in court, the judge said to Gillman, "You're not black. Why didn't you just say that to them?"

Responded Gillman, "Well, I don't like people who are prejudiced."

As Chargers coach, Gillman would not repeat the sins of the past made by less-tolerant people. He would win, and he would do it with black players. He would do the right thing at the same time.

"He wasn't self-appointed, and he didn't necessarily do it for the whole movement," said his son, Tom Gillman. "He did it for his team, and he believed it was the fairest way to go. There are different ways minorities can view other minorities. They can put them down lower than they are, or they can empathize as a minority. [With Gillman], it was the latter. It wasn't just a question of being fair, but he thought the best man should get the job. Screw all the other rules."

Gillman knew his team was close-knit, and he knew the Chargers probably could handle the new rules he was to enforce. Lance Alworth helped make up his mind. Even though Alworth, a son of the South, had made speeches on behalf of Arkansas governor Orval Faubus, who had defied the U.S. Supreme Court's decision to integrate Little Rock public schools, he was a popular figure on the team for both blacks and whites.

So, when crosses were burned above Alworth's locker after he returned from Faubus's campaign, he laughed it off. When black running back Paul Lowe led Freedom Marches and made civil rights speeches in front of Alworth's dressing area, he took the joke well. And when white linebacker Paul Maguire stepped into a team huddle with Alworth and cracked, "What's going on here? I thought this was a segregated scrimmage," the entire team got a good chuckle out of it. The team unity didn't fray.

In the early days of the AFL, the outside world infiltrated the Chargers' racial views. Gillman took his team to the movies on the day before a game, but some theater owners wanted the black players segregated to the balcony. Instead, in the spirit of unity, the entire team would move upstairs. Or the Chargers would stay at a hotel that discriminated against blacks, and instead of splitting the team into two different hotels, they'd find a place that would accept all races. Or, a racially diverse group of Chargers would enter a bar in order to shoot pool, and after the black players were invited to leave the establishment, the team would threaten not to play the next day's game unless it received an apology from city and state officials.

But until 1963, the Chargers' black players roomed with other blacks, and the white players roomed with whites.

"For you to room with a Caucasian player at that time, it was unthinkable," said Johnny Sample, a former defensive back who spent 11 years in the NFL and AFL. "They weren't going to do that."

But that's exactly what Gillman had in mind. Instead of rooming players by race, he decided to room players by position. That meant some black players roomed with some white players. And you know what happened?

Nothing.

"I didn't hear anybody complain about it," Ron Mix said. "It was massively innovative. . . . We needed the best football players and there were coaches like Sid Gillman and Al Davis who actually had a social conscience too. They threw the sport wide open for black athletes."

The AFL was the better for it. So was Sid's conscience.

For a coach who had once left a black player to sit at home alone instead of forfeiting the Sun Bowl, Gillman, in this case, recognized the right thing to do, and he did it. Did adding black players help his team succeed? Most certainly. Yet, at the intersection of winning and morality, Gillman made the right choice by integrating his team as much and quickly as possible. He wasn't interested in separate but equal. He wanted blacks and whites sleeping next to each other, hearing each other's snores, waiting for the other to finish his shower. If the byproduct of his decision was winning a few more games, Gillman could live with it.

eleven THE END IN SAN DIEGO

The first time Gillman and Al Davis met was at a football clinic in Atlantic City, New Jersey. Davis sat in the front row as Gillman lectured the coaches, and Gillman noticed that Davis took notes on everything that emerged from his lips. When his presentation was finished, Davis approached Gillman and asked question after question.

That's one way to get noticed by a big-time coach like Gillman, and when he was putting together his Chargers staff before the 1960 season, he remembered Davis's aggressiveness and offered him a job. Along with Davis, Gillman's assistants were an impressive bunch. Davis eventually won three NFL titles as the owner of the Raiders, Chuck Noll triumphed in an NFL-record four Super Bowls as the Steelers' head coach, Jack Faulkner coached the Broncos for three years before becoming an integral part of the Rams organization, and Joe Madro never really left Gillman's side.

Noll had played for the Browns for seven years, oftentimes serving as Paul Brown's play-call messenger, and after Noll retired, he called Gillman and inquired about a job. "I figured anybody who could run in plays for Paul Brown had to be bright," Gillman said. "And he really wanted the job; he was persistent."

But Davis was just as tenacious. After spending three years as Gillman's receiver coach, Davis took the Raiders head-coaching job before the 1963 season. He took some of Gillman's offensive strategies with him— Davis believed Gillman to be a football Einstein—and he developed the Raiders into a vertical stretch team that had plenty of success.

Although the two had their battles when Davis took the Raiders job, the Gillmans couldn't help but love Davis, particularly since he adored Sid.

Gillman felt the same way about Joe Madro. Gillman asked Madro to formally introduce him at his Pro Football Hall of Fame induction ceremony, because in reality, one rarely left the other's side. Madro was an offensive guard under Francis Schmidt at Ohio State from 1936 to 1939, and when he finished playing, he caught the coaching bug from Gillman. He coached at Ohio State with Gillman, and then went on to coach at Denison, Miami, Cincinnati, Los Angeles, San Diego, and Houston. Just about every step that Gillman made, Madro was right there beside him. He was an offensive line coach, and he was a damn good one.

"(Madro) was a little bitty shit," said former offensive lineman Carl Mauck, who played for Gillman and Madro in San Diego and Houston. "He was a little Napoleon. He was very smart and very sharp. He chain-smoked cigarettes, and he always talked about the stock market. He knew his stuff. He was a different breed of cat. He was a kleptomaniac. When he went through metal detectors, they'd catch him with three or four sets of silverware."

By the end of his career, Madro did have at least one regret. He never got to be a head coach. He said he never applied for a job in his life— probably because Gillman kept finding spots for him whenever he jumped to a new city—and Madro wondered what could have happened if he had been more aggressive or more career-minded.

"Maybe I had too much pride in myself and my work," Madro said. "I always felt if somebody wanted me, they knew where I was."

Always next to Gillman, always working for somebody else, always the one polishing the silverware but never getting to eat with it.

―⚬―

Even though the Chargers were consistently one of the best and most exciting teams in the American Football League and even though Gillman set the tone for the rest of the league, the survival of the AFL was still in question.

The AFL's original television deal with ABC paid each team $185,000 per year, but the ratings weren't as high as anticipated, so in 1961, that sum dropped to $125,000. By the fourth season, ABC was paying each team only $100,000.

In contrast, the NFL and CBS had struck a deal in 1962 that brought in $4.65 million annually as well as $615,000 to televise the NFL championship game. Two years later, NFL commissioner Pete Rozelle re-upped to a $14.1 million deal for the 1964 and 1965 regular seasons, the biggest contract in TV sports history at the time.

If the AFL didn't make a corresponding move, the league would be in real trouble. Considering none of the new league's teams had made a profit through the first four seasons, the league was desperate to bring in outside money to compete with the NFL. The reason the AFL was thriving at that point was because the fat-cat owners kept injecting new capital into the league. But how long would they continue to do so if that money kept swirling directly down the drain?

At the time, ABC was the third-most-popular network, and since NBC wanted to compete against CBS on Sundays, NBC gave the AFL a generous offer—$36 million over five years, an offer the AFL couldn't resist. It was a life preserver for the league, and a signal to the stodgy NFL, which was waiting for the AFL to die. Instead, the two leagues, after much discussion, merged in 1966, and by 1970, the NFL with the AFL's old teams was the only relevant pro football league.

"At that point," longtime Chiefs executive Jack Steadman said, "the NFL saw that they were in a war with people that could stay in the war."

While that TV deal saved the league, Sid Gillman—along with the way his Chargers teams played—was a big reason why NBC confidently forked over so much money in the first place. Take the 1963 AFL championship game as an example. The Chargers' 51–10 destruction of the Boston Patriots was the crowning achievement in Gillman's career and probably the best day in his coaching life, and though there was concern that the game in San Diego didn't sell out, fans across the country had access to it because there was no competition from the NFL on that day. The game was memorable, and it was highly visible. Two years later, NBC wanted a piece of the action.

But in 1960, after Barron Hilton had hired Gillman, the coach had plenty to accomplish in the fledgling league. Gillman knew how to run a football operation. He knew how to find the correct personnel. He knew how to game-plan. He was the father figure the rest of the league could admire when times were tough. The Chargers, as Al Davis once said, were the flagship franchise that the rest of the league could emulate.

"When Sid came into the AFL, Sid taught the AFL how to do business," sportswriter Jerry Magee said. "If you didn't learn, Sid would run over you. Sid was a great deal responsible for the AFL lasting as long as it did."

Even when he was fired from the Rams, one of the NFL's most popular teams, and was hired to take over a new franchise in an untested league, Gillman didn't lose that enthusiasm for coaching football. He could have said the AFL was beneath him. He probably could have taken another position in the NFL and been a head coach again someday. But no, he wanted to get started with a new challenge in a new league.

"The fact the Chargers didn't have a big fan base or a great stadium to play in," said Bill Korbin, one of Gillman's sons-in-law, "that was beside the point."

Gillman's basic idea was to draw up game plans that were the opposite of what the conservative NFL considered appropriate. He knew he needed to open up the passing game and bring in the fans with an exciting brand of football they had never seen before. Much later in his life, Gillman was asked whose idea it had been to reinvigorate the Chargers' passing game and give the rest of the league a blueprint to follow.

"I don't know whose idea that was," Gillman said with a sly smile. "But it was a splendid idea."

Not everybody was impressed. *Los Angeles Times* scribe Jim Murray, after watching the Chargers destroy the Patriots in the 1963 AFL championship game, tapped out the following: "The AFL, as you may know, is not a league so much as an exercise in geometric progression. I don't think it prepares defenses, I think it rents them, at the last minute."

But the fans bought in regardless. A typical NFL squad's mentality was to play a basic offense and win close contests with the kicking game. But in the AFL, scores of 38–35 and 42–37 were not uncommon. Field goals are hardly exciting. Waves of touchdowns, though, increase the pulse rate of a stadium full of fans. The AFL was built for Gillman; in response, Gillman built the AFL.

"He gave the league a strategic tone and a shape," said Steve Sabol, whose father, Ed, founded NFL Films. "Lamar Hunt is the George Washington of the AFL. Sid Gillman is the Thomas Jefferson."

—⁓—

While the AFL celebrated the merger with the NFL, ensuring that each team in both leagues would survive, the truce hindered the Chargers.

Veteran players like Ernie Ladd and Earl Faison wanted enormous signing bonuses, and Gillman, as the Chargers' general manager, had limited options. He could pay them their demanded salaries (costing the team as much as $525,000 and setting a dangerous precedent for himself and the rest of the league), he could trade them, or he could place them in the pool from which the expansion Miami Dolphins would draft. Ladd said he didn't care, as long as he got paid. "I'll play in Vietnam," he said. "I just want the money."

Standing 6 feet, 9 inches tall, weighing in at 315 pounds and hailing from Rayville, Louisiana, by way of Grambling State, Ladd was more than just a dominant football player who wanted all the money he could handle. He was an eater of large quantities of food, a professional wrestler, and a showman.

He was gargantuan and his talent was immense, but if you really wanted to be impressed (or simply, nauseated), you asked him about his caloric intake. During his first breakfast at Chargers training camp, he wolfed down ten eggs, eight pieces of toast, three glasses of juice, and four cartons of milk. For lunch, he sucked down a couple of hamburger steaks, beef stroganoff over wild rice, and a few other noshes before pointing out, "I don't eat too much at noon."

If he wasn't in the mood for eggs in the morning, he'd inhale a dozen pancakes (his personal best at one sitting was, no lie, 130) and a pound of bacon. If he desired a heavier lunch, he'd munch on ten pork chops, three helpings of rice and green beans, three peach cobblers, three dishes of ice cream, and a half-gallon of milk.

One night as he showed off for New York newspaper reporters, Ladd dominated two shrimp cocktails, three dishes of cole slaw, three servings of spinach, three baked potatoes, eight rolls with butter, a half-gallon of milk, and three desserts. And four 16-ounce steaks. The performance didn't impress Chargers halfback Irv Roberson, who said, "He's lost his appetite. You should see him eat when nobody is watching."

But when the world *was* watching, that's when Ladd was the best in the gastronomical galaxy.

One day, at the age of 22 when he still had much to prove, he sat down to dinner with a 48-year-old tuna fisherman named Nick Cordileone—a 5-foot-8, 268-pound specimen—in the ballroom of the U.S. Grant Hotel in San Diego. Together, the two dined on about 40 pounds of food and ingested nearly 22,000 calories. The two men didn't know each other until that night when they went head to head in the inaugural Golden West eating classic, but they became well acquainted during the eight-course meal in which they swallowed Roquefort salad, lobster tails, spaghetti and meatballs, fried chicken (though Ladd would have preferred chicken cacciatore), baked hams, prime ribs, sirloin steak, ice cream, and cake.

Ladd washed down his food with a soft drink—one reporter claimed it was actually Kool-Aid—while Cordileone sipped on wine and tried to digest the fried chicken (his Italian stomach disagreed with this intruder). At the end of the competition, Ladd failed to finish a roll, a pat of butter and a small piece of cake. But since that was 3 ounces less than Cordileone's leftovers, Ladd was declared the winner, the one with the elevated esophagus and the sturdier stomach.

Cordileone wasn't so sure. He noticed that after each course, while Cordileone drank scotch and soda to help aid his digestion and mingled among the crowd, Ladd slipped out of the ballroom. "I am positive he heaved between courses," Cordileone alleged. "I do not like to accuse a man on limited evidence but several of my friends heard a distinct 'a-a-ar-r-r-ojam-p-h' coming from the wash room. I am positive he lost weight between the lobster tails and the prime rib. He looked peaked when the chicken came."

That's why Cordileone—who was heard to ask about dessert after the proceedings were complete—suggested that organizers should have weighed the contestants before and after the event rather than measure the leftovers. Alas, his protest did not overrule the results, and Ladd claimed triumph.

So much of the time, that's what Ladd did. He put on tremendous performances. And he won. Whether it was with the Chargers or the Chiefs in pro football or putting the three-count on his pro wrestling opponent, Ladd used his big body and exceptional athleticism to build himself into a larger-than-life character. Sure, he answered his telephone with a greeting of "Jesus loves you," but he was also such a scary figure that opposing offensive linemen often tracked him down before games to glad-hand him and pat him on the back, hoping that would be enough to soothe the beast that boasted a 52-inch chest, 20-inch biceps, a 19-inch neck, and size-18 shoes. As his four-time Pro Bowl career attests, that transparent strategy rarely worked on the man nicknamed Big Cat.

Since it wasn't unusual for football players to moonlight as pro wrestlers in the offseason, a grappler named Dick "The Destroyer" Beyer invited Ladd to an event in 1961, challenging him, "Why don't you come down and join a man's sport?" Ladd did, and though it angered Gillman, Ladd became a semi-regular on the mat. Because he was so ridiculously huge and because he was strong, quick, and graceful, he built an immediate fan base.

After a few years of in-ring performing, Ladd was making so much money in the off-season that he didn't have to play football. Ladd signed a $57,000 deal with Houston after leaving San Diego, but once he retired from football at 30 years old, he made $98,000 his first year in pro wrestling and never less than six figures after that.

He began his career as the good guy, but he was too big to elicit much sympathy when he took a beating from his opponent. So, he turned villainous and drew tremendous heat from the crowds. He was scary and mean, and that gave the crowd permission to jeer him all night. Ladd wrestled into his late 40s when the bad knees that would cause him to walk down stairways backward for the rest of his life forced him to retire.

But he could give a good beating and take a good joke. One night, as he prepared for a show in Albuquerque, New Mexico, he noticed a magnetic chessboard in the bag of his opponent that night, NWA world champion Dory Funk Jr. Ladd challenged him to a game. Funk accepted.

After a few minutes, Funk sensed victory.

"I manipulated my Queen into position and said to Ernie, 'Check,'" wrote Funk after Ladd died in 2007 at the age of 68. "Ernie moved his King to safe and I followed up by sliding my Rook into an advantageous position feeling the thrill of victory on the next move.

"Ernie had stacked his Queen behind his Bishop. Sliding his Bishop to the right giving check by exposure with his Queen and trapping my King with the same Bishop, Ernie said, 'Checkmate.'

"Ernie was happy, he smiled big, his eyes opened wide and his forehead extended back slightly. He was thrilled to have beaten the NWA World Champion in a game of chess."

In the wrestling match that night, after more than 30 minutes of grappling, Ladd attempted to body-slam Funk, but instead, Funk underhooked his arm and used Ladd's momentum against him, rolling him into a cradle for the three-count. As the referee's hand slammed on the mat for the third time, giving him the win, Funk looked Ladd in the face and said, "Checkmate." Ladd could do nothing but smile.

Ladd could intimidate as well. One day, after signing with the Chiefs, he sauntered into a dorm room while some of his teammates were in the middle of a poker game, and with his naked body blocking out the daylight of the doorway, he snarled, "All right, I can't believe that you guys are some sorry ass guys that would do the nasty, dirty thing that you did to me. Somebody stole my toothbrush. I am gonna find out who it is and when I do, you're going to answer to me."

He turned around to leave, and that's when the players in the room noticed the toothbrush. Stuck between Ladd's ass cheeks.

—∞—

Before the 1966 season, though, Ladd, searching for money, went to the Oilers, and Earl Faison signed a contract with the Dolphins. Gillman didn't mind losing Faison. In his view, it had been at least three seasons since Faison had played at a Pro Bowl level—and, in fact, 1966 was Faison's last year in pro football—but Gillman knew the loss of Ladd was a bad blow. In all, the Chargers lost two offensive and three defensive starters to the Dolphins, and with Lowe and Lincoln growing older and less explosive, the Chargers' decline was noticeable. Particularly from 1966 to 1969, when they embarked on a four-year run of third-place finishes in the AFL West division (the Chargers also finished third in 1970 and 1971 in the AFC West after the leagues merged).

Making matters worse, Gillman was about to lose the best owner for whom he'd ever worked. In 1965, Barron Hilton—the man who basically gave Gillman license to do whatever was necessary to turn the Chargers franchise into a winner—became president and CEO of the Hilton Hotel Corporation. Since he needed to devote more of his time to the family business, he relinquished his majority ownership in the Chargers. When Hilton sold his share to Gene Klein and Sam Schulman, one of Hilton's stipulations was that Gillman had to remain head coach and general manager for the remaining two years on his contract and that he would receive a $100,000 bonus as a condition of the sale.

After Hilton gave up his majority share, the decline of the franchise continued. Klein and Schulman restricted the money that could be used to sign the top players of the day, and instead, they targeted less-talented (and less-wanted) players that fit into the team's budget rather than Gillman's system. Klein—who, as one San Diego writer put it, "was the tycoon who knew how to live the role"—had begun his career by selling cars in the San Fernando Valley until he made his way into the insurance and theater businesses. He, for all intents and purposes, was an absentee owner, but when he made a decision, he didn't dwell on whether it was the right call. He moved on to the next decision. And while Gillman must have enjoyed not having Klein's input at all times, he wasn't pleased by not having Klein's money.

But in his recollection, sportswriter Jerry Magee—who covered Gillman's Chargers squads—said the organization actually improved when Barron Hilton was no longer the majority owner.

"They became better," Magee said. "Toward the end of his time with the Chargers, Barron Hilton had cut back with how much he was willing to invest in the team. Klein was a damn good owner. You couldn't push that son of a bitch around."

Said Carl Mauck, who was traded from Miami to San Diego before the 1971 season: "Klein was a good guy, but he was a movie guy. He made movies, and then when he sold that out, he had race horses. He had successful endeavors, but I wouldn't say he was a hell of an owner."

Either way, with Klein involved, the Chargers suddenly lacked talent in a league that was perpetually improving, growing larger through expansion, and beginning to catch up to Gillman's game plans. But Gillman still had quarterback John Hadl, and Hadl was smart and strong enough to always give the Chargers a chance.

Hadl also had a contentious relationship with Gillman. He always believed the Chargers were not satisfied with his play—for instance, when they signed Tobin Rote in 1963—but he stayed in San Diego and, with Lance Alworth, they became one of the top quarterback-to-receiver combos in all of pro football. "John Hadl to Lance Alworth? Aw man, that was trouble. Trouble," said George Atkinson, a Raiders defensive back from 1968 to 1977.

Or as the overzealous narrator of a 1970 Chargers highlight reel put it: "Hadl is more than statistics. He's a rugged roustabout—a rambler, a gambler, a hip-slicking, brazen ball shark with the hands of a Vegas dealer and the guts of a Hollywood stuntman." It didn't impress his 9-year-old son—who, when signing up for Pop Warner football, was asked if he wanted to wear the same jersey number as his father and declined by saying, "My hero is Lance Alworth."

Though he felt an iciness from the Chargers front office, Hadl stuck in San Diego until 1972. The team and the Chargers parted ways at that point. Hadl played five more seasons in the NFL, but after a standout 1973 with the Rams as a 33-year-old, he clearly wasn't the same player afterward.

Hadl asked Gillman to be his offensive coordinator when he was hired by the USFL's Los Angeles Express in 1984. Gillman accepted, stayed on for a year, and helped the team to a 10-8 record and a Pacific Division title. These days, he calls Gillman "a dear friend." But he, like some of his teammates from that era, won't elaborate on their time together or talk about Gillman at all. He doesn't say why.

—∞—

By the end of the 1966 Chargers season, after the team went 7-6-1 and finished in third place in its division, Gillman wanted to improve a defense that finished seventh in the league in yards allowed. Chuck Noll, the former defensive coordinator, had left for an equivalent NFL job after the 1965 season. Noll had turned the Chargers into the top defensive team in the league, and a year later, Gillman was searching for another coach to shore up the defense. He turned to Bum Phillips for help.

Phillips had spent his entire coaching career in Texas, mostly in the high school ranks, and he had begun to win positive reviews for the two years he spent as the defensive coordinator at the University of Houston. One day, he received a call from the Chargers. Gillman said, "I'm looking for a defensive coordinator and you've been recommended. Are you interested in a job?" Phillips was. "Get on a plane and come out here then," Gillman said.

Phillips had never seen a picture of Gillman and didn't know what he looked like, so when Phillips stepped off the plane in San Diego, he was lost. He stood in a little holding area and watched as his planemates began walking down the long hallway that led to the main terminal. With only three or four people left in the holding area, Phillips noticed a man wearing a bow tie. Phillips walked over and asked, "Are you Sid Gillman?" Responded Gillman, "Are you Bum Phillips?"

"And that," Phillips said more than 40 years later, "is how we met."

It didn't take Phillips long to figure out that Gillman was the best offensive mind he'd ever met. But it also didn't take him long to realize that Gillman believed defense was something only to tolerate until you got the ball back on offense—which is why Gillman didn't provide much help to his new defensive coordinator at practice.

"From the time I started, he never let the offensive line work against the defensive line," Phillips said. "I had to put my defensive guys as pass protectors and rush them with my other defenders. I did that for five years. He wanted his offense to be spending time on offense. We never got to turn loose and run stunts against good blockers. We had to do it against ourselves."

With Phillips in charge of the defense, the team got a little better, posting an 8-5-1 record in 1967 and a 9-5 mark in 1968, but the Chargers still finished behind the Raiders and Chiefs both seasons in the West division. Before the 1969 season began, Phillips told Gillman he wanted to make a change. The team, Phillips said, didn't have four good defensive linemen. But he knew the Chargers owned four talented linebackers, and he wanted to change the defensive scheme. Instead of running a 4-3 base (four linemen with their hands in the dirt and three linebackers behind them), he wanted to switch it to a 3-4 (three linemen and four linebackers, two of whom could rush the passer off the ends). Phillips had some experience running a 3-4, and he wanted to give it a chance in the pros.

At the time, the 3-4 was unheard of as a permanent scheme at the pro level, but Gillman said simply, "OK. Go ahead."

"He didn't know what a 3-4 was," Phillips said many years later. "And he didn't care."

But Gillman began to notice after the Bears destroyed the Chargers' defense late in the preseason and made Phillips's 3-4 scheme look like a high school defense. As San Diego prepared to open the regular season against the Chiefs, Gillman called Phillips into his office.

"Bum," Gillman said, "I want you to go back to the 4-3."

"Coach, we can't go back to the 4-3," Phillips said.

"Bum," Gillman repeated, "I want you to go back to the 4-3."

Gillman wasn't interested in arguing the point, and Phillips had no choice but to acquiesce to his boss. So, the Chargers went back to the 4-3 and then allowed Kansas City to score 27 points in Week 1 and Cincinnati to score 34 points in Week 2. The Chargers rebounded, winning four straight, then lost four straight and ended the year on another four-game winning streak to finish 8-6. Phillips's 3-4 experiment would have to wait for another time and another place.

Gillman, though, would not finish the 1969 season with his team. Gillman had more important things to worry about. His life, for instance.

—⁂—

Gillman felt the first pang of pain during the September 28 game vs. the Jets in the third week of the 1969 season. He got ill in the locker room, and during the game, he slumped onto the bench complaining of chest pain. Team doctor Jay Malkoff, who also happened to be Gillman's son-in-law, immediately arrived at Gillman's side and helped him through his bout of distress. Malkoff ordered him to cancel a dinner party he was scheduled to attend that evening and go home to rest. The Chargers had won their first game of the season, and even though astronaut Wally Schirra was inside the locker room, Gillman received an even louder cheer when John Hadl handed him the game ball.

But Gillman still didn't feel right, and as he spoke to *San Diego Union* sports editor Jack Murphy, Gillman said, "Sit here with me. I've got this awful pain in my chest." Murphy caught Malkoff's eye and waved him over to Gillman. Malkoff put his arms around Gillman and held him close. "Father-in-law," Malkoff said softly. "You are a great father-in-law."

Later that night, Murphy called the coach at home to check in, and Gillman said, "I feel wonderful. I'm the healthiest, happiest man in the world."

The next week, he got sick again vs. the Bengals, and he had to call on Charlie Waller, his offensive backfield coach, to leave the press box and run the team in his absence.

Privately, owner Gene Klein urged Gillman to give up coaching and focus solely on his general manager job, but Gillman resisted the notion. His father, 83-year-old David, nagged his son to back away from his occupation. "He should quit," David said. "He works too hard." But Gillman had no thoughts of quitting at the time. He expected to go on coaching into infinity. Only when he got sick again, during the November 9 contest vs. the Chiefs, did Gillman begin to take his illness seriously. Malkoff ordered him to undergo an intensive physical exam, and after seeing the results, he pleaded with Gillman to stop coaching.

The 58-year-old finally listened.

"I was just glad he took my advice," Malkoff said. "I was afraid he would ignore me."

Gillman had been diagnosed with a hiatal hernia and a stomach ulcer, but later, it was determined that Gillman actually suffered from angina, which is oftentimes a symptom of coronary heart disease and causes chest pain if the heart muscle isn't receiving enough oxygen-rich blood. No matter the diagnosis, Gillman had to resign from his coaching job. After a staff meeting on November 11, he walked up to Waller, offered him the head spot, and said, "I don't want to shake you up. How much time do you need to think about it?" Said Waller: "I don't need to think about it."

At 12:32 p.m. Gillman walked into the locker room as the team's head coach one last time that season. He wore brown slacks and a brown polo shirt, and aside from the speech he was about to give, the next biggest issue on his mind was where in the hell he'd left his pipe. When he began speaking, the locker room was silent. Some players looked at the ground in front of them; some looked Gillman in the eye. All wondered what

Gillman would say, and his next words surprised them. He told them he was quitting.

"I wanted to stay until the day I dropped," Gillman told the Chargers. "But if I did, they told me I'd drop, so I have to get out."

Then, he immediately assumed a hardline general manager position. He didn't have to worry about dealing with the players as a coach anymore. So, he let loose.

"I've given 45 years of my life to this game, and I've been completely dedicated," Gillman said. "And I mean, completely dedicated. We have some men in here who don't know what it means to be completely dedicated and they're missing out. They just don't know what the hell they're missing."

If there was any sympathy toward Gillman, that attitude evaporated as quickly as those words were spoken. But it was an attitude that was completely Gillman nonetheless.

—⁂—

Charlie Waller had his chance. With a successful campaign to finish the remaining five games of the 1969 season and an impressive showing in 1970, Waller perhaps could have stayed as San Diego's head coach. Maybe, if the Chargers had made a big splash in the first season of the merger, Gene Klein would have been forced to keep Waller at the head spot and maybe Gillman wouldn't have been tempted to think he could do it better than his successor. The truth is, Waller *was* successful at the end of 1969. He lost his head-coaching debut to eventual AFL West champion Oakland, but the Chargers managed to win the final four games of the year. In 1970, though, with Gillman overseeing from the general manager's office above, the Chargers recorded a 5-6-3 record, only the second time in the organization's existence that they finished below .500 (and it actually started a run of eight straight seasons in which the team didn't finish *above* .500).

Gillman had seen enough from Waller. He was ready to make a change, and he wanted to hire an experienced coach who knew the Chargers inside and out. He wanted to hire himself. After Gillman underwent an intensive physical in which he was declared to be in excellent health and after Klein pondered his decision for 10 days, the owner gave his blessing. After only 19 games away from the job that had caused him so much stress and discomfort—and, at the same time, rewarded him with another shot at the game he so badly craved—Gillman took over the team once again. He had agreed to give up the general manager position even though he probably could have stayed in that job for life, and the demoted Waller stayed as an offensive assistant and never ascended to a head-coaching job again.

The players were split on whether they wanted Gillman back running the practices and prowling the sidelines. As Jack Murphy wrote in the *San Diego Union*, "The hostility is so fierce, the resentment runs so deep, that Gillman is portrayed as a man who embodies the virtues of Attila the Hun and Joseph Stalin."

Klein eventually gave his support to the idea because he had so much respect for Gillman's coaching acumen. Where else, Klein thought to himself, can I find a better coach? The answer was easy. He couldn't.

Gillman, it appeared, had changed as well. He wasn't as gruff as usual. He was calmer and more even-tempered. He was less Sadistic Sid and more Sid the Sweetheart. Away from coaching, Gillman had plenty of time to reflect on his tenure and to think about what he could have done differently, and he wanted to change for the better.

"Sometimes, you can't see the forest for the trees," Gillman said. "I learned a great deal about a lot of things."

Gillman also vowed to delegate more, to allow scouts to call the shots on player personnel more often, and to listen to his players' concerns. His bout with angina seemingly had made him a new man, and it appeared to the players that Gillman had lost some of his bite. Almost immediately, they felt more comfortable around him.

One of Gillman's first duties was to invite Hadl into his office so they could have a real conversation about the state of the team. If a player had a grievance or a suggestion, Gillman wanted to hear it, and Hadl got the first shot to tell him. "I came out of Sid's office with a good feeling," Hadl said. "We were pretty frank with each other . . . I think he has changed. A year away from coaching has given him a different perspective."

Even though Gillman asked a number of players to keep him informed on the locker-room atmosphere and how to improve the team's morale, San Diego's fortunes didn't improve. The Chargers beat the Chiefs to open the 1971 season, but then lost four straight. Gillman somehow had lost his touch in the organization, and he wasn't immune from the criticism bestowed upon him by San Diego's fans. Or their kids. In the midst of that slump, Gillman received a handwritten letter from adolescent siblings Tommy and Karen, who wrote, "My dad gets uptight when you lose a game. He yells at me, my brother, and my sister. So fare (sic), it's been every time you play. How about winning a game for us so we can have a pleasant weekend."

Even with the urgings of those who were under the threat of verbal abuse from their parents, the Chargers fell to 3-5 after losing to the Giants at Yankee Stadium. Afterward, Gillman paced the aisles on the team's flight back home. He didn't have much to say. He just kept replaying the game, his decisions, and the team's execution over and over in his mind. Said one player who noticed him, "The saddest thing about it is that Sid pours his blood into it. Damn, he wants it."

Though Gillman was less abrasive with his players, his feelings hadn't softened about overbearing owners with no football background who wanted to make football personnel decisions. So, on October 26, when Klein told Gillman he wanted to trade receiver Jerry LeVias for a first-round draft pick—a potential transaction that excited Klein because the Chargers didn't have a first-round pick in the upcoming draft—Gillman vetoed the idea. At that point, Gillman was still trying to save the season. "How can I go to my people and tell them I've traded LeVias for a draft choice?" Gillman asked. "They'll look at me and say, 'Great, but how does that help us this season?'"

Gillman's insolence enraged Klein, especially since LeVias wasn't a top-line player. Thirty minutes before the trade deadline, Klein called

Gillman out of practice, and he asked him to reconsider the trade request. Looking back on it, if Gillman would have bent to that request, he probably would have kept his job through at least the end of the season. But the stubborn Gillman said no. Klein ordered him back to practice and slammed the phone into its receiver.

A few weeks later, Gillman knew he needed a confrontation with his boss. On the flight to Oakland on what would be the final road trip of his Chargers coaching career, Sid, in his aisle seat leaned across Jack Murphy to give his bride a good-luck kiss. "Just be sure you don't kiss me," Murphy quipped. "Why not?" Gillman said. "I kiss my sons-in-law. I kiss my son." And after the Chargers lost 34–33 to the Raiders, Gillman confided in Murphy that he was set to kiss goodbye his job in San Diego. He would approach Klein for a meeting in his Beverly Hills office and find out exactly where he stood with his owner. "Whatever happens," Gillman told Murphy, "I don't want sympathy."

Klein hadn't planned on making a coaching decision until the end of the season, but the rumors that Gillman's days were numbered ran rampant. Gillman was under the impression that he had signed a lifetime contract with the Chargers, so he had false confidence in the amount of leverage he held against Klein. He didn't like what Klein had to say.

"I think it is apparent I've been moving away from one-man rule for some time now," Klein told reporters, referring to the fact that Gillman held the coaching and general manager duties for most of his time with the Chargers. "I think the day of one-man rule in professional football is gone. I just don't think that one man is big enough and strong enough and able enough to work 80 hours a day and take care of all the details necessary to run a pro football franchise.

"We did part of it last year when we divorced the general managership from the coach. Sid has the full authority as far as the field is concerned. But we intend to segregate the duties as they should be segregated."

Klein didn't want Gillman to be able to veto a trade that made sense for the long-term health of the club. Gillman's five-year contract was actually set to expire in December, and Gillman wanted to talk about it right away. Klein said they could evaluate it at the end of the season. That was unacceptable to Gillman. Gillman offered to stay on the rest of the year. Klein said Gillman would have to scrap some of his players, including Hadl, to do so. That also was unacceptable to Gillman.

Throughout their time together, Gillman and Klein generally got along. But Klein got impatient with Gillman in 1971 and became critical of his coaching methods. Gillman didn't want a boss who butted in.

There really was no other solution. Gillman needed to leave in something between a forced resignation and a firing.

"Dad said, 'If I start making trades in the middle of the season, it looks like I have given up,'" said Lyle Gillman, his oldest daughter. "Dad said, 'How do you think that will look to the players?' Klein said, 'I'm the owner.' Dad said, 'I'm the coach.' Klein said, 'You're fired.'"

Said Bum Phillips, San Diego's defensive coordinator, "Sid went to talk to Gene Klein and he handed him his resignation letter and told him, 'Now, here's what I want to do. If you don't want to do it, turn me loose.' He told him what he wanted, and Gene accepted his resignation. What he was doing was trying to impress on [Klein] the way things had to be. He wanted to make sure that that guy wasn't going to butt in, because lots of owners try to tell you what to do."

Of course, when those owners tell you to pack up your things and vacate the premises, you generally have to listen. Klein thought Gillman was metaphorically putting a gun to his head, and he couldn't let that stand. Despite what Gillman believed was a lifetime contract, Klein countered that by saying the lifetime contract wasn't to be the Chargers head coach. Instead, he meant that Gillman could always have a job in the organization.

Big difference, but it produced a great line from Gillman at his farewell news conference at the Kona Kai Club. "I have a message for the youth of America," he said. "I'd put my faith in a lifetime contract. Just say, 'Thank you. But please put it in writing.'"

"It was a terribly bitter time," said Tom Gillman, Sid's son. "When you had trust in somebody and somebody's word and they have broken it, and considering what they broke it about, it was not a pleasant time. It was a terrible surprise. When bad things happened to my dad, he moved on. He certainly moved on from that, but it was one of those rockier times."

Once again, Gillman faced an uncertain future, and as he walked away, his players weren't sure how to feel. To this day, some still haven't figured it out. As Wells Twombly wrote in the *San Francisco Examiner* after Gillman lost his job, "Few coaches have produced such a furious love-hate ambivalence in their players as Gillman did. They cursed him. They praised him. They loved playing for him. And they couldn't wait to get away from him."

And now, he was gone, leaving his job in the hands of general-manager-turned-head-coach Harland Svare—who had coached the Los Angeles Rams from 1962 to 1965 and had finished with a record of 14-31-3 and fared no better with the Chargers, going 7-17-2 as the head coach.

But what would Gillman do now? He, once again, was unemployed, though unlike during his tenure in Los Angeles, Gillman had made the Chargers franchise his own and had made an enormous impact on pro football. He could walk away satisfied, like he accomplished what he set out to do. Maybe, just maybe, he could relax for a while. "I've got a big rear end," Gillman said. "I'm going to spend the rest of my life sitting on it. I'm out of football and enjoying life."

A month later, Gillman was on his way to Dallas. For a new coaching job.

twelve   HOUSTON

Without a football job and without a new league that could hire him, Gillman went back to show business. After nearly four decades on the sidelines and at the age of 60, he restarted an old career in front of the camera. Unlike the last time, when he appeared in a Western TV show following his departure from the Los Angeles Rams, there was a journalistic twist. He joined KCST, Channel 39 in San Diego, and become a celebrity sports reporter.

Two NFL clubs went after Gillman to serve as their offensive coordinator after his Chargers reign ended, but Gillman simply couldn't stomach the thought of becoming an assistant again and serving under another head coach. He hadn't done so since Earl Blaik at West Point, and he wasn't going to demote himself again. One opportunity came from his old assistant coach Chuck Noll, then the head coach for the Steelers. Gillman flew to Pittsburgh to talk to Noll about the position, but ultimately, Gillman declined Noll's advances. Instead, he donned makeup and reported the news of the day.

"Sid will be content in whatever he does if he does it well," Esther said. "As a matter of fact, he is kind of excited about his new life."

In reality, though, the new position bored him. He attended press conferences but didn't ask questions. He just sat there, listening and looking unhappy. He made more news by showing up rather than actually relaying any of it.

But as usual, when somebody called with a new football challenge— not just an assistant job, but a real *challenge*—Gillman dropped everything to accept it. He couldn't expel football from his bloodstream; his love for the game grew stronger after every passing year. He was an addict, and when the Cowboys called and offered him a job, he couldn't resist. He plunged the needle into his arm and prepared to enjoy the football high that was to come.

"Football must be some game if he needs it so much he's leaving four children and seven grandchildren," Lyle Gillman said in 1972. "But I know my father and I'm glad he's going to Dallas, because he can't be happy away from football."

Tex Schramm, the president of the Cowboys who had been Gillman's original general manager in L.A., told Gillman his role was to analyze the personnel and tendencies of Cowboys opponents, assist with game preparation, and work on the team's offensive scheme. Gillman would brainstorm ideas and present them to coach Tom Landry. Gillman would not be on the field during games. Instead, it was a quality control position that left him in charge of research and development, and it allowed him to look at game film for everything and anything.

"What's this all about, Sid?" his old buddy, Los Angeles sportswriter Melvin Durslag, asked after he took the job. Said Gillman: "I'll tell you about quality (control) coaching. You're all right as long as your quarterback is all right. When the quarterback goes down, you can take quality coaching and throw it in the crapper."

Responded Durslag: "Well, if all else fails, Sid, you can get a job playing the piano at a whorehouse."

The Cowboys position under Landry was a stopgap for Gillman. Under the NFL-AFL merger rules, Gillman needed one more season in pro football in order to qualify for the pension that eventually paid him $168 per month. Schramm knew this and wanted to help out his old buddy. Since Gillman considered Dallas to be the most progressive franchise in the NFL—creating a position for him a year after the Cowboys' first Super Bowl title was one example of that forward thinking—the decision to join Landry's staff was an easy one.

This was not a job that Gillman could stay in for the rest of his career. He said he wanted to leave coaching, but in reality, he never would. In some ways, quality control was the perfect job for Gillman's brain. But not his heart. Because this wasn't truly coaching. It was analyzing and brainstorming.

Gillman took the job anyway. Sid and Esther were comfortable, but he was no millionaire. He still wanted a paycheck. If he had hired an agent sometime during his career, someone who could have helped him earn more money in marketing and endorsement deals, he could have had a bigger bank account. If he had hired a financial advisor, he could have invested more. But he refused to hire an agent, because he didn't want to put himself in the spotlight. And he declined to hire an advisor, because he didn't want to take the risks.

"The fact he didn't have an agent killed him financially," said Lyle Gillman. "He stayed very conservative. That's the only thing he was conservative about. . . . If he had gotten an agent then, this book would have been written in the 1970s."

Throughout his post–San Diego life, Gillman had been offered financial deals from friends and colleagues. But Gillman was always averse to taking the chance. In fact, Sol Price approached Sid and Esther about becoming one of the 10 original investors in a little warehouse store called Price Club. That little warehouse store eventually merged with another company called Costco. It was an investment that would have made the Gillmans millions of dollars. All Gillman needed was $100,000 for the initial investment.

He couldn't do it. He told his daughters he couldn't sleep at the thought.

"He was not a gambler," said Bobbe Korbin, his second-oldest daughter. "He was not an investor. He was not a gambler, even with his future."

Not with his money, perhaps. But with his coaching choices, Gillman had proven he would take a risk. Leaving the safe haven of Cincinnati for a job with the one of the highest-profile pro teams and, later, accepting a job in the unknown AFL were not slam-dunk propositions. So, when Bud Adams, the owner of the Houston Oilers and Gillman's heated rival in the AFL, called and asked him to take over his general manager job, Gillman didn't hesitate. Sitting in the GM office had to be better than watching film in a darkened room, even if the Cowboys and Oilers might as well have been in different leagues.

—⚎—

It didn't take long for Gillman, in his new Cowboys job, to hear the whispers that Adams wanted to hire him as the team's general manager and as an assistant under Oilers head coach Bill Peterson. Landry gave his permission for Gillman to interview for the GM job but not for any assistant position. Despite Adams's troubled past with Gillman when he was at San Diego—"They were like water and oil, no pun intended," said Bobbe Korbin—Adams said he was willing to give Gillman everything he wanted.

"I told him I wanted him to take over completely," Adams said. "I told him it was his baby and I wanted him to run it."

How could Gillman refuse? The simple answer: he couldn't. Thus, after Dallas' 10-4 regular season in 1972 ended in an NFC conference championship game loss to the Redskins, Gillman made preparations to move four hours south to Houston. He was entering a cesspool of terrible football. The Oilers had recorded a winning season only once in the past 10 years, and from 1970 to 1972 with three separate head coaches, they'd won a combined eight games, tied twice, and lost 32. Adams was so desperate to change the course of his franchise, he was willing to hire an old enemy and give him full authority to help clean up the Oilers.

The first problem, as Gillman saw it, was that the franchise had no talent and, therefore, no prospects for winning in the future. As the general manager, he immediately began making trades, swapping Oilers draft picks for current talent. Exchanging future potential to win games today. Gillman knew he had to build a winner right away, because he recognized Adams's impatience (before the 1971 season, he gave first-time head coach Ed Hughes a five-year deal, and after a 4-9 mark that year, fired him with four years left on the contract).

The second problem was with Peterson, whose career head-coaching career record was 1-18 with 240 points scored and 553 points allowed. It wasn't simply that Peterson was incompetent as an NFL head coach. It was that he was perceived as a hopeless oddball who had no control over his team. Peterson had worked under Gillman protégé Paul Dietzel on LSU's 1958 national title squad, and he parlayed that into a relatively success-ful decade-long stop at Florida State, where he coached Fred Biletnikoff to All-American honors and where he helped mold the minds of Bobby Bowden and Joe Gibbs.

But in Houston, Peterson was completely in over his head. His game plans were too long—his players called it "The Grab Bag Offense"—and when he spoke, he made strange, disjointed comments that made little or no sense. Unlike Gillman's mentor, Ohio State madman Francis Schmidt, Peterson's teams didn't win. He wasn't an eccentric genius. He was just eccentric. After Adams hired Gillman as the general manager, Peterson knew his days were numbered. During practice, he stood off to the side and talked to his taxi squad players. He glanced over the shoulders of his assistants as *they* coached practices. He was invisible, and after Gillman took over the offense before the team's fourth game, Peterson had no credibility and no impact on his own team. He just sort of faded away.

When Peterson announced to his team that Gillman would run the offense, he simply said, "I've asked Sid to help us." Then, as Gillman be-gan with the pep talk, Peterson walked over to the corner of the room and sat in a fetal position. It was, to say the least, a sad sight.

The 1973 team was in shambles. One *Houston Post* reporter wrote that covering the team was like "visiting friends doing eight to 10," and in the paper's weekly predictions section, another reporter picked the Bal-timore Colts to beat the Oilers by 100 points (strangely, Houston upset the Colts that week for its only win of 1973). After the Oilers lost 31–26 to the L.A. Rams in Week 4, Gillman went to the hospital to visit starting center Bill Curry, who had broken his leg. "If there's anything bothering you," Gillman said, "let me know." Responded Curry, by then on pain-killers, "As a matter of fact, something's bothering me now. When's the charade going to end?"

Gillman took that point to heart, because the next week, after losing to Denver by four touchdowns, he mercifully relieved Peterson of his duties and made himself the head coach. During one of his initial meetings, he told his team not to expect miracles. "I didn't come here to be a prophet," Gillman said. Muttered one of his players, "No, you came here to be a god."

But Gillman was right. He wasn't a miracle-worker. The Oilers won a single game and, and for the second straight season, Houston finished 1-13. That, though, is to be expected when a team employs, in the span of four years, four head coaches, four defensive line coaches, three defensive backfield coaches, four offensive backfield coaches, three linebacker coaches, three receiver coaches, three offensive line coaches, three trainers, three general managers, and three team physicians.

It led some players, like offensive guard Tom Regner, to consider other lines of work. After the 1972 season, following six years in the Houston organization, Regner decided he'd had enough and began helping to run an Italian restaurant across the street from the Oilers' practice field. When his forlorn former teammates came into the restaurant for a bite to eat, Regner sympathized, telling them, "You don't have a future here. Head coaches don't have a future here. . . . The only thing you've got to look forward to each year is a new coach and a new system." Then, Regner looked out the window at the team's practice facility and wiped his hands on his apron. "I," he said, "would rather be making sandwiches."

Heading into 1974, Gillman remained in his dual role of general manager and coach, but before the season began, the players union enacted a work stoppage. When the strike was settled 42 days later, Gillman made himself a lightning rod for criticism. In one of his first team meetings of the season, he warned, "This is not a democracy. This is a dictatorship, and I'm the dick." He then pointed to seven veterans—including linebacker Paul Guidry, who had driven 26 hours from Buffalo to be at camp on time—and because they were union player representatives who supported the strike, he immediately cut them from the roster. "You guys," Gillman said addressing the team again, "are a bunch of losers. We're going to change that attitude right now."

The attitude Gillman wanted apparently was for everybody to hate the head coach—and for Gillman to be the only one to take the heat if the team performed poorly again. But his players burned with intense emotion at Gillman. "It is people such as Gillman who cause the players to ask for all sorts of freedom they normally wouldn't need that they would not even think about if it weren't for people like Gillman," said one wonderfully poetic Oilers player. But Gillman didn't care, and some theorized that because Gillman believed the Oilers were too friendly and nice when they were losing, he could be the person they could all band together against and hate for extra motivation. "I don't know about that," Gillman said.

Gillman didn't necessarily like his players either. In his Houston office, he hung a plaque on the wall that read, "Illegitimi noa carborundum"—faux-Latin for "Don't let the bastards grind you down." When he was in San Diego, he hired a doctor named Bruce Ogilvie who specialized in counseling pro athletes, to analyze the entire coaching staff. One of the first questions asked by Ogilvie was how Gillman felt about football players in general. "I hate them," Gillman said.

"If you hate them," Ogilvie asked, "why are you coaching?"

"Because," Gillman said, "I need them."

His players needed him too, and he realized that as well. That's why Gillman, despite his reputation among many of his players, tried to help them off the field. With owner Gene Klein in San Diego, Gillman secured an investment counselor for his squad, and he advised players and their families how to budget their money.

Though quarterback Dan Pastorini vehemently disliked Gillman when he chewed him out in front of the rest of the team, he also appreciated the fact that Gillman defended Pastorini from the owner. Pastorini had originally signed a six-year contract worth $250,000, and by the 1974 season, Pastorini was in the fourth year of his deal.

"Not for nothing," Pastorini told Gillman, "but I'm starting quarterback, and I've been your punter and backup kicker. I'm making one-third of the money of some of the linemen who aren't blocking for me."

Gillman pulled out Pastorini's contract, and after skimming it, he stormed out of the room. When he returned, Gillman had a new two-year deal that bumped Pastorini's base salary from $30,000 a year to $110,000. "Sign it," Gillman said.

"There were no negotiations," Pastorini said decades later. "But I appreciated that."

But by the time the 1974 season began, Gillman was 62 years old, and some wondered if the game had passed him by. Some wondered if the innovation that had carried him from Ohio State in the late 1930s to the successful Chargers teams of the 1960s had grown stale. "His ideas on the field are current, but off the field he's not a modern-day coach," Pastorini said during 1974's training camp. "He doesn't adapt to the 'now genera-tion.' He feels he's dealing with unintelligent people and he isn't."

Either that or Gillman was simply fooling everybody and building the foundation for one last great gasp as a head coach.

—⚊—

While Gillman figured he could begin to rebuild the Oilers offense, he also called to an old colleague for help in mending a defense that al-lowed 31.9 points per game in 1973, the worst in the NFL. After Gillman was fired in San Diego in 1971, his defensive coordinator Bum Phillips took a job as an assistant at Oklahoma State. But by 1974, Gillman need-ed him again, and this time, Phillips—one of the biggest pro innovators of the 3-4 defense that Gillman ultimately rejected in San Diego—had leverage.

Before he accepted Gillman's offer to become the Oilers defensive coordinator, Phillips told Gillman, "Coach, I want to run the 3-4. Would you be willing to run whatever defense fits our personnel?" Gillman said he would, and just like that, Phillips was one step closer to his first non-high school head coaching job.

But after falling 51–10 to the Vikings in a loss that dropped the Oilers to 1-4 on the 1974 season, Gillman reneged. He called Phillips and told him the team was returning to the 4-3 scheme. Phillips had no recourse, because Phillips wasn't the boss.

"Sid was a great guy—one of the best people in the world—except when he wanted to do something, he wasn't going to listen to reason," Phillips said. "He got to be so successful by doing it his way."

The next week after the Oilers fell behind 21–13 to the undefeated St. Louis Cardinals, Gillman had another change of heart. At halftime, Gillman approached Phillips and asked, "You reckon we can go back to the 3-4?" Phillips said that the team could, and though Houston lost 31–27 that day, the Oilers won six of their final eight games of the season. In four of those wins, they held their opponent to 10 points or less, and Phillips's defense was a major contributor.

It led to a 7-7 season and the AFC Coach of the Year award for Gillman. He had continued learning patience, and though the team was split on whether it despised him, he clearly reached his squad that season.

"He was trying to build a football team, and I think Esther had a lot to do with his temperament," Pastorini said. "She was his soothing force over him. She got him to stop and take a deep breath every now and then. He accepted mediocrity. Mediocrity was 7-7. But for us, it was a turnaround season."

Entering the last game of the year, the Oilers were 6-7 and coming off a humbling loss to the Broncos, and in order to win its seventh game, Houston needed to beat Cleveland for the first time in its last 10 tries. Entering the season, the Oilers were so bad that the Browns coaches threatened to trade underperforming players to Houston's squad, but by the time of the December 15 game, Cleveland was in the midst of its worst season in club history.

Despite falling behind on two occasions, the Oilers put together a pair of valiant comebacks and managed to squeak out the win. After the game, Browns owner Art Modell found Gillman in the Oilers locker room, stuck out his hand and said, "Congratulations, Sid. Good job." Feeling the effects of two long seasons in Houston, Gillman pulled in Modell for an appreciative embrace. In the middle of the party, quarterback Dan Pastorini led his teammates in the singing of "Happy Birthday" to Gillman, a joyful tradition that had been repeated five other times that season. The team didn't actually play on Gillman's birthday of October 26 that season, but on October 27, Houston ended a five-game losing streak by beating Cincinnati. Then, every week, after the last "Happy Birthday" note had faded away, Gillman said, "Not this week. My birthday isn't until next week."

It was truly a remarkable outcome for Gillman and the Oilers. Considering the organization had won just two of the previous 26 games before the 1974 season, Gillman's accomplishment that year ranked as one of the most satisfying of his career. Sure, he couldn't push the Oilers above a .500 record, but he set the organization on the path to winning at least 10 games in four of the next six seasons.

"I sought out Sid Gillman to turn the Oilers around, whether it took . . . even five years," Adams said. "And he did it in two years."

True, Gillman had raided the team's future drafts in order to build a modicum of present success, but it was also clear the franchise wasn't a lost cause. Still, he managed to anger owner Bud Adams, who had to pay a $15,000 fine because Gillman kept 63 players on the regular-season payroll. While Gillman conceded he had exceeded the 47-man roster limit, he said he miscalculated only by a player or two. Either way, Adams was upset.

"I made it understood that if there were any fines like that this year, it's going to come out of somebody else's pocket," Adams said. "It makes me look like a poor owner, and I do not want to be the laughingstock of the owners around the league."

No, but in the views of many, Adams didn't need anybody's help in becoming a laughingstock.

—〰—

If some in the Oilers organization hated Gillman, Oilers fans utterly despised Adams. Especially after he moved the team to Tennessee following the 1996 season and renamed it the Titans, leaving an oil field void in Houston. Like his father, Boots Adams, Bud Adams was a successful oilman. But he wasn't a good football owner—the fact that no team Adams has owned ever won the Super Bowl is one good indication—and for many years, some observers believed the only way Adams could save the franchise was to sell it.

"It was bad management right to the core," Gillman said when asked how the Oilers had fallen so far into the abyss. "The success of a pro football team starts with the front office, with ownership, and works down."

One reason for the lack of success was that Adams meddled unnecessarily in the business affairs of his underlings. Bill Peterson felt so hamstrung by the team's organizational model that he sent a memo to Adams following the 1972 season in which he explained that the head coach needed to have the ability to make daily decisions that affect the franchise. "Often on the slightest matter," Peterson wrote, "I must waste a day seeking out someone in authority." Peterson also wondered why the head coach had to compete with the owner for loyalty within the organization. For his trouble, Peterson was cuckolded and then fired the next season.

"Bud knows football," said one Adams associate, "but he doesn't know too much about people."

Or how to properly reward a successful season. In 1978, Adams gave each Oilers assistant coach a $3,000 bonus for beating Miami in the playoffs. The following week, after Houston upended the Patriots, the assistants received $2,000. "If we win the Super Bowl," one assistant said, "we could wind up paying the owner."

Adams must have known that Gillman, first as the general manager and then as the GM/coach, would spend money to make the team a winner as quickly as possible. Gillman pulled the same maneuver at Miami (Ohio), at Cincinnati, and with the Chargers under Barron Hilton. Adams might have been embarrassed about having to pay a $15,000 fine for Gillman's roster maneuvering, but he also let Gillman get away with overspending the team budget by $800,000 and by making Adams the only NFL owner in 1973 to lose money.

"I don't care what he says: there is no way that $600,000 worth of movies can make us a better team," Adams said. "I wouldn't say Sid and I are having problems. That isn't true. We just aren't talking."

After their breakup in the beginning of the 1975 season, there was never reason for them to speak again.

—ɷ—

Bum Phillips looked at Gillman and saw an immensely talented coach who massaged his offensive schemes and ideas to fit the personnel of his team. Gillman impressed him in that way, especially during the 1974 season when, as Phillips said, "he had nothing as far as talent . . . Then he took those same players and made them into a 7-7 team. Now, *that* is utilizing your personnel." Phillips could relate, and part of the reason he originally installed the 3-4 defense with Gillman's Chargers in 1967 was because the team had much better linebackers than defensive linemen.

With Houston's turnaround still in its infancy stage under Gillman, he decided, once again, to retire from head coaching and stay on as the team's general manager. He wanted Bum Phillips to succeed him and offered him $125,000 to seal the deal.

Phillips was a clear departure from the coaching style of Gillman. The old coach's playbook was as thick as a Stephen King novel, but early in his tenure, Phillips thinned out the offensive scheme. He instead preferred a smaller number of plays the team could actually run correctly. Phillips was a folksy ex-Marine with a plug of tobacco in his cheek, and when he coached on the sideline, he wore powder blue ostrich-skin boots and a Stetson (though not in the Astrodome because his mama had told him never to wear his hat indoors).

"All he needed," Gillman said, "was a holster."

His given name was Oail, but he went by Bum because "can't nobody spell it or pronounce it or anything." And unlike most coaches of yesterday and today, including Gillman, Phillips took delight in talking to the press (he made the beer cooler in his office just as accessible, scoring him major points with the beat writers). He also turned down $15,000 to do a beer commercial because he didn't want to risk influencing some teenager to drink too much and then drive.

Gillman ran a tight organization, but life in a Phillips regime was hardly regimented at all. "That was like Camelot for us," said lineman Carl Mauck, who became a Phillips assistant coach in New Orleans. Said Pastorini: "It was like going to Disneyland with Bum. He really made football fun. . . . I don't know of a man who was more loved."

History proved that Gillman made the right call by promoting Phillips, because he took the Oilers to the playoffs in three of the next six seasons he was in Houston. But Gillman sealed his own fate by elevating Phillips to that position. When he hired Phillips as the head coach, Gillman expected to have ultimate control over personnel. Maybe he figured Phillips would be subservient to Gillman's every wish and demand. Maybe he underestimated Phillips's own desires. But Gillman was wrong. A magazine writer compared Phillips to Douglas MacArthur playing the role of Pa Kettle, and like Gillman in San Diego and Houston, Phillips needed absolute control of the team he coached.

"I'd make a good one-term politician," Phillips said. "I'm afraid I wouldn't get re-elected, 'cause there ain't but one way to do something and it's got nothin' to do with gettin' votes."

Gillman offered Phillips a contract that contained a clause giving Phillips responsibility for player-personnel and policy-making decisions, but all of it was subject to approval by Gillman. Phillips wasn't surprised. He had seen Gillman meddle with Charlie Waller in 1969 and 1970 after Gillman retired from coaching following his health scare, and he knew that in Houston, Gillman interrupted Bill Peterson during practice to give his own instructions. Phillips couldn't have that hanging over his head.

This is where the story gets two-sided.

Taken from multiple reports and multiple interviews, Phillips approached Adams when Gillman was out of town and told him that he wouldn't coach unless the Gillman clause was removed from the contract. He also said he wanted Gillman barred from the locker room and the practice field.

"Bud Adams had to let me have it," Phillips told *Sports Illustrated* in 1980. "He couldn't get anybody else to screw it up much worse than it'd already been screwed up before Sid. But Sid had to know my feelings. I was going to run this football team."

Said Dan Pastorini more than 25 years after the fact: "Bum wasn't going to be like Bill Peterson. He had to have full control or nothing. He figured if Sid caught (the removal of the clause) in his contract, he would be fired. If Sid didn't catch it, he would have full control."

Gillman didn't catch it, and after the contract was finished, Phillips, unbeknownst to Gillman, had control of the team and who could watch practice. When Gillman discovered he'd been outflanked, he went in search of Adams. When it was clear that Adams sided with Phillips, Gillman had no other choice. He was a general manager who had less power than the head coach, so he resigned.

"We had a tough time getting along with the owner of the club, Bud Adams," Gillman said many years later. "So, we decided it was time to leave. Every once in a while, you coach for somebody that wants to maintain control, that doesn't want to turn over control to his coach and general manager. This gentleman, Bud Adams, owned the club and had every right to want to control the coach. But as a coach, I figured the only way I could succeed was to run it myself."

Gillman's family has never forgiven Adams—who rarely does interviews and whose PR people didn't respond to multiple phone messages for this book—or Phillips. In their view, Phillips went behind Gillman's back to delete the original clause that gave Gillman ultimate control of the roster.

"[Gillman] turned everybody around and the city," said Tom Gillman, Sid's son. "What made it even more was the betrayal by Bum . . . He gave [Phillips] everything. He gave him a good shot at his back."

But these days, Phillips, close to entering his 10th decade of life, said he did nothing wrong, especially because Phillips had already told Gillman he needed control and that Gillman agreed with him.

"I had control of the team," he said. "I had the right to draft, waive, trade. I had the control I needed. That's what [Gillman] gave me. I told Sid that's what I wanted, and he said that was fine. We didn't have any disagreement over that. Evidently, the disagreement was with Bud."

As for going behind Gillman's back and indirectly causing Gillman to quit his job, Phillips said, "There was a whole lot of stories running around, I guess. Believe me, I'm telling you what happened. I worked for him for six years, and I enjoyed it for six years. If he wanted to draft somebody that I didn't want to draft, we wouldn't have drafted him. I had no problem with knowing my responsibilities."

Either way, Gillman was gone, and for Phillips, it was probably for the best.

"Bum knew Sid. He knew if they were both there, they weren't going to get nothing done," said Mauck, a center on the 1975 squad. "Spin it any way you want."

While the Gillman family bristles at the mention of Adams and Phillips, the latter has nothing but nice things to say about Gillman. And it seems that Gillman forgave Phillips, because in 1980, Gillman attended a dinner honoring Phillips. In a photo taken at the event, Gillman, dressed in a tuxedo, wore a wide grin as he was embraced by Mauck—clad in a derby hat, overalls, a bow tie, and a tuxedo jacket complete with boutonniere. Mauck was laughing maniacally next to Phillips, who sported a coat, large glasses, a buzz cut and a bemused grin.

At the time, though, the rebuke hurt Gillman, and he, once again, was out of a job. It was time for Gillman and Esther to look ahead. "It was time to retire," Esther said. "In quotes."

He'd never hold another NFL head coaching or general manager job. At the age of 64, he had to wonder if his relevance to pro football had begun to erode for good.

thirteen   FAMILY LIFE

Sid Gillman loved football. He spent much of his life inside darkened film rooms, on sweltering practice fields, or entrenched on icy stadium sidelines, and when he wasn't engaged in actual football activity, he talked about football and he thought about football. Gillman was so engrossed in his love that he barely could find his way out of his obsession, and when he couldn't, he tuned out the world. It wasn't unusual, if the conversation at a dinner party turned away from football, for Gillman to fall asleep in his chair.

"The last time I was at his house, he became so engrossed in a football discussion he didn't notice that the steaks he had placed on the outside grill had caught fire," said a Gillman friend named Dick Heekin in 1955. "It didn't upset him, though. He just put on some more steaks and continued the conversation."

This is a fine line for a coach to walk. Vince Lombardi, for example, was so focused on his job that his lonely wife fell into depression and took to alcohol to fill the void of an absent husband; his children long felt the burden of a father who paid more attention to his players than to them. Gillman's football preoccupation affected his household, but on the bright side, there weren't many other families that could succinctly explain how an offensive guard could successfully trap-block an opponent on the inside handoff. Yet Gillman's children loved him passionately, and when he was gone coaching or recruiting or when he was *thinking* about coaching and recruiting, they missed him dearly. He tried to include them in his obsession.

"How many kids are so involved in their father's profession?" asked Lyle Gillman. "Usually, Daddy goes to work, and he comes home. I don't care if he owns General Electric, they have activities indigenous to the

231

family, not his profession. With us, we lived and breathed his winning and losing. We lived and breathed for Saturdays in college and Sundays in the pros."

If Gillman's team had lost that weekend, he was usually even-keeled when he returned home. The rest of the family was heartbroken—"It wasn't a loss," said Bill Korbin, Bobbe's husband, "it was a wake."—and Gillman oftentimes was the one to cheer up his wife and kids. He had left his emotion at the office, and since he knew nothing else could be done that day, he usually let go of a bad result. Those moments were tougher for his family than for him.

"It's not a great way to raise kids," Korbin said. "That's why we're very black and white, right and wrong. You either win or lose, because there weren't many ties."

Said Terry Hill, his youngest daughter: "It was the good news and the bad news. He was very even-keeled, but there was a degree of absence all the time. He was really absorbed with football. I think he was always thinking about football. He was an incredibly kind person. I don't remember him ever being an angry person in our house. But I also remember that it would have been very hard to sit and have a stupid conversation with him."

It's not that he wasn't smart and aware of the world, but football usually came first. And while it was rare, Gillman showed his kids the temper he possessed. With Terry and Tom attending University of California-Berkeley for college, both took a sharp left turn from their father. He was an old-school Democrat, but when Terry and Tom opposed the Vietnam War, they drew their father's ire. In fact, the only time Gillman yelled at Terry was when she actively supported the end of the conflict as a college senior.

"He thought it was terrible that anybody should ever question the U.S. government," Terry said. "I took great offense to that. I thought he was being very narrow-minded."

Gillman was rather narrow-minded on the issue of facial hair as well. During college, Tom had an awakening and grew a mustache in protest of

Vietnam, leading to the most intense family situation he ever experienced. Sid told him that no son or player of his grew a mustache. "You do," Tom countered, "if your son wants to have one." Sid wouldn't budge. Tom wouldn't budge. But unless Sid was going to strap his son into a chair and physically shave his mustache for him, there was little chance for Sid to win this battle. So, Sid exhaled and let it go.

While Gillman's football-crazed mind was always whirling in different directions, he still managed to make his kids laugh.

"Dad had a great sense of humor," Lyle Gillman said. "We got that from him, because all of us are very funny."

Responded Bill Korbin: "He thought he was funny. He wasn't very funny."

Zoom in on the skeptical faces of Lyle and Bobbe.

"No, he was not," Bill continued. "He laughed before he could finish the joke."

Lyle: "He cracked himself up."

Bill: "I know. That was funny to you. He tried to be funny."

Bobbe: "He *was* very funny."

What's clear these days is that his kids appreciate a good joke or story and, like their father, are prone to fits of humor. And while Lyle and Bobbe settled down early on with husbands and children, Terry took a different route to happiness.

—⁂—

Out of all of Sid and Esther's children, Terry knows the least about their football lives. While Lyle, Bobbe, and Tom can recite old games and the emotions those results brought at the time, Terry doesn't have such recollections. These days, Terry and her husband, Larry, live in the Richmond district of San Francisco, and inside their home, the scrapbook Gillman's mother created nearly a century ago is stored. Their son, Trevor Hill, currently living in Japan, will take possession of the priceless heirloom when he returns to the States permanently. For now, though, Terry holds her father's memories inside her home.

Terry and Larry have lived an adventure since meeting when Terry was in college at Berkeley and Larry was at medical school in San Francisco. When the two got to know each other, Larry told his father—Irving Hill, a longtime federal judge—that he had met the daughter of Sid Gillman. "Marry her," Irving told his son. "We'll get a parking pass."

On their third date, they attended a Raiders-Chargers game at Frank Youell Field in Oakland and sat in the bleachers to watch Sid at work. The Chargers had already clinched the AFL West championship and had begun to prepare to face Buffalo in the 1964 league title game. During the contest, Esther leaned across Terry and, without checking with her daughter first, invited Larry to travel to Buffalo with the family for the championship contest.

"Yeah," Terry said, "I barely knew the guy."

Esther, though, had spotted a winner. Terry and Larry took in their fourth date watching the Chargers fall to Jack Kemp and the Bills, and more than 45 years later, the two still revel in their marital bliss in their beautiful home in that beautiful city.

After they were married, they lived in San Francisco for a year and Los Angeles for two. Larry then became a doctor in the Foreign Service, and for 16 years, they lived in Mali, Bangladesh, South Africa, Beijing, the Philippines, and Washington, DC.

"They," Esther said, "are the wandering Jews of the family."

And while they were largely absent during Gillman's later career, the Hills, like all of the Gillman children, are quick to defend him from his harem of detractors.

The most passionate defenders in the family, though, are Bobbe and Tom. Even if a Gillman slight was minor and not malicious, the Gillman children took to their pens and paper to write letters to the editor to correct what they felt was a wrong.

Said Tom: "Hell yes, we write letters. We've written a number of letters to editors. He deserves it. He really, really deserves it. But he did a few things that weren't so great, and we're happy to talk about that, too.

"It comes naturally. Bobbe, Terry, and I lived through it more intensely. My family was about my dad's job. It wasn't a complaint. It's just the way it was. Things were centered around that. We've always learned loyalty is very important anyway. We can empathize with our friends as a result when they win or lose. We're very, very quick to defend. It's partisanship, but I don't feel it's a blind one. There's so much more that goes on than him just being a football coach. We want to make sure it gets told."

And told correctly.

"We," Lyle said, "have been very busy making truth out of history."

—⁂—

While Gillman has plenty of critics and detractors, it's impossible to find anybody who will describe Esther as anything other than sugary-sweet. A former player would rant and rave about Gillman, but when the topic turned to Esther, the voice softened and the edge disappeared. Gillman's biggest enemies couldn't stop themselves from raving about the No. 1 lady in his life. This was the power of Esther, the antidote to Gillman's asperity, the one who could calm Gillman, and the one who made him more palatable to those who couldn't stand him. She could be your grandmother, your mother, your best friend. But she was Sid's wife first and foremost, and Sid's career was her career as well.

"It defined her," Larry Hill said.

When she and Sid began dating, she didn't know much football, other than that she had a special affinity for Red Grange. Boxing and hockey were the sports she enjoyed, but soon enough, with Sid's patient help, she discovered that she had an aptitude for understanding the intricacies of Sid's game.

"I guess I was a tomboy all my life," Esther said. "I loved sports from the beginning."

She didn't see football players as brutes who simply looked to pound their opponents into submission. Maybe because of the cultured way in which her parents raised her, she saw the artistic achievement in the game that few others thought about. She appreciated the preciseness of 11 men performing 11 different functions at the same time in order to achieve the same goal. To Esther, this was like a symphonic performance, a ballet even.

That's why, when she studied film with Sid or saw a game live in the stadium, she didn't watch the entirety of the play unfold. Instead, she preferred to isolate one player to see how he interacted with his teammates. She likened it to focusing on one instrument in an orchestra and concentrating on how the bassoon played off the violins and cellos to make that beautiful sound.

In truth, Esther was glad her husband of 67 years was not a 9-to-5 businessman. She thought that kind of life would bore her. She also quickly learned that telling Sid to come in the house from watching film didn't work. She was the one who had to be flexible. So, after dinner, she'd go out with coffee, dessert, and her knitting and sit with him as he studied the game. At one point, she figured that she must have set a world record for football wives who created afghans.

She was also a popular interview with the press. It seemed like there was a feature on Sid Gillman's wife every year, and the photos accompanying the stories usually featured her posing with a film projector. It helped that she was pretty, friendly, polished, philanthropic like Bono, fashionable like Jackie Kennedy, knowledgeable about the game like her husband, and a damn good quote.

"She was an angel," said quarterback Dan Pastorini. "She was the soft hand in that whole deal. She was like the den mother. To put up with that guy for that many years, she had to grow wings."

She was more than a football wife, though. She read to the blind when the Gillmans lived in Philadelphia in the late 1970s and early 1980s. She volunteered at the famed MD Anderson hospital in Houston when Gillman worked with the Oilers. She was a sophisticate, and she was interested in everything that was happening in a visitor's life. In their San Diego home, she hung marvelous paintings, many of which went back to the work her uncle, Peter Krasnow—an American modernist—completed before he immigrated to the U.S.

"She could talk about anything and always could talk about football," longtime NFL executive Carl Peterson said. "After Sid was gone, I would call her and she'd say, 'Carl, some of the football being played in the NFL right now is atrocious. They don't execute. The passing game is not there.' She was just beautiful. When you came into her home, she made you feel so special. She could talk about anything. She was up on everything. You marvel at how right she was, and she was right until the very end."

Most of all, though, she was married to the love of her life. From the moment he noticed her at the Sweet 16 party until the day he died, their love was storybook. He worshipped the ground she walked on, and she whispered the names of big-time team boosters he couldn't remember when they shook his hand. He couldn't go on a road trip without her, and she laid out his clothes every day. He spoke constantly of her beauty, and she made Jewish Spaghetti.

She could deal with Sid's quirks and obsessions and the peccadillos of just about anybody else.

While participating in a tennis tournament at the La Costa resort one year, chess master Bobby Fischer demanded fresh clothes, but the laundry service at the country club was closed. Esther volunteered to wash and iron his tennis attire. Later, Sid knocked on Fischer's door with the cleaned and folded laundry. He waited. He knocked. He waited. And waited some more. Finally, the door opened a crack, a hand emerged from the darkness within, grabbed the laundry and shut the door. Not a word was spoken, and Gillman shrugged and walked away. But the power of Esther didn't wane. Fischer, who later grew infamous for his anti-American and anti-Semitic ramblings, made sure to track down Esther and thank her personally.

In the end, Esther's job was, simply put, to make people feel good. Sid's players and their spouses and girlfriends, but most of all, her husband and her children. For nearly seven decades, that was her calling.

"This has been my career," Esther said. "These are my people. You have to understand. There has to be love to begin with. And understanding. Sid made it very easy for us to love football. He made it so interesting for us by bringing film home and teaching us this play and that play. You have assistant coaches who have wives who are sitting at home as much as I am. You have the players who are alone. Someone (needs to) pick them up and tell them what has to happen to be successful; that you can't be on your own.

"It's an old-fashioned phrase, but I think we were a happy family, and I think that contributes to his success. The man can't do it alone and the woman can't do it alone. I didn't do it because I was supposed to do it. You do it because that is *the way* to do it."

And the love between Sid and Esther and the attraction they shared never died. That was made clear one night when the Gillmans went to dinner with Carl Peterson and his wife after Sid retired from coaching. The Kansas City Chiefs were in town to play the Chargers, and the Petersons picked up the Gillmans in a limousine. After the dinner was over, the Petersons walked the Gillmans to their front door, and just as the Gillmans were about to enter, a massive power failure knocked out all the lights in the house.

Peterson said, "Geez, maybe you guys want to come back to the clubhouse and wait until the power is back on. I don't want you stumbling around in the dark."

Esther looked him in the eye. "We'll be just fine," she said and then looked at Sid. "We might even get lucky tonight."

That was all Sid needed to hear.

"Good night!" he exclaimed and slammed the door shut.

—⚏—

Tom Gillman is on the phone, and he's choking up. He's about to begin weeping, and he stops talking for a moment to catch his breath. He's the son of a football coach, and the sons of football coaches aren't supposed to cry. So say the stereotypes, at least. They swallow their feelings. They stop the tears. They push their emotions back into their gut where nobody can see them. Then, they go outside and toss around the football.

But that's not Tom Gillman, and when he gets emotional, his voice cracks, and he has to halt himself, lest he begin bawling on the phone with a virtual stranger.

Tom is a gay man living in Los Angeles. This would be unremarkable if his father spent his life in a classroom or in an office designing buildings or in a three-piece suit handing out loans to bank customers. But he's the son of Sid Gillman, the All-American from Ohio State, the one who other football coaches idolized, the one who never failed to show his players who was boss.

"Sid was the portrait of the masculine man," said longtime Los Angeles writer Melvin Durslag. "He wasn't a ruffian or anything, but he was a tough man."

Tom's a tough guy, too. He's suffered through seven different bouts of chemotherapy. He's burned through radiation twice. He'll ingest at least 30 different types of medicine per day for the rest of his life. His most recent health concern was a back surgery that put him out of commission for many months. But he's still alive.

"I didn't expect to live this long," Tom said. "Down deep inside, I never thought it would lose. I didn't think it would happen."

Yet he's still here and fighting, almost 30 years later.

But that's not why Tom, overcome with emotion, stops talking on the phone. That's not why he's struggling to keep the tears from popping out of their ducts. No, he's become emotional because he's talking about Tommy Lasorda and his son, Tommy Jr. He doesn't mention Lasorda's name, but in this Google age, it's not hard to determine who Gillman means.

"There is a former manager in the Los Angeles area in the field of baseball who's very well known," Gillman said. "He had a gay son. His gay son was a flamboyant queen, to the extent that those two were estranged. There was no familiarity there. There was no family there. The kid got AIDS, and there still wasn't any reconciliation. The son died from AIDS."

The truth is that when Tommy Jr. was a teenager in the 1970s, he hung around the Dodgers locker room and befriended outfielder Glenn

Burke, who later emerged from the closet after his career was finished and died in 1995 of AIDS-related complications. Burke believed Lasorda traded him to the Oakland A's in 1978 because Lasorda thought Burke was a bad influence on his son.

Tommy Jr., nicknamed Spunky, spent much of his time at the bars and clubs in West Hollywood, smoking cigarettes out of a long holder and attracting male attention. Though his father detested his lifestyle, Lasorda was at his son's bedside when he died in 1991 of pneumonia and dehydration. Lasorda had privately accepted his son's cruel fate and at the end of Spunky's life, he made amends. But he never let on in public. He didn't disown his son—not at the end, at least—but in an interview with *GQ* in 1992, Lasorda denied his son was gay at all. "My son wasn't gay," he said. "No way."

Billy Bean wasn't surprised. As another ballplayer who announced he was gay after he retired from baseball, Bean wrote the following in his autobiography: "Having spent most of his adult life in the world of gladiators, Tommy must have found it difficult to be truthful about his son."

And that's why Tom Gillman was on the precipice of a temporary breakdown during that phone call. It's because his dad didn't act like that when Tom came out to him in 1970. It's because Sid and Esther tried their best to understand why Tom was gay and what that meant. It's because this rough-and-tumble coach treated his gay son just the same. There was no estrangement, no need for reconciliation. Only love.

"I knew I was gay when I was 5 years old," Tom said. "I knew where to keep feelings like that, even though I didn't know what it was. It came time to tell him after I graduated from college. The worst part about it is that you're living a lie. He could ask me, 'Where are you going?' and it's always some fabrication. That's how I felt. We got closer after I told him. When the lie is gone, everything is a lot closer. That's how I felt with him, and that's how he felt with me."

When Tom made the decision to announce that he was gay, he first told each sister one by one. Then, he told Esther. And then, though Esther was uncomfortable about Sid's possible reaction, Tom broke the news to his father during dinner one night on a Chargers road trip. At first, Sid was unhappy about the revelation, and Tom could understand why. The news had come as quite a surprise. But almost immediately, Sid and Esther were advised to call the UCLA psychology department and ask for Dr. Evelyn Hooker, one of the foremost experts on homosexuality. After the three met with Hooker, she told Sid and Esther that their son was completely normal. Not abnormal in any way.

"From then on, it was OK with my dad," Tom said. "He did have some time thinking that it was his fault. It wasn't his fault, and he finally accepted it. He didn't feel guilty about it."

When Tom first introduced Ron, his partner of 23 years, to Sid, the most masculine of football coaches treated him the same way he treated his other sons-in-law. With love and affection. In some cases, he treated Ron better. Sid liked Tom's current partner, Bill, even better than Ron. "My dad was even crazier about him than the first," Tom said. "He always made sure Bill was invited to everything he did."

Thirteen years after his father embraced him and his identity, Tom had even worse news—news that he knew would eventually kill him. When his doctor told him he had AIDS in 1983, it didn't register with Tom. Hardly anybody knew what that acronym even meant, and at the time, HIV hadn't been identified yet. This was in the infancy of the disease, and Tom was one of the forefathers of the hell that was to be unleashed.

Tom might as well have been diagnosed with death, and even if the disease wouldn't kill him immediately, he would become a pariah. Living with AIDS in the 1980s was like living as a Communist in the Joseph McCarthy era. You couldn't let on. You couldn't be seen. Otherwise, your friends would know. Slowly, those friends melted away.

Tom knows only two people who were diagnosed with AIDS about the same time as him who are still alive. He knows hundreds who didn't make it. He watched heartbroken as his beloved Ron got sick and died. Tom watched as an entire generation of gay men fell victim. He watched but somehow survived. For this, he credits his father.

"I had some fairly remarkable things happen to me," Tom said. "I attribute a lot of why I'm living to my folks. Gene-wise, for sure. But also the idea of making it as a metaphor. We're all about winning and losing. This is a game I wanted to win. I never could believe I was going to lose it. Having that kind of mentality and having that point of view, it helped me know what I had to do to win. I was very hands-on with everybody. I was a very hands-on patient. I learned that all from my folks. I'm also lucky. You have to have some luck in this."

One of Tom's biggest incentives was to stay alive long enough for his parents not to have to bury their youngest child. But some of his endurance is unexplainable. He's lived nearly 30 years with a deadly disease. He can never relax. It's like he's perpetually running a race, and he always has to sneak a peek behind him to see how far death is trailing. Yet Tom also knows this: he has to keep running. That's why he took the experimental drugs when his doctors had no idea about the potential outcome. That's why he went to psychologists who taught him how to visualize the happy ending. That's why he endured the chemo and the radiation.

When he told his parents about the AIDS diagnosis, Tom believes they simply didn't understand. He doesn't blame them for that either. After all, who wants to think about their son dying of AIDS? But when he had his medical triumphs, they celebrated with him. When he went through another illness, they supported him through that as well.

But Tom has perspective on himself. He lives with AIDS, and in spite of the disease, he thrives.

"You say one in a million, and that's me," Tom said. "Don't think I don't know it and remember it and am appreciative of it. But it doesn't matter why. That's one of the reasons I accepted my homosexuality. Why? Because. You have other things to worry about. Where are you going to school next year? What are you doing tomorrow? The lie isn't a false promise, but it's not enough to ask why. Now, get on with your life."

Before he finishes his story to the stranger on the other side of phone, Tom thinks back to Tommy Lasorda and his son, Spunky. He ponders the denial—even after Tommy Jr.'s death—that the baseball manager's son was gay. He remembers how Lasorda denied his son . . . well, just about everything.

"My dad couldn't be further from somebody like that," Tom Gillman said. "That is not being a father. As little as I saw of my dad in my life, he was a loving father. He was there for me when I needed him."

And with that, Tom Gillman begins to cry.

fourteen   CAN'T GET AWAY

Al Palmiotto thought his boss was crazy. United States International University needed a new athletic director in December 1978, somebody who could build a football program to forge a big-time atmosphere for school athletics. School president William Rust had a wild idea. Call Gillman, he told Palmiotto, and see if he'll take over the position. It was a fishing expedition, and Palmiotto had been asked to catch a whale using a wooden pole and a tiny net.

About one-third of the 3,500 USIU students were foreign, but the San Diego–based school wanted to make a name for itself in American collegiate athletics, moving from the National Association of Intercollege Athletics to NCAA affiliation. Tom Walsh, who had been teaching physical education classes at a local high school, was hired as the football team's head coach.

The school needed an athletic director. Why not give Gillman a call? Why not set the bait and see if Gillman would bite?

"I was practically laughing when I phoned Sid," Palmiotto said. "I mean, Sid Gillman, the father of modern offensive football. I said, 'You wouldn't by any chance be interested?' He said, 'Sure, why not.'"

Gillman, after leaving the Oilers, had spent the rest of 1975 scouting for Al Davis's Raiders and then worked as an advance scout for the Redskins in 1976. But he felt anxious to return to the field, and when Jack Pardee, who played for Gillman in L.A. and was the Chicago Bears' head coach, called to offer Gillman the offensive coordinator position before the 1977 season, Gillman didn't hesitate.

"I wasn't interested in the details," Gillman said. "I just wanted to know when I could report for work."

But life in Chicago quickly turned sour for Gillman. Though the Bears, behind the expertise of running back Walter Payton, made the playoffs for the first time in 14 seasons, Gillman couldn't handle Pardee's conservative football nature and the way he simply ignored Gillman's advice.

"I was hired to come in and control the offense, but the way it was finally resolved, I had no control over it on game day, calling plays," Gillman said. "That just kind of completely turned me off."

Gillman needed a new turn-on. He needed, at least temporarily, to go back to the bottom where the budgets were anemic and the football talent was, too. He would go back to college, but at a place hardly anybody knew, at a school that no longer exists. At least the commute was easy.

Enter a nonplused Al Palmiotto, whose offer of the athletic director's job at USIU (now known as Alliant International University) was quickly accepted by Gillman.

The job appealed to Gillman because he'd been building programs for much of his career—at Miami (Ohio) and with the Chargers and the Oilers—and since the school was located in San Diego, he didn't have to worry about leasing another apartment in another city. It might have been football at an elementary level, but hell, it was still football.

Gillman immediately went to work, finding a quarterback named Bob Gagliano, who was reading gas meters for the city of Glendale, and a cornerback named Vernon Dean, to commit to USIU. Obviously, his eye for talent was still on target. Those two played in the NFL a combined 14 seasons.

Gillman still needed to find help for Walsh on the coaching staff. One day, Mike Sheppard—a graduate assistant at BYU under legendary college coach LaVell Edwards—was waiting to interview for a high school coaching job when he saw a copy of the *Los Angeles Times* and read that USIU had hired Gillman and had begun looking for coaches.

Sheppard placed a call to the school and was surprised to learn that he had no trouble reaching Gillman. There was no red tape getting the legendary coach on the phone, and Sheppard couldn't believe that no PR person had been dispatched to protect him from the probing public. Instead, before Sheppard realized what was happening, Gillman picked up and said hello. Sheppard introduced himself, told him where he had come from, and explained that he was interested in a job.

"Well," Gillman said, "you were at BYU. Tell me about the offense you guys ran." Before they concluded their talk, Gillman said, "You know, the head coach is going to coach the quarterbacks and the receivers and run the offense, so I don't know if we'll really need that. But if you're in the area, come on by."

Said Sheppard 30 years later, "So, I just happened to be in the area at 7 the next morning."

Gillman and Walsh were already conducting interviews in trailers on campus, and when Sheppard walked in, three potential hires were waiting in chairs while Gillman and Walsh interviewed two other candidates. Sheppard sat and waited until only he and a redheaded fellow remained. Gillman popped his head out of his office and said, "Hey Tom, which one do you want?"

"I'll take the redhead," Walsh replied.

Sheppard walked into the office, reminded Gillman of their conversation, and Gillman said, "Yeah, it's good you made it down here. Now, tell me about those speed cuts at BYU." The two talked, and Sheppard instantly made a good impression. Thank goodness, Sheppard said, much later, that Walsh was the one to select the ginger-haired applicant.

"You know something; we have to hire you," Gillman told Sheppard. "How much money do you need?"

Sheppard made a quick calculation. He was making $181 a month, his wife was pulling in $500 a month at her bank job, and they were saving $200 a month. Sheppard didn't know what to tell him. "Coach," he said, "I don't know. I'm just happy to be here."

"How's $5,000 sound?" Gillman said. Then, Gillman walked to his door, poked out his head and said, "Tom, get rid of that red-headed guy. We've got a guy over here we have to hire."

Turns out Gillman hired three coaches who would make their way to the NFL. Sheppard was a longtime Cincinnati Bengals receivers coach before he moved on to the Jacksonville Jaguars in 2011, and Mike Solari has been an NFL assistant coach for most of the past 25 years. The most famous USIU coaching alum, though, is John Fox, who took the Carolina Panthers to the Super Bowl before moving to Denver to coach the Broncos and won the 2011 AFC West title in his first season.

Fox originally didn't have any desire for the big time. Instead, he wanted to work as a teacher and a high school coach. But California passed Proposition 13, which put a freeze on all California state hiring and meant Fox couldn't get a job after spending five years in college earning his teaching credentials. He had to settle for Gillman.

"It was awesome; we were like little kids in a candy store," Fox said. "We'd come to work every day, and he was just a wealth of knowledge. To spend 12 hours a day with Sid Gillman, even though it was only a four- or five-month span, that was incredible. We all look back on it as being a real catalyst for our drive, the way we coach, the way we work, and our methods."

Here's what Sheppard and Fox learned from Gillman during their time with him: no matter how complicated the scheme that's in place, simplify the terminology; don't ever be satisfied with anything less than winning; remain young at heart. Gillman, after all, was 67 at the time, but he still drove a red Corvette convertible and didn't ever plan to retire from football.

"Why do you keep doing this?" Fox asked Gillman one day.

"Foxy, life is not any fun when your biggest decision of the day is when your tee time is."

Once practice began, Gillman couldn't help himself from returning to his former coaching function. While the USIU receivers ran routes one day, Gillman wandered out of his office to watch, and after a multitude of dropped passes, he blew his whistle and said, "Hold it. Hold it right there. All you receivers—or you guys that call yourselves receivers—stand over there." He summoned over the defensive backs and made them line up and run pass routes to see if any of *them* could catch the ball. Fox, who worked with the defense, was steaming mad, so much so that he softly implored his charges to "drop it. Drop it. Whenever he throws it, you drop it."

Gillman didn't stay at USIU for long. After only a few months in his new job, the NFL came calling once again, and Gillman soon after was on a plane to Philadelphia. Once he left, Walsh upgraded Sheppard to offensive coordinator and made Fox the defensive coordinator. The team finished 8-3 that season, but the school dropped the program afterward. Walsh later left football, winning the Swan Valley, Idaho, mayor election, while Fox, Sheppard, and Solari embarked on long NFL coaching careers. None ever forgot Gillman's impact on them.

"What you did was you kept your mouth shut and you wrote and you learned and you listened," Sheppard said. "You tried to absorb it all, reread it, think it through, and then carefully ask questions. He was such a great teacher that you really didn't have to ask a lot of questions. He made it simple.

"I interviewed him before he left and went to the Eagles. One of the questions I had for him was what was his philosophy of football? He said, 'Young fella, the purpose of football is to get more people to an area of the field faster than your opponent.' You could look at that and think about the BYU (goal) of getting three on two in a pass situation or the Houston veer (scheme) of getting two on the edge against one. If you start thinking about defenses, they want to get somebody unblocked to the point of the attack. That philosophy fit every phrase of football. That was the genius of it. He thought about things like that. I was trying to understand things like that, much less think them."

Not all of Gillman's coaching rubbed off on Fox, though. Gillman told the USIU staff that if he had to choose between his worst pass play and his best run play, he'd go for the pass every time. In his career, though, Fox has always relied on a strong defense and a powerful running game. Fox, in effect, would rather call his worst run play than his best pass.

"Gillman," Fox said, "would be bored."

—⟋⟍—

Gillman decidedly was not bored by the thought of his next job offer.

Dick Vermeil first met Gillman in 1960 at a football clinic in Reno, NV, that featured a Vince Lombardi chat as the main event. Vermeil happened to be sitting next to Gillman in the first row, and during Lombardi's clinic, Vermeil—who had just graduated from San Jose State—feverishly transcribed Lombardi's thoughts. Gillman asked what Vermeil was doing, and Vermeil explained that his wife would type up his handwritten notes. He would then diagram the plays and turn it into a poor man's textbook for his coaching friends. That impressed Gillman.

Eighteen years later, Vermeil realized he needed help. By then, he was the Eagles head coach, and in 1978, his third year in Philadelphia, the team made the playoffs for the first time in 18 seasons. But the Eagles struggled offensively. He had built them into a team that played well on defense and special teams, but Vermeil, who called the plays on offense, needed more innovation. He thought back to the Lombardi clinic. He thought Gillman could assist.

First, though, Gillman had to take care of an emerging health issue. After his bout with angina in 1970, Gillman's health had been relatively good, but by 68 years old, doctors told him he needed heart surgery. Gillman wasn't sure about the risks. While he was deciding, hospital employees showed Gillman film of the planned surgery, and for a guy who spent so much of his life studying celluloid, this was something he could understand and appreciate.

"Bring in the first team," Gillman said in response.

When doctors opened him, they determined that Gillman needed a sextuplet bypass surgery that would delay his arrival at Eagles training camp. Three weeks after surgery, he showed up at a Chargers-Rams scrimmage in La Jolla, California. Doctors had told him to limit his walking, so for the scrimmage, he rode in a golf cart with longtime NFL executive Don Klosterman. A week later, he attended Chargers practice and walked the field the entire time. Gillman was a fast healer and stubborn as hell, and he didn't like getting old.

"My dad had a hard time figuring out and accepting the health thing and how it prevented him from doing what he wanted to do," said his son, Tom Gillman. "I don't know if it was a denial thing, but he had a ter- rible time accepting the fact throughout his later life of getting older and becoming more physically incapacitated. He couldn't lean back and say, 'Well, I've done my thing.' Even at that time, he didn't. He still went back to coaching afterward. He always had more to do. He never had a feeling of being finished. That's why he kept on looking at film, even when he was doing nothing. He thought there was always something to contribute."

His official title in Philadelphia was director of research and quality control, but unlike the 1972 season in Dallas, he actually had on-field responsibilities with the Eagles. In reality, Gillman was Vermeil's de facto offensive coordinator and quarterbacks coach, and even before his bypass surgery, Gillman began upgrading the Eagles organization, starting with the coaching staff. He didn't care only about schemes, game plans, and clock management. From his perspective, he also had to teach the as- sistants about practicing, about fundamentals, about teaching, and about how to teach and practice the fundamentals.

Despite all the scheming, film-watching, and game planning in his life, Gillman never lost sight of the importance of fundamentals. He had learned that early in his coaching career, and he never wavered from the importance of maintaining those basic football skills. Of course, he still knew how to formulate a winning offense, which is why Vermeil wanted him in the first place. Vermeil was tired of having most every result hinge on a play at the end of the game. He wanted Gillman to help the Eagles increase their winning margin.

"We were being held hostage by one play," Vermeil said. "The hell with winning by one point. I wanted to win by 14. We took Sid's coach- ing, our scheme, and his thoughts, and—like he said—we've got to 'put some shit in the game.' That's what he said—PSSITG. Put some shit in the game."

That acronym was successful in splattering points all over the score- board. In 1978, when the Eagles went 9-5 to earn a wild card spot into the postseason, they scored 270 points, the 18th-best total in the 28-team league. The next year, with Gillman's advisement, they recorded 339 points (12th-best in the NFL), and in 1980, the year Philadelphia went to the Super Bowl, they notched 384 points (6th-best).

Gillman and Vermeil worked on receiver patterns and how to use the running game more effectively, and he taught the assistant coaches how to teach the scheme better. The Eagles never became a fancy passing team like Gillman's Chargers squads of the 1960s, and the offense didn't really change much. But Gillman helped tweak it enough to make it much more effective.

"The greatest thing about Sid is that he's a very opinionated person, a great idea guy with a great work ethic," said Tom Coughlin, who worked with Gillman in Philadelphia and has won two Super Bowl titles as the head coach of the New York Giants. "Here was this Hall of Famer, 70 years old, down on the field 15 minutes early waiting for practice to start."

It was what Gillman actually did at practice that helped turn Ron Jaworski from an underwhelming quarterback into the NFL player of the year and helped transform a once-moribund franchise into a Super Bowl contender.

—m—

The first time Jaworski was within touching distance of Gillman, he was a 13-year-old kid who had just watched his hometown Buffalo Bills win their first AFL title. While the Bills carried Jack Kemp off the field in triumph of the 20–7 win against the Chargers, Jaworski, along with hundreds of others, broke through a War Memorial Stadium snow fence and rushed the field in celebration. Buffalo center Al Bemiller handed Jaworski his chin strap as a souvenir, and then, the 13-year-old noticed Gillman just a few feet away, miserable and despondent about his team's performance.

"He brushed past me for a fleeting moment, and then he was gone," Jaworski wrote in his book *The Games That Changed the Game*. "[I] certainly didn't feel sorry for him—I was exhilarated about my team winning a title. But I will never forget the heartsick expression on Sid's face."

Jaworski had been selected in the second round of the 1973 draft by the Los Angeles Rams, but after starting just three games in his first three seasons, L.A. shipped him to Philadelphia, and two years later, one of Vermeil's goals for Gillman was to improve Jaworski's performance. In one preseason game, Jaworski fumbled three center-to-quarterback exchanges, and Vermeil told Gillman he didn't want to lose games because of something so basic.

So, Gillman laid on the ground with his head underneath center Guy Morris's bottom, watching Jaworski take the exchange from the dirt's point of view. Gillman ordered it filmed from six different angles. Then, he and Jaworski studied the film on how to improve the snap.

"It was an exercise in the meticulousness of coaching to the nth degree," said Carl Peterson, an assistant coach on those Eagles teams. "We laughed about that as a staff so much, but Sid got it straightened out. I don't think Ron had another drop the rest of the year."

In 1980, Jaworski was ready to break out and become the NFL's top player. Earlier in his tenure with the Eagles, Gillman watched Jaworski make his first throw of the day during an off-season practice. Gillman asked to see Jaworski's grip on the ball, and although Jaworski had thrown the ball the same way for the past decade, Gillman took one look at it and decided he needed an immediate makeover.

"Let's see your fingertip control," Gillman said. "Shit, Ron, your palm's touching the leather!"

The two spent the rest of the season working on his mechanics, his drop, and the correct way to take the hike from the center. And, of course, how to hold the ball. Gillman performed the same maneuver a half-decade earlier with Dan Pastorini in Houston. The Oilers also had a problem with the center-to-quarterback exchange between center Sid Smith and Pastorini. So, Gillman positioned his camera on the ground to film the exchange, and immediately, he saw the problem. Whenever Pastorini took the snap, his hands separated to the width of the ball, and combining that with Smith's snapping inaccuracy, the exchange was oftentimes a disaster. Gillman's solution was to have Pastorini interlock his thumbs, and that forced his hands together, keeping the ball safely off the ground.

Gillman wasn't officially coordinating the Eagles offense under Vermeil, and he wasn't installing the weekly game plan. But he was supplementing the scheme with his knowledge, and he was making sure the quarterback understood his role down to the tiniest detail. At this point in his life, Gillman was more a consultant than anything else.

In 1980, though, Gillman was persuasive enough to sell Vermeil on the philosophy that a two-tight-end set could make a difference in the Eagles offense, because that formation gave a more balanced look. That meant there was no strong side (where the extra blocker, usually the tight end, would line up) and no weak side. That made it more difficult for the defense to read the offense before the snap, and it meant the offense could run right or left with equal authority because each side had a blocking tight end.

Gillman, by this time, had mellowed as a coach. He didn't blast Jaworski the way he would have smoked John Hadl for making mistakes two decades earlier in San Diego. And for a guy who never wanted to stop watching film, Gillman approached Vermeil, who used to sleep in his office, and say, "Remember, no matter how many times you run that film back and forth, there's only 11 on your side and 11 on the other side. It's not going to change."

He also made peace with Pastorini, his quarterback for two seasons in Houston. With Pastorini on the downside of his career, his squad visited Philadelphia, and as he warmed up before the game, he and Gillman locked eyes. Pastorini walked over to Gillman and said, "You know what, I want to thank you and I want to apologize. You're one hell of a coach. Your people skills suck, but I owe you a lot. I wanted you to know that." Gillman loved him for saying that, and the two discovered a newfound mutual respect for each other.

"He just loved the game," Pastorini said. "He loved being around it. I can sympathize with that. I can feel that. I'm the same way. I miss the game and I miss the camaraderie and I miss the excitement. It's a sickness. We are sick fucking people who play that game."

The great payoff for Gillman in 1980 was that for the first time in his career, he participated in the Super Bowl. He invited the whole family—his daughters, their husbands, their kids—to New Orleans for Super Bowl XV, and after the Eagles' first practice in the Superdome, the team was scheduled for a press event.

"We figured maybe 50 or 100 guys would show," Gillman said. "They opened the doors and the media started pouring down the aisles. Thousands of reporters, hundreds of photographers. I've been around this game a long time, but I never saw anything like that."

The game wasn't quite as uplifting. With his three daughters flanking his wife in the Superdome stands, they watched the first play from scrimmage, and as soon as the tackle was made, "We looked at each other, and the three girls all shook their heads," Esther said. "We just felt it." They sensed a loss on the horizon, and sure enough, the Raiders posted a 27–10 win.

A few days later, Gillman turned in his resignation letter. Football was a young man's game, Gillman told reporters, and the 69-year-old was returning home to San Diego.

"I probably will miss coaching," Gillman said at the time. "I've done nothing all my life except coach football. It's a game you don't turn on and off. Oh, I'll do something out of my house. I don't want to move anymore."

Yet, he couldn't stay away. After the 1981 season, new Eagles quarterback coach Ed Hughes—who played for Gillman with the Rams in 1955—resigned, and Vermeil called Gillman again to ask if he'd make an encore appearance in Philadelphia. Naturally, Gillman said yes. "I thought," Vermeil said, "he was going to jump through the phone."

Gillman stayed for 1982, and even after Vermeil retired from coaching, citing burnout (a word that was not in Gillman's vernacular), he returned to Philadelphia in 1985 for coach Marion Campbell. His job—his final on-field coaching job in the NFL—was to help offensive coordinator Ted Marchibroda tutor rookie quarterback Randall Cunningham.

Even after his final Philadelphia gig was finished, Gillman had more to give. He still had coaches who needed his help. He still couldn't stay away.

That's why Gillman accepted the general manager's job with the United States Football League's Oklahoma Outlaws in June 1983 (he quickly was dismissed when he and the team owner clashed on how much money the team should be spending on personnel). It's why Gillman accepted an offensive coordinator position for the USFL's Los Angeles Express, where he'd work under his former quarterback John Hadl and instill knowledge in a young kid named Steve Young that being a quarterback was more than just about dropping back and throwing the ball. There was attitude, confidence, and the knowledge of how to lead a team. There was film-watching and opponent-scouting. Gillman told Young about Norm Van Brocklin, John Hadl, and Ron Jaworski and about what made them successful quarterbacks. Not what made them *good* quarterbacks, but what made them *great* quarterbacks.

"I want to take from him as much as possible," said Young, who was inducted into the Pro Football Hall of Fame in 2005, surpassing the likes of Hadl and Jaworski and, at the least, equaling Van Brocklin's career. "I hang on his every word because I think he's that great a coach. He doesn't mince words, doesn't try to make me feel good. He tells it the way it is."

Which is exactly why University of Pittsburgh coach Mike Gottfried wanted Gillman for the 1987 season—the last season Gillman would ever coach.

Gottfried barely knew Gillman, but they both were former coaches at the University of Cincinnati. Gottfried knew Gillman well enough to know that he wanted Gillman's consulting help.

"I'd like for you to come to Pittsburgh for a week and visit with us," Gottfried told Gillman when he reached him at home.

Gillman put down the phone and said, "Esther, I'm going to Pittsburgh."

Gillman was there all year. The two grew close, and following an upset win against Notre Dame, Gottfried presented Gillman with the game ball, a souvenir Gillman kept until his dying day. Gillman, because of NCAA rules, wasn't on the payroll as a coach. Instead, the 76-year-old was basically a volunteer offering advice whenever asked but not ever extending himself if he wasn't.

"All too often," Gottfried said, "people tend to forget that people are still the best research material you can find."

Said offensive coordinator Mike Dickens: "It's like a guy who is interested in history being sequestered in the Smithsonian."

With Gillman as the visiting professor, the Panthers finished the season 8-4. Along with upsetting Notre Dame, Pitt also squashed Penn State. Gillman wasn't a major reason for the team's success that year—the best of Gottfried's four seasons at Pitt—but he added tips here and there and made a few suggestions that had a meaningful impact. That was especially true for a 25-year-old tight ends coach named John Harbaugh.

"A lot of the football stuff I owe to Sid," said Harbaugh, now the Baltimore Ravens' head coach. "He basically taught me how to coach the tight ends. I learned some offensive ideas and concepts from him, but I wasn't at that stage yet. I was just learning how to coach a position.

"The thing I'll never forget is that he taught me it's your job to get that right. It's your job to get the best player on the field. That's what he told me. Whoever the best player is, it's your job to get him on the field and playing. You owe that to the head coach and to the team. And if he can't or won't do it—if he's so far gone you can't get the most talented guy coached up—then he has to be off the team. Then, he's recalcitrant, and that would be a word he would use.

"So it was like: Just get it done. Keep them before practice. Keep them after practice. Bring them in at night. Whatever it takes, help him be the player he should be . . . That's what a coach does. A coach does everything possible to help you be what you don't even see in yourself."

Harbaugh remembers those lessons today. Whenever he knows he needs to stand firm, he tells himself, "I know this is right. This is one thing I know is right." That's what he said Gillman ultimately taught him. What would Sid have said? How would Sid have responded? Those are the questions Harbaugh asks himself. Gillman taught him how to answer correctly.

After the final game of the 1987 season, after his work with Gottfried and Harbaugh and the rest of the Panthers was finished, Gillman and Esther disappeared back to San Diego. Back to their house in La Costa. Back to his office of memorabilia. Back to his football film library. Back to the rest of his life.

"Then," Gillman said, "we really did retire."

Said Esther: "Well, there weren't any more football teams."

fifteen LEGACY

Sid Gillman never truly left the game of football. By the end of his visiting professorship at the University of Pittsburgh, he was 76 years old and ready to stay at his two-story, four-bedroom home at the La Costa resort outside San Diego. But the phone in his house kept ringing and ringing. It was NFL owners and executives who were loyal to him asking for more help. It was coaches still interested in Gillman breaking down film on their respective teams. It was former players who gave him a holler when they were in town and somehow later found themselves persuaded into his film-watching lair. And it was reporters. Good God, the reporters that called on the phone and visited him in person.

Gillman never tired of talking about football. So, he helped his friends, he broke down film for the coaches he didn't know, he got excited to show his old players game tape from 40 years earlier, and he welcomed reporters for interview sessions that could last for hours.

Gillman was treated like a sage, like a walking, talking Google search before anybody had the foggiest idea of what a Google search was. Dick Vermeil asked him one day during a Philadelphia session about the first time he had ever seen a quarterback take a shotgun snap, made famous by Cowboys coach Tom Landry and quarterback Roger Staubach. "Well, Dick," Gillman said, "I think we used it in 1934. We called it the short punt."

Gillman's football obsession had mellowed after he returned from Pittsburgh. He no longer thought about it every second of his life. His day usually began early in the morning with a four-mile walk on the golf course outside his home. He ate breakfast with his buddies in the club-house, or he tended to his tomato garden that local bunnies devoured as easily as a pass-rusher sacking a bruised quarterback. In the afternoons, he played nine holes of golf, walked another mile on his treadmill, or swam 10 laps in his pool.

His pool, naturally, was shaped like a football, complete with brown tiles on one side that looked like laces. He had wanted to put Pete Rozelle's autograph on the pool floor, just like an NFL regulation football, but he didn't think of the idea until the installers had begun filling it with water. "If Liberace can shape his pool like a piano," Gillman said, "I can have a football."

What Gillman really wanted, though, was to never slow down.

He was also a never-ending source for reporters who needed a history lesson. During the middle of an in-person interview with *Sports Illustrated* in 1991, the telephone rang and Gillman answered. "You're doing a *what?*" he asked. "A history of the American Football League?" Under his breath, he muttered, "Oh God, another one."

"Everyone's interested in the past, the good old days, the Golden Age," Gillman said, turning his attention back to *Sports Illustrated.* "God almighty, football is so much better now, the technique, the players. The games are great now. I'm part of the good old days, and they weren't worth a damn."

Yet people wanted his take on all the information he collected during those good old days. That's why he was such a popular speaker on the coaching clinic circuit. He was one of the most knowledgeable football men around, and he could take the tiniest topic and expand it into a discussion on why the game's minutiae represented the sport as a whole.

"He was just marvelous to listen to because he was so good and articulate with what he said," said longtime NFL executive Carl Peterson. "He could explain it to the smallest detail and to the largest generalization."

It's been three decades since Steve Mariucci, then a quarterbacks coach at Cal State–Fullerton, watched Gillman headline a coaching clinic in Southern California, but to this moment, the former coach of the 49ers and Lions is still enthralled by what Gillman spoke about that day. For an hour, Gillman discussed the center-to-quarterback exchange. For 60 minutes, Gillman broke down and built up the most basic, most fundamental action in the game. True, you couldn't start a play without the center snapping it somewhere, but to an outside observer, spending that much time on a singular motion was overkill.

Unless, of course, you were Ron Jaworski or Dan Pastorini and had been filmed by a camera underneath you, because Gillman was obsessed with getting the snap exactly right every time.

"It was fascinating," Mariucci said. "I had never seen anybody discuss one thing for so long. And he kept it interesting. I was a young coach, and it led me to believe that being detailed and being specific with coaching points was the way to coach. It gave me an idea what it is to coach the details of each position."

Mariucci used those lessons when he tutored a second-year player named Brett Favre in Green Bay in 1992 and when he coached Jeff Garcia in San Francisco.

"I could be much more detailed in everything I teach," Mariucci said. "What everybody in that room—and there were 1,000 coaches sitting there—got out of it was to be detailed. You would never spend an hour teaching your quarterback the exchange because you didn't have that kind of time, but to take the coaching points and make the most important ones yours. I came away with something that day."

Those who learned from him and remained fond of him were all too happy to honor him in their own special way. When Ara Parseghian finished his successful tenure at Notre Dame, he was invited to coach in the final Chicago College All-Star game in 1976. He, in turn, invited Gillman, who was knocked out cold by Bronko Nagurski in the All-Star game's debut in 1934, to be his assistant on the sideline. Gillman was still getting over his acrimonious departure from the Houston Oilers, but Gillman accepted his former player's offer. It was Parseghian's way of honoring his coach, and the fact that it was the final College All-Star game made it all the more appropriate.

Gillman, of course, would stick around football as a consultant for another decade. But it was a sport that would have been unrecognizable to him when he first started coaching. The outside world had changed and the circumstances around the sport had begun a transformation, but he couldn't turn off his passion for the game itself. That was why he couldn't stay away. That was why he never failed to pick up that ringing phone.

But every once in a while, as Gillman advanced into the last 15 years of his life, he'd walk to the window of his home office, draw back the shades, and stare into the sun. "Why am I doing this?" he'd ask himself. "I'm almost 80 years old. Why am I evaluating quarterbacks?" And as the curtain fell away from his fingers and the darkness once again enveloped his domain, the answer was clear: the game kept him alive.

—⁓—

While Gillman kept himself busy throughout the rest of the day, walking the golf course, swimming in his Liberace-inspired pool, or chasing rabbits from his garden, he left the late morning open every day to continue his lifelong study of football. He wasn't as obsessive as he was when he coached, but he still couldn't fill whatever organ in his body craved the need to watch football film.

The fixation started in the summer of 1935 when his theater-owning cousin rounded up illegally cut football film from the Fox newsreels, and from then on, Gillman was enthralled. He stayed that way for the rest of his life. "I watched him one time go through the film, and it was like a little kid seeing a movie for the first time," said former Oilers quarterback Dan Pastorini, who met Gillman 40 years after his initial introduction to film. "He was mesmerized."

Those early film-watching exploits shaped his football philosophy for the rest of his life. Because the old Fox and RKO film reels didn't show teams playing successful defense, Gillman studied only the plays that resulted in offensive triumph. If those reels had shown nothing but goal line stands and interceptions, Gillman might have made his mark as a defensive wonder. Even in the 1930s, watching offense was just more exciting, and as a result, Gillman showed throughout his career that he believed defense to be an afterthought.

Gillman never relinquished those cans of film. Instead, he stored them in his home office, and he could pop in a reel or a videotape whenever he wanted to make a point to a visiting player or reporter. Gillman collected film from the past and present out of fear.

"It would disturb the daylights out of me if someone were to call me up and say, 'What about this? What about that?' from a technical football standpoint and I couldn't provide an answer," Gillman said.

Gillman avoided that dishonor, because a half-dozen teams sent him film each Monday to evaluate. He also utilized both VCRs he owned to record games on Sunday, and he still owned three film projectors. His youngest daughter, Terry, had a satellite dish, so whatever he couldn't watch on network TV, she tracked down and recorded for him.

"I try to keep up with what everybody is doing," Gillman said, "so if the phone rings, I'll be ready."

When he was 86, Gillman made a fascinating discovery. He realized he could activate his entire film-watching setup (a Sony Betacam DT, a Panasonic VHS, and a 24-inch Sony monitor) by flipping just one switch on a surge protector—quite a difference from tacking a white sheet to the wall and watching grainy footage. That, for Gillman, was a good day.

When he wasn't recording or watching film, he daydreamed about new offensive passing plays that he dutifully jotted into a notebook. When *Sports Illustrated* writer Paul Zimmerman visited in 1991, he estimated that Gillman's office was decorated with 500 cans of film (gray cans that showed passing plays and blue cans that showed rushing plays) and about 100 loose-leaf notebooks, some 150 pages thick. Meanwhile, Gillman's hand remained on the remote control, and the film went forward and backward only to stop and begin again at regular speed. Then, a stop, a start, a flick of a pencil in a notebook, a rewind, a stop, a play, and an exhale of satisfaction. That was how Gillman spent nearly every late morning, and after a day of watching film with him, Zimmerman wrote that a casual observer would "stagger out into the La Costa sun like a drunk, your brain reeling."

"He found his true love in life," two-time Pro Bowl quarterback Phil Simms said. "He loved it. It was never work to him. This is the way you stay close to the game. He had so much information and so much knowledge, you'd be crazy not to go over and see what he had to say about you."

And people cared about what Gillman had to say.

After Carl Peterson took the Chiefs' general manager job in 1989, he invited Sid and Esther to Kansas City once a year to be his guest at a game. Peterson was one of the admirers who sent Gillman game film every week, and one year, after the Chiefs had slipped by their opponent on a late field goal, Peterson invited Gillman to go down to the field level and congratulate head coach Marty Schottenheimer on the victory.

As soon as Schottenheimer saw Gillman, he said, "Sid, it's great to see you. Sid, I want you to tell me. I know you've been looking at our offense. Tell me about our offense. What do you like about our offense?"

"Marty," Gillman said, "you have no offense."

He wasn't always that harsh, but Gillman spoke the truth. When it came to analyzing football, even well past his coaching expiration date, nobody knew more than Gillman.

"Film is the coach's best friend, you know," he said. "Without it, he's just another guy with a bad seat at the game."

———

Sid Gillman was nowhere near Super Bowl XVII—in fact, he sat 2,500 miles away from Pasadena, California—but he was excited to watch the Redskins and Dolphins tangle nonetheless. He was at a Super Bowl celebrity gala in Atlantic City, making speeches and signing autographs. Willie Mays sat on one side of Gillman, and Lou Groza stationed himself on the other side. Every one of the other nine men who had joined Gillman was either in the Pro Football or Baseball Hall of Fame.

About 10 minutes before kickoff, a messenger approached Gillman and told him he had received a long-distance phone call. Gillman told the messenger that he would return the intruder's call at a later time. The messenger insisted it was important, and as Gillman walked to the phone to take the call, he thought to himself, "If I miss even one play, I'll slit my throat."

The knife would have to wait. The phone call was from a Pro Football Hall of Fame representative. He had been elected for induction, Gillman was told. He would join the rest of the class from 1983 in Canton, Ohio, and he would be honored forevermore for his contributions to the pro game.

Gillman hung up the phone, walked back into the banquet hall, found his cohort of almost 50 years, put his arms on Esther's shoulders, and said, "Take it easy now. But I have to tell you, we've made the Hall of Fame." Esther immediately began weeping, and Gillman returned to Mays and Groza and boasted, "I don't have to take a back seat to any of you guys anymore."

After he heard the news, he told a reporter, "It's fantastic. I can't believe it. I pinch myself every five minutes." By the time of his induction ceremony that summer, Gillman knew to keep his speech simple and to the point. But he allowed himself a little hyperbole.

"When I sat in the back of that car in the parade, I thought I was General MacArthur returning to the Philippines," Gillman proclaimed. "It seems to me I made a great contribution to the parade because there seems to be a tremendous amount of senior citizens out there and they wanted to know who that nut was that still played kids games." Mostly, Gillman spent his induction speech thanking all the people who made it possible for him to be standing on that dais in Canton, Ohio, on a day that was so hot the inductees were told to shed their yellow blazers.

He thanked his wife, his children, his grandchildren, Tom Rogers, Francis Schmidt, Joe Madro, Tex Schramm, Ollie Matson, Bum Phillips, Ron Mix, Jack Kemp, John Hadl, Tobin Rote, Dan Pastorini, and Dick Vermeil. To read his induction speech is similar to listening to an Oscar winner thank his agent, his manager, his supporting actors, and his parents without the benefit of an orchestra to play the "get off the stage" music.

In fact, Gillman later believed he made one mistake with his induction. He later confided to his family that he regretted not asking Al Davis to introduce him to the crowd, rather than Madro. Davis, instead, sneaked into the section reserved for the families of the inductees five minutes before the ceremony began and sat next to Tom Gillman. Tom asked Davis how long he was staying, and Davis—all conflicts with Sid long forgiven by that point—said he had flown in to see Sid's induction and was immediately flying out to return to Oakland's training camp.

Sid Gillman made no grand proclamations during his speech, and he kept his remarks modest, because it was such a humbling experience. For all he had been through in his career—the high of impacting the game forever with his offensive innovations and the low of a trio of job losses— he had been validated as one of the game's most important figures.

"It was the greatest experience I ever had," Gillman said. "It was one of the greatest thrills of my life."

Another of those moments occurred 16 years later when the living Hall of Fame members took a trip from Canton to Cleveland to celebrate the new Cleveland Browns Stadium. A large party was held in one of the stadium's banquet rooms, and before the festivities began, officials attempted to corral the large group of football legends into a single-file line so they could walk across the stage one at a time.

"It was young guys with clipboards, saying, 'Mr. Ditka, could you please get behind Mr. Davis?'" longtime *Houston Chronicle* sports writer John McClain said. "Mike Ditka is sitting there, drinking and smoking a cigar, and some 21-year-old kid is trying to get him to move."

In the middle of the confusion, Davis got down on one knee in front of Gillman's wheelchair, took Gillman's hand in his, and began speaking to him in a low voice. It was a gesture of respect, a show of reverence. McClain never forgot it.

"It was an unbelievable scene seeing Al down there, holding his hand," McClain said. "After Al got up, it was like Sid was the Pope. All these Hall of Famers, most of them drunker than skunks, were coming up to Sid. They crowded around him and talked to him one at a time. To see the high esteem the greatest of the great held him in was unbelievable.

"I bet that was one of the best moments of Sid's life."

It might have felt like vindication for those who thought his ideas from long ago wouldn't work, for those who called his scheme a "bullshit offense," for those owners who wouldn't or couldn't give him what he needed in order to build a franchise.

But perhaps his biggest sense of absolution occurred in 1991.

Gillman had already been inducted into the College Football Hall of Fame—making him the only coach who had been selected for the pro and college halls—but when Miami (Ohio) officials finally decided he was worthy of inclusion in their hall, that was a moment of deep satisfaction.

"Miami was known for its coaches. Cradle of Coaches, they call it," Gillman said. "I started that . . . For some unknown reason, Miami didn't acknowledge that. It took them a while before they decided, 'Well, hell, Sid started all this. We should put him in the hall of fame.'"

The campaign to induct Gillman began in earnest when members of the 1947 Sun Bowl team traveled to Oxford for a 30-year reunion to celebrate that undefeated season—one of the best years in Redskins football history—and the program's first postseason game. The subject of Gillman and the fact that he wasn't in the school's Hall of Fame was broached, and the players agreed it was a travesty that Gillman hadn't been included.

"There was a very strong flavor for his induction," said Ara Parseghian, an All-American halfback on that squad. "People recognized what they had learned from Sid and didn't think about the negative things, where he got his ass in a jam."

Since there hadn't been much movement to get Gillman into the Hall of Fame by 1977, the 1947 team hatched a plan. They would start a letter-writing campaign to force Miami to induct their old coach. The target was John Dolibois, Miami's vice president of development and alumni affairs, and in the summer of 1977, the letters poured into Dolibois's mailbox. Inside the envelopes were requests—on workplace stationery, mostly—for Miami to do the right thing and induct Gillman.

Dear John: In recent conversations with members of the Miami football team of 1947, it was brought to our attention that Mr. Sid Gillman has not received the honor of being inducted in the Miami Hall of Fame [wrote Paul Dellerba] . . . It was certainly a pleasure to renew acquaintances with you at the recent Sun Bowl reunion. It was one of those rare evenings in a man's lifetime that I personally will remember with a great deal of pleasure [wrote Jim Jones on Northwest Local School District (Ohio) letterhead] . . . I believe the most enjoyable part of the weekend was our reunion of the 1947 football team at Bill Hoover's home. A rare collection of truly fine people, including many Miami 'Hall of Famers' [Jack Carmichael on Stevenson Photo Color Company letterhead].

I am writing to recommend Sid Gillman to Miami's athletic Hall of Fame [Dave Putts on GlenOak (Ohio) High School letterhead] . . . I can think of no one more eminently deserving than Sid [H.E. Stahl on General Motors Corporation letterhead] . . . Not to do so would be a travesty of justice and an absolute blot on the good name of Miami. Everyone in the United States knows that Sid Gillman is single-handedly responsible for the Cradle of Coaches. More importantly, every one of us who has attended Miami knows it . . . [Nick Vracin on Century 21 letterhead].

I am aware of the efforts and pressures that have kept Sid from this honor but I also find it increasingly difficult to believe that a man as qualified as he is for such an honor should be shut out because of personal or professional things that happened 30 years ago [Robert Kappes on Ohio University athletic department letterhead] . . .

I am sure that you will be receiving similar letters of this kind, as this was a general topic of discussion among those attending the Sun Bowl reunion [Hal Paul on Central Reserve Life of North America Insurance Company letterhead] . . . It is true that he did not graduate from Miami but he certainly played an important part in its formation and I should certainly like to suggest he be enshrined . . . while he is still alive [Paul Dietzel on Indiana University athletic department letterhead].

Soon after he began receiving the steady stream of correspondence, Dolibois penned a quick note to Dick Shrider, the Miami athletic director. "I was literally besieged at the Sun Bowl party about Sid Gillman. I now agree . . . that his time has come. Definitely! [Signed] John"

And it did happen. Only 14 years later.

The honor didn't keep some former Miami players from disliking Gillman or how he handled his departure in 1948. But now, nobody could deny that Gillman's influence reached everywhere he had coached.

—⁂—

When Gillman was a young man, still playing football and in fantastic shape, he donated his body to science. Well, to a book on science, anyway. For a study on the human anatomy, Gillman's body was photographed for the book and his muscles were labeled. He kept that book—which obscured his face and groin but, unfortunately, not his rear—for the rest of his life. "It shows you just how weak a football coach can be," Gillman joked when pointing it out to a reporter many decades later.

At one time, he was a storybook specimen, but through years of coaching, sitting for hours in a film room, eating meals at midnight, and snacking on bad food, Gillman wasn't in great shape. He was not fat, but his food consumption habits were less than healthy. He didn't begin exercising until later in life, because, as his oldest daughter Lyle said, "He walked so he wouldn't die. We put the fear of God in him."

But that didn't stop him from indulging in his favorite foods, oftentimes behind Esther's back. She tried to corral him, but her suggestions rarely worked. One day, as Gillman munched on salami, Esther tried to convince him to stop. "Don't eat that," she said. "It's so bad for you." Larry Hill, one of their sons-in-law, turned to her and replied, "Esther, you don't have to practice preventative medicine at 85 years old."

Other times, Gillman got his kids to cover for him. One year, at an NFL-sponsored Super Bowl party, the family got in line at a glorious buffet that featured any kind of meat Gillman could have wanted. Esther went first, followed by Sid, Ralph (Lyle's second husband), and Lyle. Gillman grabbed what he wanted, and handed it to Ralph on the sly. Then, Ralph passed it to Lyle, who kept all of the taboo goodies in a napkin. It was, to say the least, an innovative maneuver.

"Talk about the center-to-quarterback exchange," Lyle said. "It was the salami and prosciutto. Oh my gosh, did we cater to him."

"He was an overeater," said Bobbe, his second daughter. "He ate salami, bad stuff. He lived to 92 because of Mom."

Aside from the heart scare in 1970 and the sextuple bypass surgery in 1979, Gillman had maintained good health as he entered his 90s. But while working out with a personal trainer at his La Costa home on August 3, 2000, Gillman collapsed. He was rushed to Scripps Hospital where he underwent emergency surgery. He had suffered a rupture of an abdominal aortic aneurysm (when the vessel that supplies blood to the lower half of the body becomes abnormally large and bursts). Considering he was nearly 89 years old and on the medicine Coumadin (which prevents blood clots), his chances of survival were slim. But the hospital was 10 minutes from his house, and the vascular surgeon was available to help immediately. Originally, doctors thought the aneurysm was leaking, but when they surgically opened him, they discovered the vessel had ruptured.

Though still sharp in mind, Gillman was beginning to slow. A week before he passed out in his home, Gillman attended a Pro Football Hall of Fame celebration in Canton. Gillman's hand was not strong enough to sign his full name for the autograph collectors, so he simply wrote, "Sid." But knowing that fans had paid $78 to collect autographs that day, Gillman rallied. He began signing his full name until he could write no more. Slowly, Tom Gillman took the pens away from him.

A week later, Gillman was on life support, and somehow he survived. "It was," Lyle said, "miraculous."

Gillman remained hospitalized for two months after his surgery. He was in the intensive care unit for several weeks, and he underwent several more weeks of physical therapy. He had lost leg strength, and he would spend most of the rest of his life in a wheelchair. But he was alive, and on a Saturday, he finally came home. On Sunday, he was watching football.

"He's adjusting," Esther said the day after Sid's return home. "He watched a few football games yesterday; three of them, to be exact—morning, noon, and night."

Gillman, though, never fully recovered from his hospital stint. As Lyle says, "that was the beginning of the end." Esther's mission in life was to care for Sid, a lofty goal for an 88-year-old woman who had health issues of her own. Gillman had taken to a wheelchair, so he could get around faster, and he still watched film. But he was becoming weaker and frailer.

"Seeing him deteriorate like that really took a toll on her," Lyle said. "He was a burden for her."

In 2001, Sid and Esther moved to Century City in Los Angeles to be closer to their kids. In their home, they set up a trophy room to display all the plaques, game balls, and mementos they collected during a football career that lasted more than 55 years. It was Gillman's favorite room, and when the couple had a hospital bed delivered on January 2, 2003, there was only one area in the home big enough to accommodate it. So, for one night, he lay in his bed surrounded by his essence.

By then, Gillman was suffering. He was confined mostly to his wheelchair, and his caregiver, a Filipino man named Ike Belem, was a constant companion. Gillman had a touch of dementia, and he had developed a small tremor that made his hands shake. Esther had the hospital bed brought in so Gillman could be more comfortable, and with the NFL playoffs set to begin on January 5, Gillman needed his rest in order to focus on the action in front of him.

Belem had never stayed overnight in the Gillman household, but with Gillman in a new bed in a new room, he had been asked to remain until the next morning. During the night, Gillman, every once in a while, lifted his head and looked around his room at his mementos. As he studied his football possessions, a grin creased his weathered face and he rested his head back onto his pillow. Gillman did that a few times that evening. He raised his head and looked from corner to corner. His eye caught on the game ball presented to him by the Pitt football team after beating Notre

Dame in 1987. Or on the photograph of 1955 Los Angeles Rams players carrying him off the field. Or on the autographed glossy of Gillman lip-kissing Goldie Hawn on which she had written, "Happy birthday, Sid. I love you."

"I don't know if he remembered," Belem said. "But he had a smile on his face."

Around 4 a.m., Gillman asked Belem for a drink, and Belem walked the short distance from Gillman's office to the kitchen and back to fetch him a glass of water. Gillman finished, and Belem asked if he wanted a refill. Gillman said yes. Belem walked away, and Gillman closed his eyes. When Belem returned with the second glass of water, he realized Gillman was still. Belem tried waking Gillman, but he was unresponsive and not moving. The caregiver summoned Esther and said he thought something was wrong.

A few minutes later, the phone rang in Bobbe's house. Esther was on the other line. "Bobbe," she said. "I think he's gone."

"We were relieved for him," Bobbe said. "He was this pillar of strength until three years before. The last year was just awful. It was a blessing. The guy had had enough."

When the paramedics arrived, they noticed that Gillman's arms were covered with bruises. They looked to Bobbe for an explanation. He's on Coumadin and aspirin, Bobbe told the suspicious medics, and soon after, convinced she was telling the truth, they wheeled him away. Later that day, word leaked out, and Esther began taking phone calls from reporters looking for comment on the death of her husband of 67 years.

"The whole time, he was never in pain," Esther told the Associated Press. "He was in a room with all the plaques and all the footballs and the mementos from all the years. It was a wonderful room. And he was aware of that.

"He had such a nice smile on his face. That was the best part."

Said Belem almost a decade later: "The only thing I really noticed after he died was there was a glow, something was glowing on his face. He was really at peace. You could see the difference from when he was still alive. He just left so quietly."

It was clear that Gillman was at peace with himself, at peace with the world, and at peace with his place in it. He wasn't the only one relieved to be out of his misery. When Gillman had suffered his ruptured aortic aneurysm, Esther's life got much tougher. Without her husband, Esther could finally take a breath.

"Her mission in life was to take care of Dad," Lyle said. "When he died, she resolved to have a life."

Esther wanted to travel abroad—she never could with Sid, because he hated traveling so much—but at 89 years old, she was diagnosed with ovarian cancer. At the time, she and Sid lived in San Diego, and after going through chemotherapy, she beat the disease. Five years later, it returned. Esther insisted on more chemo, because she felt better on it than off it and because she had resolved that cancer was not going to kill her. "She," Lyle said, "had my dad's survival instincts."

She was still a dynamo as well. She had shrunk to 4-foot-8—in her prime, she was closer to 5 feet—but she didn't take guff from anybody. When she moved into a Santa Monica assisted-living home, she was assigned to a dining room table filled with women who complained nonstop. This hurts, that hurts, why am I in this pain? Every meal, every day, she had to listen to the kvetching. Finally, Esther grew tired of the morbidity, and one day, she made an announcement to her tablemates.

"If each one of us would read the editorial pages of the *Los Angeles Times* and *The New York Times*," Esther proclaimed, "we would have something else to talk about."

"She wasn't going to put up with that 'poor-me shit' from those people," Lyle said. "And don't you know, they all did. She completely changed everything at that table."

She still kept in touch with old friends and Gillman's old players. The holiday card she wrote in 2007 stated, "Had my 95th with my whole family. Do you think that I am blessed! Look forward to seeing you. Still watching lots of football. Love." A year later, she sent greetings to former University of Cincinnati co-captain Nick Shundich in which she wrote simply and beautifully, "I think of you and the gang often." Enclosed was a picture of Esther, snapped on her 96th birthday, with her arm hanging around a bust of her husband and a photo of the two of them together in front of the ocean.

Her personal stationery read simply, "A note from Mrs. Sid Gillman," and she never thought of herself as anything but that. She was Mrs. Sid Gillman who loved her husband more than she could explain and who, after marrying Sid, loved football nearly as much.

Once a month, invariably while he was watching a game on TV, Dick Vermeil called Esther to say hello. Esther would answer, and Vermeil would say, "Hi, do you know anything about football?" Immediately, she'd go into her rant about the quality of modern-day coaches. "I don't know who is calling the offense for this team," Esther would yell, "but he doesn't know shit. What the hell is he doing?"

Her spirit carried her through two bouts of cancer, and osteoporosis, but on February 3, 2010, Esther Gillman died at the age of 97.

Two weeks before she died, she was watching playoff football on TV. She was analyzing each game and complaining about the play-calling. She probably noticed that the fundamentals were lacking. She probably believed her husband could have made any of those teams better.

She was her husband's better half, the one who kept her family bonded together, and when she died, the love story between Esther and Sid went with her.

And when Al Davis, the day after Gillman died, said, "The great ones, time never ends for them. Immortality is real when it comes to those people," he could have talking about Esther as well.

—m—

In 1965, Gillman was speaking at a Chargers booster club meeting, and somebody asked him about the kind of money the players made in those days. It was obviously a sore point for Gillman, the coach and general manager, and he stiffened and scowled at the thought.

"With some of them, football is a vocation. With some, it's an avocation," Gillman said. "You know what football is to me? It's blood."

If coaches and players took away anything from an encounter with Gillman—even if it wasn't about techniques or game-planning or how to run a team—they could never say Gillman wasn't obsessed with the game. And when he was asked, at the age of 80, how long he could keep coaching and watching and analyzing and thinking about it, he argued, "How about forever? I'll never walk off the field."

His spirit and innovation still haven't exited the game, even nearly a decade after he died. Though players today don't know much, if anything, about Gillman, the coaches remember. The coaches know the impact he's made. The coaches know that the offenses run today are a testament to his vision.

Today's NFL is a passing league. A team led by a non-elite quarterback hasn't won a Super Bowl since 2002, and only two (the 2000 Baltimore Ravens squad with Trent Dilfer and the 2002 Tampa Bay Buccaneers team with Brad Johnson) have triumphed since 1991. Sure, a top-notch defense is a wonderful attribute to have, but it's no longer imperative to win a title.

The trends keep pointing toward the running back becoming less important—only one rusher was selected in the 2011 NFL draft, and Mark Ingram wasn't taken until the 28th pick. The passing game, meanwhile, continues to expand at a rate never seen before. In 2011, for instance, Saints quarterback Drew Brees and Patriots quarterback Tom Brady blew away Dan Marino's 27-year-old record for passing yards in a season, and neither of them won the MVP award. In fact, four of the top six passing seasons in NFL history occurred in 2011. And none of them were Green Bay's Aaron Rodgers, who might have had the most impressive season by a quarterback ever.

It's not just quarterbacks who have taken over football. One of Gillman's biggest loves were his tight ends, and his use of them in the passing game, rather than just to block, was unseen before Gillman thought of it.

In 2011, New England's Rob Gronkowski and New Orleans's Jimmy Graham beat the tight end receiving record—in fact, five of the top 15 pass-catchers in 2011 were tight ends, the first time that had happened—and those two are as dangerous as any wide receiver in the game. Gillman would have loved them. They don't necessarily have to stick to the seams of the field, like Gillman envisioned for his tight ends. They're fast enough to dominate linebackers dropping back into pass coverage, and they're too big and strong for cornerbacks to have a chance to stop them.

"I think the reason it wasn't as prevalent before was because if you have a 6-foot-6 Gronkowski-type guy, guess what, I'm putting him at defensive end and having him rush the quarterback," said future Hall of Fame tight end Tony Gonzalez, who likely will finish his career as the second-leading pass-catcher in NFL history behind Jerry Rice. "Tight end was not a glorified position, but now guys want to go out and catch 100 balls and 15 touchdowns a season.

"You're going to see the whole league start to move to that, because it's such a matchup problem. Even if you're guarded, it doesn't matter. Just throw it up there, give me a chance, and most of the time, I'll come down with it."

Some decry the passing display—"I fear we may be losing the essence of what makes this game special," former coach Brian Billick wrote in 2011—but there's no doubt Gillman would love today's game with the spread, no-huddle offenses that rely on quarterbacks to throw 40-plus times a game.

"Are you kidding me, *this* is Sid Gillman's NFL," CBSSports.com football writer Pete Prisco said. "He has to be looking down from high above with a big Sid Gillman smile on his face."

One rule that tilted momentum toward the offense was the decision by the league in 1978 to loosen the definition of offensive holding and to outlaw a defensive back's ability to hit a receiver five yards past the line of scrimmage. Before, a cornerback or safety could crack a receiver whenever he wanted, but with the advent of the new rules, crossing patterns became less dangerous, and quarterbacks suddenly found a more open field. The current-day rules, including the ultra-conservative protection for quarterbacks against rushing defenders, have tilted greatly toward the offense.

And those changes helped a coach named Bill Walsh establish an offense that, in some ways, is an homage to Gillman.

—⚲—

Gillman first caught Walsh's interest in a San Diego hotel room the night before the Chargers were to face the Raiders during the 1966 season. Walsh, then an Oakland assistant, was relaxing and watching TV when the *Sid Gillman Show* appeared on the screen. His guest that night was receiver Lance Alworth, and the two sat in front of a projection screen and waxed on about the Chargers' offense. Walsh, because he knew more than just about any other viewer who happened to catch the show that evening, sat transfixed.

"Sid was describing the slant pattern," Walsh said. "He ran the film back and forth, breaking down this play. That had a major influence on me. The attention to detail the man took with this one play was unbelievable."

Like Gillman, Walsh's offense in San Francisco was based on timing patterns, where the receiver had to reach a certain spot on the field in an exact amount of time. Walsh believed his team could play ball control with his system of passing because many of the passing routes were 10 yards or less and because he could exploit holes in a zone defense with crossing patterns that were run underneath linebackers.

This was the foundation of what became known as the West Coast offense. When Walsh got the 49ers' head coaching position—the job in which he won three Super Bowl titles and made himself a legend—he implemented his offense with quarterback Joe Montana, receivers Dwight Clark and Jerry Rice, and running back Roger Craig. From time to time, Walsh called Gillman to gain his insights into Walsh's scheme.

Gillman wasn't a big fan of the West Coast offense. Though he tried to hire Walsh in 1974 for a job in Houston, Gillman didn't appreciate the quantity of crossing patterns, and he felt Walsh's system was too horizontal. But whenever anybody gave credit to Walsh for revolutionizing the offensive game, he always made sure to point the finger back at Gillman.

"He's always believed in controlling the ball with those short passes," Gillman said in 1982. "He hasn't converted me, but he's made me think. . . . I can't think of giving up the deep-pass concept, but I believe if I were coaching a team now, I'd add some of his high-percentage passes."

He would, because he truly believed in the axiom that the goal of football was to get more of his players into an area on the field faster than his opponent could. Walsh could do that with his West Coast scheme, and Gillman appreciated that.

But what distinguishes Gillman nearly as much as his high-flying offense is the kind of play-calling today's normal fan wouldn't think odd. A seam route or five receivers lined up wide or the pass setting up the run. Gillman's innovations made sure the game was never the same when he was finished with it.

"You know, people hated Gillman for his innovation," Prisco said. All these NFL snobs never could understand it."

But Gillman, when he left his last full-time consulting job with the University of Pittsburgh, was comfortable in what he had accomplished. He was a humble man, but it also pleased him greatly when colleagues like Al Davis and Bill Walsh credited him with making the game into what it became. When somebody called him the father of the passing offense, he blushed with pride.

Sid and Esther had seen the world—not just the world of football, but the world in general—change so drastically. Sid lived 91 years; Esther 97. They were married 67 of those years. They rarely slept in different beds. They were as close as a couple could be. They experienced the world and all of its changes hand in hand.

During a 1996 sit-down interview, the questioner asked Sid and Esther about the changes they had experienced. Esther talked about the world in general, about computers and e-mails and faxes. You can probably imagine Gillman's subject choice.

Sid—who would have been in heaven with today's computer film-work technology—described the biggest change he'd seen, and it was about football and the dramatically increased weight of linemen and the drastically increased money the players made.

That was Sid. It always came back to football. It had always been that way. It always would.

"You've changed a hell of a lot," Sid said, turning to his bride. "I don't think I've changed. I'm pretty much the same."

EPILOGUE

Some of his former players have a hard time describing the impact Sid Gillman made on their lives. Gillman was beloved by many of those he coached in college; he was despised by many of those who played for him professionally. Some talked for hours about Gillman and why they loved him so much. Some refused to answer the phone.

A man like Dan Pastorini hated him when they first worked together. By the end of Pastorini's career, his contact with Gillman was enjoyable. He learned more football from Gillman than any other coach, but he also learned that Gillman was the kind of person he didn't want to become.

Gillman, you see, was a man of incongruity and a man of paradox. He was a football coach who wanted to do the right thing but couldn't let his humanity get in the way of winning. He was a family man who was obsessed by football at every waking moment, a father who loved his kids but had to abandon them because the film just couldn't wait. If a reporter's family was going through a crisis, Gillman came running, but if a player's wife just had a baby and needed a couple of extra days before arriving in camp, Gillman cursed his name and then traded him away.

He was, without a doubt, a man of contradiction. And it's appropriate that his final resting place is exactly that as well.

Hillside Memorial Park is in Culver City, situated between downtown Los Angeles and the Pacific Ocean, and driving into the park is like entering a peaceful refuge in the middle of a city of madness.

Only a few miles away, a line of airplanes many miles long wait to land at Los Angeles International Airport, and from a hillside inside the park, you can see the pilots making their final approach to the runways of the stars. But you can't hear the jet engines. The chirping birds drive them away.

On this day, it's a bright, sunny morning, but there's a nice breeze that mitigates the sun rays that are beginning to bake a visitor's jeans. The 405 is only a few hundred yards away, but those sounds seem far off, like they're in a different dimension of life. All you notice in here are the Hillside workers in their golf carts and the weed-whackers that maintain the park's appearance.

This is a Jewish memorial garden, and resting inside are many of the stars who pioneered this town into what it has become—actors, comedians, TV producers, and lingerie magnates.

There are no headstones in this 48-acre park, because it's a memorial garden and not a cemetery. Some markers have flowers, some of which are not so fresh.

In the Jewish tradition, visitors place stones on gravesites, a symbolic and physical act that indicates the deceased has not been forgotten. But at Hillside, there are no rocks. Not one. It's as if the grounds crew has deliberately rid the garden of any pebbles to place. Instead, the office will give you a clear plastic bag containing Jerusalem stones (limestone that has been used in buildings in Israel since ancient times) because they disintegrate easier than a pebble.

Outside the garden, the outside world is buzzing, and this huge park of eternal rest is surrounded by glass-windowed buildings (a mall, a business office, a hotel or two). But in here, with the breeze blowing, the birds singing and swooping, and the fronds of the palm trees shimmying, it's peaceful. The outside world just doesn't matter.

Yet, the outside world waits. There are people to meet, interviews to transcribe, appointments and schedules to keep. But it's hard to pull away. Here, life's problems are kept at bay by the sound and sight of the water fountains being lit by the bright sunshine. Outside these walls is life. Inside, there's only peace.

—m—

Before Sid and Esther made the final move of their lives, before they packed the trucks that would take them and their lifetime of possessions from San Diego to Los Angeles for their last years, Esther decided one day to pick out the couple's Hillside plots. Sid wanted nothing to do with the errand. Instead, Esther took Bobbe with her, and when they returned from their outing, Sid pulled his daughter aside and asked, "What did you get?"

"We got an up-and-down," Bobbe said. "A tandem."

In Hillside, because there's a finite amount of land and because the plots are expensive, many future residents buy one grave site for two people. When the plot calls for a tandem burial, Hillside will install two vaults, one on top of the other separated by a layer of dirt, and dig a 10-foot hole into the earth.

"When it's a double burial, we take out the first vault and cover that with a green tarp," said Sheila Weiss of Hillside Memorial. "We remove the earth, unseal the second vault below, and raise it up. Then, the bottom one goes down, and families can move earth on top of the casket or on top of the vault (in the Jewish tradition). We seal the vault below and layer it again with 18 inches of earth. Then, the second one is placed on top of that."

That's how Sid and Esther would be buried, and after hearing those plans, the claustrophobic Sid had one simple request for Bobbe. "Remember," he said, "I want to be the one on top."

After Sid and Esther bought their plots, one of their daughters suggested that they buy a plot for Tom nearby. Tom didn't learn about this plan until more than a decade later, but it's clear to him that the assumption was that when he eventually died from AIDS, he could be near his parents in Hillside. Esther later confirmed the plans with her son. "Very strange," Tom said. "Not because they all thought the same about my then-immediate future but because none of them broke the confidence they shared for all those years."

When Esther died, Tom sensed the pain felt by Lyle, and in order to make her feel better and because he plans to swim with porpoises and whales when he's gone, he offered her his plot. One problem: the plot didn't exist.

"It turned out," Tom said, "she never did buy one. She felt—and she was—entitled to be with Dad by herself."

Thirteen months after Esther had been laid to rest, the garden's visitor on that March morning still heard the words of Esther from a 1996 interview ring in his head as he walked to his rental car. "Don't lose sight," Esther said, "that love is the most important thing in life." For though this was the story of a football coach, one of the greatest and most underappreciated of all time, it's something more than that. It wasn't just about Sid. Really, it never was. For Sid and Esther, it was also a love story come to life. And that is what their kids remember most of all.

—m—

Sid and Esther's grave site sits on the north border of Hillside Memorial, and it's only a Jerusalem stone's throw from the fence that separates the garden from Doverwood Drive. Maybe 20 yards away from the grave—a short pass from John Hadl to Lance Alworth—are condominiums and townhomes, and on this sunny mid-March morning, at least four DirecTV satellites are pointing toward the heavens.

This means that there are people inside The Diplomat condo complex who subscribe to the only satellite provider that features the NFL Sunday Ticket and the Red Zone channel. This means there are certainly football fans in that complex that, through their satellite provider, can witness every single touchdown scored on the day, seconds after it's occurred. And it's a decent bet that the majority of people who have DirecTV in the complex do so simply so they can watch every NFL game possible.

These are the people who hunger to watch touchdowns instead of field goals, those who pay the exorbitant fees the NFL knows it can charge, those who are helplessly and hopelessly addicted to the most popular spectator sport in this country. They don't live in the 1950s. They live in the now, and they are the people who want their football offensive-minded with quarterbacks who can throw for days. Their neighbor in Hillside Memorial would have loved that.

Those fans might not know who Gillman was. They might have forgotten about the vertical stretch and the AFL and the innovation. They might not have ever known it in the first place. But they know his ideas, because they unknowingly see them performed every week on DirecTV. They know his essence. They watched it in Super Bowl XLV when Greg Jennings ran that fourth-quarter seam route to help seal the game for Green Bay, an old Gillman innovation come to life in the 21st century.

Less than a football field away from the complex, there lies a grave marker with two freshly placed Jerusalem stones sitting on its face, just underneath the epitaphs that read "Devoted family man, coach & friend" and "Loving wife, mother and friend." Sid and Esther rest, among the thousands of other Jews who have had their own full lives, among the hundreds who have made a long-lasting impact on the world around them. There are no monuments built to the most important professional football coach who hardly anybody remembers. Just a simple plaque on the ground.

He's no better than anybody in this 48-acre slice of heaven, and he's no worse either. Sid and Esther sleep without any fanfare.

In a few months from that March moment, the 2011 NFL season would begin, and the most prolific passing performances ever would be recorded. The people living inside The Diplomat would watch with rapt attention. Twenty yards away rests one of the men who made all of it possible.

Hardly anybody knows he's here.

SOURCES

WIRE SERVICES
Associated Press
United Press
United Press International

NEWSPAPERS
Allentown (PA) *Morning Call*
Boston Globe
Buffalo News
Canton (OH) *Repository*
Charleston (SC) *Post & Courier*
Chicago Tribune
Cincinnati Enquirer
Cincinnati Post
Cincinnati Times-Star
Cleveland Plain-Dealer
Columbus Dispatch
Columbus Journal Dispatch
Coshocton (Ohio) *Tribune*
The Daily Californian
Dayton Daily News
Denver Post
Elyria (Ohio) *Chronicle Telegram*
Hamilton (Ohio) *Daily News Journal*
Houston Chronicle
Houston Post
Houston Press
Long Beach (CA) *Independent*
Long Beach (CA) *Press-Telegram*
Los Angeles Herald and Express
Los Angeles Times
Massillon (OH) *Evening Independent*
Milwaukee Journal
New York Post

The New York Times
Newark Star-Ledger
Ohio State Journal
Olean (NY) *Times Herald*
San Diego Evening Tribune
San Diego Independent
San Diego Jewish World
San Diego Union
San Francisco Examiner
Sandusky (OH) *Register*
Wall Street Journal
Washington Star-News

MAGAZINES

Collier's
Inside Sports
Minnesota History
New York Times Magazine
The Ohio State University Monthly
Pro Football Weekly
San Diego Magazine
Saturday Evening Post
Sport
The Sporting News
Sports Illustrated
Tablet
Time

WEBSITES

225 Baton Rouge
AOL Fanhouse
CFL Scrapbook
Comcast SportsNet Philly
ESPN.com
Grantland.com
Minnpost.com
NFL.com
NFLUK.com
Online World of Wrestling
Philadelphiaeagles.com
Steel Belt Wrestling

BIBLIOGRAPHY

Bean, Billy. *Going the Other Way: Lessons From a Life In and Out of Major League Baseball.* New York: Marlowe & Company, 2003.

Danyluk, Tom and Paul Zimmerman. *The Super '70s: Memories From Pro Football's Greatest Era.* Chicago: Mad Uke Publishing, 2005.

Dietzel, Paul F. *Call Me Coach: A Life in College Football.* Baton Rouge, LA: Louisiana State University Press, 2008.

Fowler, Bud. *Loser Takes All: Bud Adams, Bad Football and Big Business.* Atlanta; Longstreet Press, 1997.

Full Color Football: The History of the American Football League. NFL Films, 2009.

Greatest Sports Legend: Sid Gillman. Dir. Matt Gibson. Steve Rotfeld Productions, 1985.

Grizzard, Lewis. *If I Ever Get Back to Georgia, I'm Gonna Nail My Feet to the Ground.* New York: Ballantine Books, 1990.

Harris, David. *The Genius: How Bill Walsh Reinvented Football and Created an NFL Dynasty.* New York: Random House, 2008.

Jaworski, Ron. *The Games That Changed the Game.* New York: Ballantine Books, 2010.

Katzowitz, Josh. *Bearcats Rising.* Wilmington, OH: Orange-Frazer Press, 2009.

Kemper, Kurt Edward. *College Football and American Culture in the Cold War Era.* Champaign, IL: University of Illinois Press, 2009.

Kurz, Bob. *Miami of Ohio: The Cradle of Coaches.* Troy, OH: Troy Daily News, Inc., 1983.

Lombardo, John. *A Fire To Win: The Life and Times of Woody Hayes.* New York: Thomas Dunne Books, 2005.

Lost Treasures of NFL Films: Volume IV. Dir. David Plaut. NFL Films, 1999.

Maiorana, Sal. *Buffalo Bills: The Complete Illustrated History.* Minneapolis: MVP Books, 2010.

Massing, Phyllis and Rhoda Lewis. Lifestories/A Video Legacy. Jan. 16, 1996.

Miller, Jeff. *Going Long.* New York: McGraw-Hill, 2003.

O'Toole, Andrew. *Paul Brown: The Rise and Fall and Rise Again of Football's Most Innovative Coach.* Cincinnati: Clerisy Press, 2008.

Park, Jack. *The Official Ohio State Football Encyclopedia.* Champaign, IL: Sports Publishing LLC, 2003.

Perkins, Brett. *Frantic Francis: How One Coach's Madness Changed Football.* Champaign, IL: University of Nebraska Press, 2009.

Pont, Sally. *Fields of Honor: The Golden Age of College Football and the Men Who Created It.* New York: Harcourt Inc, 2001.

Quirk, James and Rodney D. Fort. *Pay Dirt: The Business of Professional Team Sports.* Princeton, NJ: Princeton University Press, 1997.

Rappoport, Ken. *The Little League That Could.* Lanham, MD: Taylor Trade Publishing, 2010.

Steidel, Dave. *Remember the AFL.* Cincinnati: Clerisy Press, 2008.

Stram, Hank and Lou Sahadi. *They're Playing My Game.* Chicago: Triumph Books, 1986.

Tobias, Todd. "A Bolt from the Past: Sid Gillman As Head Coach in the American Football League" (master's thesis, University of San Diego, 1999).

NOTES

INTRODUCTION

During Super Bowl Media Day, I asked 10 offensive players . . . Various interviews, Feb. 1, 2011.

"There's a little separation in time. . ." Interview with Brian Billick, Feb. 1, 2011.

"There seems to be an inordinate focus by the media . . ." Interview with Ron Mix, March 10, 2011.

"Dad always refused . . ." Interview with Lyle Gillman, March 7, 2011.

"I don't know. I don't know. . ." Interview with Gil Brandt, Feb. 2, 2011.

"Most teams did not run down the seam," . . . Interview with Greg Cosell, June 9, 2011.

"Sid was one of the first people to lengthen the field, . . ." Interview with Keith Lincoln, June 14, 2011.

CHAPTER 1

On his way to the biggest game . . . Interview with Keith Lincoln, June 14, 2011.

The Rip Van Winkle of American cities. Murphy, Jack. "Despite Gate Losses, Chargers Investing Heavily in the Future," *San Diego Union*, Dec. 22, 1960.

There's always a lot of suspense going to San Diego these days . . . Murray, Jim. "Rented Defenses," *Los Angeles Times*, Jan. 7, 1964.

"San Diego was kind of in the doldrums in this period." Interview with Jerry Magee, May 18, 2011.

"Tobin Rote is about as great a quarterback . . ." Tobias, Todd. "A Bolt From the Past: Sid Gillman as Head Coach in the American Football League" (master's thesis, University of San Diego, 1999).

He also was pretty special . . . Malich, Rob. *CFL Scrapbook*. 1996 < http://cfl-scrapbook.no-ip.org/Rote.Tobin.php >.

An example: during the 1963 season . . ." Perkins, Steve. "Chargers Won Rote On Toss of a Coin," *Houston Post*, Dec. 13, 1963.

"Tobin Rote had all the stuff." Interview with Keith Lincoln, April 21, 2011.

"He was greatest guy in the world to be around." Interview with Tom Bass, March 21, 2011.

On the second play of the Chargers first exhibition game of 1963 . . . Tobias

"How many points did you want to score, Sid?" King, Bob. "Jack Boils as Sid's Chargers Turn It On," *San Diego Independent,* Dec. 26, 1963.

"Replied Faulkner, 'Thanks a lot, Sid, you son of a bitch.'" Zimmerman, Paul. "When Sid Was Caesar," *Sports Illustrated,* Feb. 1, 1988.

"How many points did he want to score, anyway?" King

In reality, nobody in the league . . . Ahern, John. "Pats Best on Defense, Gillman Says," *Boston Globe,* Jan. 2, 1964

"Hell, we blitzed a lot because we could get away with it." Jaworski, Ron. *The Games That Changed the Game.* New York: Ballantine Books, 2010.

Perhaps in an attempt to save himself from himself . . . Miller, Jeff. *Going Long.* New York: McGraw-Hill, 2003.

Another problem for the Patriots . . . Miller

"What one man in motion does to this defense . . ." *Greatest Sports Legend: Sid Gillman.* Dir. Matt Gibson. Steve Rotfeld Productions, 1985.

But Lincoln could see how effective the game plan . . . Interview with Keith Lincoln, April 21, 2011.

In the first series . . . Jaworski

"The whole game plan was (centered) around . . ." Tobias

"We showed them motion." Int. with Lincoln, April 21

"I'm just about convinced the boy is a pro misfit." Murphy, Jack, "Gillman Happy to Be Wrong; Lincoln Does Everything Right," *San Diego Union,* Aug. 18, 1961.

On the next play, the Chargers called for a "Toss 78 Y-Man 0" . . . Jaworski

And since the Grambling marching band was playing halftime . . . Miller

"The 1963 AFL championship is a game . . ." Jaworski

As the embarrassed Patriots trudged off the field . . . Miller

After this latest embarrassment . . . Collins, Bud. "Defense Deserts Pats," *Boston Globe* Jan. 6, 1964

"Everything we did was perfect." Interview with Ron Mix, March 10, 2011.

George Halas had finished watching the AFL championship game . . . Murphy, Jack, "Chargers vs. the Bears? 'We'd Love to Play Sid's Team,' Says Halas," *San Diego Union,* Jan. 7, 1964.

In the note, he referenced the decision . . . Jaworski

Instead, the Chargers had to be content with the $2,498.89 . . . Steidel, Dave. *Remember the AFL.* Cincinnati: Clerisy Press, 2008.

Many years later, when Gillman was an assistant coach to Dick Vermeil . . . Jaworski

"I think it meant the world to him." Int. with Lincoln, April 21.

"That was the game he won." Interview with Tom Gillman, April 6, 2011.

CHAPTER 2

David Gillman lived a long fruitful life . . . Massing, Phyllis and Rhoda Lewis. Lifestories/A Video Legacy. Jan. 16, 1996.

"She was a doll." Massing and Lewis

"I didn't belong to the French club." Massing and Lewis

"We played practically every wedding in Minneapolis." Tobias, Todd. "A Bolt From the Past: Sid Gillman as Head Coach in the American Football League" (master's thesis, University of San Diego, 1999).

"One afternoon, the gang wouldn't wait . . ." Hoffman, Jeane, "Gillman Glad to Stay in Football Hot Seat," *Los Angeles Times*, Feb. 5, 1960.

"She was a beautiful person." Massing and Lewis

"I cried for days when Dempsey lost." Massing and Lewis

In 1880, about 100 Jews lived in Minneapolis. Weber, Laura E., "Gentiles Preferred: Minneapolis Jews and Employment 1920–50." *Minnesota History*, Spring 1991.

"The telephone companies, the banks . . ." Interview with Budd Guttman, May 7, 2011.

The editor of the *Saturday Press* . . . Nathanson, Iric. *Minneapolis in the Twentieth Century: The Growth of an American City*. St. Paul, MN: Minnesota Historical Society Press, 2010.

"It was a blow to the city's solar plexus." Anthony, Michael. "From anti-Semitic Hotbed to Healing," *Minnpost.com*, April 25, 2008.

"I did have aspirations." Massing and Lewis

"Sid was the first Jewish kid . . ." Int. with Guttman

"As a basketball player, I would have made a good goalie in hockey." Furillo, Bud, "Ram Coach Prep Star with 'Biggie' Munn," *Los Angeles Herald and Express*, Jan. 29, 1955.

"My brother, Don, used to walk home from school with Sid." Int. with Guttman

And that, as Esther liked to tell her daughters . . . Interview with Bobbe Korbin, March 7, 2011.

". . . She was the prettiest girl in Minneapolis." Massing and Lewis

A man named George Hauser . . . Lawson, Earl, "Football's Man Without Mercy," *Saturday Evening Post*, Oct. 8, 1955.

"I felt that she and I had to separate for a while." Massing and Lewis

"He knew it was most important that he get his degree first . . ." Massing and Lewis

CHAPTER 3

"She was smarter than I, honest to goodness." Massing, Phyllis and Rhoda Lewis. Lifestories/A Video Legacy. Jan. 16, 1996.

The day before the Buckeyes . . . Young, Clarence, "Buckeye Football Players Ready to Answer Sam Willaman's Call," *Ohio State Journal*, Sept. 14, 1931.

Every night, after his work day was complete . . . "Filling Stadium Football's Question Mark," *Columbus Journal Dispatch*, Oct. 1, 1931.

As the team set to open the 1931 season . . . Scheibeck, Irven C., "Bucks and Bearcats Set For Grid Tilt," *Columbus Dispatch*, Oct. 2, 1931.

The first day of Gillman's step into manhood was dreary . . . Young, Clarence. "Weather Interferes, Russ Embrey Reports." *Ohio State Journal*, Sept. 15, 1931.

That was proved when, after a few days of practice . . . Young, Clarence, "Sophs holding key to Buckeye destiny." *Ohio State Journal*, Sept. 17, 1931.

Before his team scrimmaged for the first time . . . Scheibeck, Irven C., "Ohio State Gridmen sent through First Scrimmage of Season," *Columbus Dispatch*, Sept. 19, 1931.

Howard Rabenstein, the other end, was not performing up to expectations . . . Associated Press, Oct. 14, 1931

Gillman "strengthened the end position considerably . . ." Scheibeck, Irven C., "Buckeye Grid Machine Needs Smarter Generalship," *Columbus Dispatch*, Oct. 12, 1931.

Willaman had made up his mind about Gillman early in the Vanderbilt game . . . Rosensweet, Alvin, "End Situation Is Worrying Ohio State Coaching Staff," *Columbus Dispatch*, Oct. 16, 1931.

On a wet, rainy day in a 20-0 win against Navy . . . Harper, Robert S., "Buckeye Line Carries Load of 20-to-0 Win," *Ohio State Journal*, Nov. 8, 1931.

His piano work, though, didn't seem to suffer. Gillman family scrapbook

When a sophomore named Kenneth Rasmussen was added to the squad before the 1933 season. . . *Sandusky Register*, Sept. 20, 1933.

One June before summer classes let out . . . Gillman family scrapbook

As one United Press International reporter wrote . . . Kirksey, George, United Press, Nov. 10, 1932.

Willaman declared in October that Sid was "the greatest end I have ever coached." Danzig, Allison, *The New York Times*, Oct. 19, 1933.

The first choice was one of the titans of the coaching industry, Notre Dame's Knute Rockne . . . Park, Jack. *The Official Ohio State Football Encyclopedia*. Champaign, IL: Sports Publishing LLC, 2003.

During the Northwestern game, Willaman looked to his bench and saw Ohio State legend Chic Harley . . . Penisten, Ed, *Columbus Journal Dispatch*, Oct. 29, 1933.

Considering Ward also performed the play-by-play duties over WOSU . . . Hooey, Robert E., "Ward to Broadcast Game," *Ohio State Journal*, Oct. 28, 1933.

What also might have gotten their attention was Ward's insistence . . . Associated Press, Oct. 28, 1932.

"There you go. He was doing it all the way back then." Interview with Bobbe Korbin, March 7, 2011.

Much of the acrimony began in an Oct. 26 editorial . . . "The Athletic Issue," *Ohio State Lantern*, Oct. 26, 1933.

But in December, after the successful 7-1 season was finished . . . Becker, Fred J., "Lantern Editorial Attacks Willaman," *Massillon Evening Independent*, Dec. 7, 1933.

The next week, after performing well against the University of Pennsylvania . . . Gillman family scrapbook

While Gillman dined on crème of chicken soup reine . . . Gillman family scrapbook

"After the game was over, all these guys went down to Hollywood to get into the movies . . ." Massing and Lewis

"She would do everything she could to facilitate Esther staying in her house before they got married." Interview with Tom Gillman, April 7, 2011.

When Francis Schmidt was a senior at the University of Nebraska, the forward pass was finally deemed a legal maneuver. Perkins, Brett. *Frantic Francis: How One Coach's Madness Changed Football*. Champaign, IL: University of Nebraska Press, 2009.

After listening to the advice of *Columbus Dispatch* sports editor Ed Penisten . . . Fullen, John B., "Introducing Francis A. Schmidt," *The Ohio State University Monthly*, March 1934.

He ran a single-wing formation, a double-wing formation and a short-punt formation . . . Snyder, Larry, "This Man Schmidt," *The Ohio State University Monthly*, October 1934.

Schmidt and Gillman first met at a luncheon after Schmidt had been hired . . . Perkins

His plays used so much misdirection and confusion . . . Snyder

"He used to come on the field with charts for hundreds of plays." Furillo, Bud, "Picked By Schmidt as Buckeye End Coach," *Los Angeles Herald and Express*, Jan. 31, 1955.

After he participated in the East-West Shrine game and the Chicago College All Star game the next summer . . . Tobias, Todd. "A Bolt From the Past: Sid Gillman as Head Coach in the American Football League" (master's thesis, University of San Diego, 1999).

CHAPTER 4

Gillman had planned to be a lawyer, the same as Schmidt . . . Perkins, Brett. *Frantic Francis: How One Coach's Madness Changed Football*. Lincoln, NE:

University of Nebraska Press, 2009.

"I haven't seen a law school yet." Perkins

"Maybe, I will," Gillman thought to himself. Massing, Phyllis and Rhoda Lewis. Lifestories/A Video Legacy. Jan. 16, 1996.

"I needed him in the business." Tobias, Todd. "A Bolt From the Past: Sid Gillman as Head Coach in the American Football League" (master's thesis, University of San Diego, 1999).

"I got paid [as an Ohio State student assistant coach], but very little." Massing and Lewis

They wed in a formal affair at the Curtis Hotel in Minneapolis . . . Massing and Lewis

On the day of the Chicago College All Star game . . . Murphy, Jack, "Gillman's Bride of 30 Years Still Faithful Football Fan," *San Diego Union,* Aug. 22, 1965.

At the time, the couple had only $25 in cash. Murphy

The reason Gillman joined the team in the first place . . . Grayson, Harry, "Pro Grid League Bars All America Jones, But Admits Club He Made," *Coshocton Tribune,* Aug. 3, 1937.

It certainly convinced one writer to exclaim . . . Braden, Ernie, "Sports Cut Short," *Elyria Chronicle Telegram,* Oct. 12, 1936.

Life was pretty good for the Cleveland franchise as well, drawing interest from the NFL. Perkins

Nearly 5,000 fans signed a petition and sent it to NFL president Joe Carr and the league's executive council . . . Associated Press, Aug. 10, 1937.

"They asked if we wanted to go to church; they learned and we learned." Massing and Lewis

The little house in Granville in which the Gillman's lived didn't offer laundry facilities . . . Massing and Lewis

They spent hours together drawing up plays and strategizing . . . Perkins

Once, a Texas Christian player named Johnny Vaught . . . Perkins

At the team banquet . . . Perkins

After the banquet, Schmidt traveled to Los Angeles . . . "Jack Stephenson to Inspire 1941 Bucks," *The Ohio State University Monthly,* Dec. 1940.

"When he came to Ohio State . . ." Perkins

His inability to stay organized eventually doomed Schmidt . . . Perkins

"I had so many children at the time, I had every [deferment] classification that the good Lord created." Massing and Lewis

"Daddy used to smoke a pipe." Interview with Lyle Gillman, March 7, 2011.

"I didn't try to avoid the service, but that's exactly the way it came out." Massing and Lewis

CHAPTER 5

"The statues are bigger than life. Then again, so were the men they depict."
Moore, Terence, "With Rocking Cradle, Miami (Ohio) Goes From Worst to First," AOL Fanhouse, Nov. 24, 2010.

"You can have him [frowning]." Moore

"We have one civilian letterman back." Dillman, Grant. United Press, Aug. 10, 1943.

In the late summer, with 42 players Redskins practice, only 10 were civilians . . . Aston, Joe, "No College Football for Cincinnati; Miami Wanted to Play," *Cincinnati Post*, Sept. 1, 1944.

"He was so into it; I don't know of anyone who was so passionate about the game." Interview with Ara Parseghian, July 12, 2011.

"We would work all week on offense, and about Thursday night, he'd say, 'OK, we'll go work on defense now.'" Interview with Paul Dietzel, Oct. 23, 2010.

"I remember on a Friday, we would go out for a light practice." Int. with Parseghian

In seven of nine regular-season games, the Redskins rushed for at least 175 yards. Miami University archives

In a letter dated March 1, 1946, an unnamed school vice-president wrote Gillman a letter. Miami University archives

The season before, the program had turned down the chance to participate in its first bowl game against Pepperdine in the Will Rogers Bowl . . . Moeller, Bill, "Bill's Board," *Hamilton Daily News Journal*, Nov. 29, 1946.

This had created a firestorm of controversy the year before at the University of Cincinnati . . . Katzowitz, Josh. *Bearcats Rising*. Wilmington, OH: Orange-Frazer Press, 2009.

The decision on whether to accept the bowl bid and the Sun Bowl's racist provisions seemingly shouldn't have even been in the athletic department's hands. Miami archives

Gillman wasn't sure which way to turn, so he asked Harris for advice. Dietzel, Paul F. *Call Me Coach: A Life in College Football*. Baton Rouge, LA: Louisiana State University Press, 2008.

"They simply had too much hustle and were too fast for us." Mothershead, Finis, "Better Team Came Through, Texas Coach's Comment," *Cincinnati Times-Star*, Jan. 2, 1948.

"It wasn't a difficult problem at all." Massing, Phyllis and Rhoda Lewis. Lifestories/A Video Legacy. Jan. 16, 1996.

It was getting late one night and the room was dark . . . Interview with Bum Phillips, June 8, 2011.

"He was supposed to take tickets, but he would stand around and bullshit." Interview with Bud Guttman, May 7, 2011.

"In the newsreels, invariably, they had a football game, the outstanding game of the weekend." Massing and Lewis

"One time, I forgot, and God almighty, what an explosion." Dickey, Glenn, "Inside Track," *Inside Sports*, March 1982.

Gillman started utilizing the film when he took over the Miami job. Dietzel

"Sid was a great copier." Int. with Dietzel

No, to Gillman, studying one's self was just as important. Kurz, Bob. *Miami of Ohio: The Cradle of Coaches.* Troy, Ohio: Troy Daily News, Inc., 1983.

Gillman knew that watching a game from start to finish lead to too much confusion . . . Cronin, Ned, "Cronin's Corner," *Los Angeles Times*, March 8, 1956.

If you looked at the side of his film canisters . . . *Greatest Sports Legend: Sid Gillman*. Dir. Matt Gibson. Steve Rotfeld Productions, 1985.

One day, after spending hours cutting and splicing and winding film . . . Danyluk, Tom, "Art Rooney Jr., Remembers," *Pro Football Weekly*, June 8, 2010.

"Everywhere you go, you see Cradle of Coaches . . ." Interview with Ben Roethlisberger, Feb. 3, 2011.

"Sid found out we had dated in high school." Int. with Dietzel

"Gillman is the guy who deserves most of the credit at Miami." Murphy, Jack. "Parseghian Recalls Gillman's Dedication, Detail at Miami," *San Diego Union*, Dec. 6, 1964.

"I searched and searched and searched." Interview with Bob Kurz, Oct. 23, 2010.

Before Stu Holcomb and Gillman took over the football program, the fan base had grown apathetic. Kurz

"You could shoot a cannon into the stands and not hit anybody." Murray, Jack, "Football's Fiddlefoot," *Cincinnati Enquirer*, Sept. 26, 1976.

"That was the only reason I was invited." Lombardo, John. *A Fire To Win: The Life and Times of Woody Hayes.* New York: Thomas Dunne Books, 2005.

"Talk about a Cradle of Coaches. It wasn't any kind of cradle when I got there." Associated Press, Feb. 8, 1979.

"We thought this was the routine." Interview with Bobbe Korbin, March 7, 2011.

"We were coming out of the Depression, people were settling down, but it was more important to be academic." Massing and Lewis

"That was a treat—showering in these huge showers and we lived in this little tiny house?" Interview with Lyle Gillman, March 8, 2011.

All of which led Gillman to this insistence: the next time the family had to break down and buy a new car, he would buy a convertible. Murphy, Jack, "Gillman's Bride of 30 Years Still Faithful Football Fan," *San Diego Union*, Aug. 22, 1965.

When he saw Gillman's variation of Fritz Crisler's speed sweep . . . Dietzel
"He was promised Earl's job. "That's the only reason they considered it." Interview with Lyle Gillman, Dec. 9, 2011.
Or, as legendary Tennessee coach General Robert Neyland, chair of the NCAA rules committee, would put it . . . Kemper, Kurt Edward. *College Football and American Culture in the Cold War Era.* Champaign, Ill.: University of Illinois Press, 2009.
While Gillman learned the importance of Blaik's theories, he was in the middle of transforming Army's undersized line into a technically precise unit . . . Furillo, Bud, "Blaik Credits New Coach Gillman with All-Conquering Army Precision Lines," *Olean Times Herald,* Nov. 22, 1948.
Every once in a while, an assistant coach at Fordham University would drive north to West Point to meet with Gillman . . . Zimmerman, Paul, "Screen Gem," *Sports Illustrated,* Sept. 2, 1991.
"I have my own department store in Green Bay." Oates, Bob, "Q&A with Sid Gillman," *Los Angeles Times,* Feb. 6, 1983.

CHAPTER 6

But he wasn't politically popular. Katzowitz, Josh. *Bearcats Rising.* Wilmington, OH: Orange-Frazer Press, 2009.
On Dec. 19, 1948, a cold, rainy Sunday evening, *Cincinnati Enquirer* reporter Dick Forbes received a telephone call at his home. Forbes, Dick, "Hall of Famer Gillman Remembered," *Cincinnati Enquirer,* Feb. 4, 1983.
Earlier in the day, he had told *Cincinnati Post* sports editor Joe Aston that he would remain at the U.S. Military Academy to coach for Blaik. Aston, Joe, "Gillman Turns Down U.C. Job," *Cincinnati Post,* Dec. 20, 1948.
Gillman called each player to the team's locker room, where they met a tailor ready to take their measurements. Interview with Ray Penno, Sept. 25, 2008.
After the Bearcats' first workout with Gillman in charge . . . Interview with Nick Shundich, March 27, 2011.
"When Sid came in, it was like night and day." Int. with Penno
"Some of the guys didn't really like Sid, some of the really good ballplayers." Int. with Shundich
"Well Paul, you don't need to go to Cincinnati with Sid." Dietzel, Paul F. *Call Me Coach: A Life in College Football.* Baton Rouge, LA: Louisiana State University Press, 2008.
"It isn't what Sid's teams do. It's the way they do it." Aston, Dec. 22, 1948.
The Bearcats first game with Gillman in charge was with the University of Nevada. Forbes
Paul Dietzel, who was in Stockton, CA, scouting Pacific, said observers were amazed . . . *Cincinnati Post,* Sept. 20, 1949.

"If you had the right technique, you got $5." Int. with Penno

Since the Redskins were so ingrained in the fabric of Oxford, local merchants had a knack for providing complimentary items for Miami players. Howard, Bob. Unpublished article, *Collier's*, 1948.

"But those were innovations that were not part of the rules." Interview with Ara Parseghian, July 12, 2011.

"He took some of the top players, but he didn't know me, because I was on crutches." Interview with Carmen Cozza, Oct. 23, 2010.

Before his team took the field, Hayes gave a simple instruction: "Take small steps." Lombardo, John. *A Fire to Win: The Life and Times of Woody Hayes.* New York: Thomas Dunne Books, 2005.

Behind the play of John Pont and Jim "Boxcar" Bailey, the Redskins snow-skied their way to a 28-0 victory . . . Pont, Sally. *Fields of Honor: The Golden Age of College Football and the Men Who Created It.* New York: Harcourt Inc., 2001.

"Most of them are playing as sophomores at Cincinnati." Aston, Joe, *Cincinnati Post*, Nov. 27, 1950.

The decision stunned Ohio State officials. Hornung, Paul, "Fesler Resigns as OSU Coach," *Columbus Dispatch*, Dec. 10, 1950.

"They called him back and said, 'I'm sorry, Sid. The board met. We cannot hire a Jew.'" Interview with Bobbe Korbin, March 7, 2011.

"I really never had any difficult times coaching." Massing, Phyllis and Rhoda Lewis. Lifestories/A Video Legacy. Jan. 16, 1996.

"Instead of 'Three Yards and a Cloud of Dust,' it could have been 'The Ohio State Express.'" *Full Color Football: The History of the American Football League.* NFL Films, 2009.

Missouri coach Don Faurot was the committee's top choice. Park, Jack. *The Official Ohio State Football Encyclopedia.* Champaign, IL: Sports Publishing LLC, 2003.

Gillman had "confided to close friends that he knew he wasn't under serious consideration . . ." Lawson, Earl. "Football's man without mercy." *Saturday Evening Post*, Oct. 8, 1955.

In fact, the hiring committee apparently was split between Brown and Hayes . . . O'Toole, Andrew. *Paul Brown.* Cincinnati: Clerisy Press, 2008.

"You were evaluated and graded." Interview with Jim Kelly Sr., Aug. 25, 2008.

"When they tried to cover our halfbacks, we shot it to our ends." Forbes, Dick, "UC Head First to Greet Team," *Cincinnati Enquirer*, Nov. 19, 1950.

At the NCAA convention in New York, local Cincinnatians were unanimous in their belief . . . Forbes, Dick, "Gillman Will Stay; Erdelatz to Rams," *Cincinnati Enquirer*, Jan. 11, 1955.

"I hope this makes it clear to people in Cincinnati that my whole future is wrapped up with the Bearcats. Forbes, Dick, "Not Candidate for Rams'

Post," *Cincinnati Enquirer*, Jan. 16, 1955.

"I was interested in pro football." Tobias, Todd. "A Bolt From the Past: Sid Gillman as Head Coach in the American Football League" (master's thesis, University of San Diego, 1999).

When Esther heard the offer, she exclaimed, "$25,000!" Interview with Lyle Gillman, March 7, 2011.

When Reeves called to offer him the job, Gillman said, "I have to tell you something. I'm Jewish." Int. with Bobbe Korbin

CHAPTER 7

When he originally denied that he was leaving Cincinnati for Los Angeles in 1955, the boosters were not surprised. Lawson, Earl. "Football's Man Without Mercy," *Saturday Evening Post.* Oct. 8, 1955.

"I'm thunderstruck. Absolutely thunderstruck." Forbes, Dick, "Hall of Famer Gillman Remembered," *Cincinnati Enquirer*, Feb. 4, 1983.

"Certainly we helped boys find jobs." "Gillman Hits Back at Cincy Charges," *Los Angeles Times*, April 28, 1956.

"We can't except to play big-time teams if we don't have a big-time stadium." Lawson

"Gillman didn't leave us in as bad shape as he did Miami." Lawson

"A lot of people at Miami were upset when I went to UC." Murray, Jack, "Football's Fiddlefoot," *Cincinnati Enquirer*, Sept. 26, 1976.

"It was a question of doing what you have to do to create a top team." Murray

"He left some bills there . . . I remember there was a lot of animosity." Interview with Ara Parseghian, July 12, 2011.

Apparently, Gillman proclaimed, Nolting must have recruited players based on what the sports writers in those players' home towns had told him. Lawson

He called Gillman to give him the heads-up that he'd be a couple of days late to training camp. Anderson, Dave, "Robustelli's Family Came First, and Giants Reaped the Benefits," *The New York Times*, June 4, 2011.

"If you are not here on time, then don't bother to come at all." Izenberg, Jerry, "Andy Robustelli Almost Never Made It Here, But He Became the Perfect Giant," *Newark Star Ledger*, June 1, 2011.

"I've been talking to the Rams about you, and they're willing to trade you." Anderson

"Fellas, the party is over." Zimmerman, Paul, "When Sid Was Caesar," *Sports Illustrated*, Feb. 1, 1988.

"I never learned to cook well. I learned to cook a lot." Beyette, Beverly, "Mrs. Sid Gillman: Football Has Been a Way of Life," *Los Angeles Times*, 1961.

He rushed to the corner drugstore, bought ice cream, smeared it over the missing pieces of pie crust and yelled, "Look kids, pie à la mode!" Hoffman,

Jeane, "Gillman's Glad to Stay in Football Hot Seat," *Los Angeles Times*, Feb. 5, 1960.

The Gillmans would host a dozen athletes at a time, and as Nick Shundich, co-captain of the 1951 Cincinnati squad, remembered, "It was the hottest stuff in town." Interview with Nick Shundich, March 27, 2011.

Pour enough olive oil to cover the bottom of a big kettle and heat before adding the following . . . "Her Spaghetti Sauce Pleases Footballers," *Los Angeles Times*, Dec. 11, 1960.

Gillman and Brown spent their summer vacations learning from Buckeyes coach Francis Schmidt, and Hayes took classes, but in the evenings, the three came together to talk football . . . Lombardo, John. *A Fire To Win: The Life and Times of Woody Hayes.* New York: Thomas Dunne Books, 2005.

Brown is credited with becoming the first head coach to employ year-round assistant coaches . . . Harris, David. *The Genius: How Bill Walsh Reinvented Football and Created an NFL Dynasty.* New York: Random House, 2008.

This mirrored rather closely Gillman's philosophy: "Write it. Learn it. See it. Do it." Barber, Phil, "To Air Was Divine," *Super Bowl XXXII Official Program*, Jan. 1998.

"The one thing that came across to anyone who was paying attention was that Woody Hayes was a lot more than a football coach." Interview with Jim Tressel, June 27, 2008.

"They all have strong suits." Interview with Ara Parseghian, July 12, 2011.

"Several of the fellas didn't think Woody's system was updated." Lombardo

"Woody would say, 'Sid Gillman sends his daughter here. Why wouldn't you come?'" Interview with Lyle Gillman, March 7, 2011.

The two wouldn't appear on the same radio or television shows when Hayes was still at Miami . . . Lawson, Earl, "Football's Man Without Mercy," *Saturday Evening Post*, Oct. 8, 1955.

Though Gillman had to be content that Gillman and Hayes split the only two games they coached against each other . . . Katzowitz, Josh. *Bearcats Rising.* Wilmington, OH: Orange-Frazer Press, 2009.

"I can understand Paul. No other person in the world can build a football team better than he can." Forbes, Dick, "Gillman Ready for Old Nemesis Brown," *Cincinnati Enquirer*, Sept. 5, 1968.

After Brown refused to exchange game film with Gillman, the Oilers coach went on a rant while talking to Ed Menaker of the *Cincinnati Post.* O'Toole

Hayes wept in appreciation. Interview with Bobbe Korbin, March 8, 2011.

Many years after their initial wars, Gillman and Hayes happened to bump into each other one morning in the coffee shop of a Chicago hotel. Lombardo

"Yeah, there are three of those. I hope that ends it right there." Massing, Phyllis and Rhoda Lewis. Lifestories/A Video Legacy. Jan. 16, 1996.

Just before he was inducted into the Pro Football Hall of Fame, the Canton
  (Ohio) Jewish Community Center threw him a banquet . . . Schrock, Art,
  "HOFer Sid Gillman Honored by CJCC," *Canton Repository,* July 28, 1983.

Esther grew up in a more religious home in Minneapolis . . . Interview with
  Lyle Gillman, March 7, 2011.

"We had great college teams, and I was an ambitious sucker." Tobias, Todd. "A
  Bolt From the Past: Sid Gillman as Head Coach in the American Football
  League" (master's thesis, University of San Diego, 1999).

Someone invariably would offer her food and drink, and Esther would say . . .
  Massing and Lewis

To Ron Mix, a Hall of Fame offensive tackle during Gillman's decade as the San
  Diego Chargers coach, Gillman was a revelation. Seymour, Joey, "Chargers'
  Jewish Forefathers—Ron Mix and Sid Gillman," *San Diego Jewish World,*
  Nov. 5-7, 2009.

During high school, there was a shortage of Jews around him. Tracy, Marc,
  "The Other League," *Tablet Magazine,* Feb. 3, 2011.

"Jews were All-American football players and leaders of the Los Angeles Rams."
  Seymour

In 1983, it was clear to Jews around the world that Gillman had broken the
  stereotypes that allowed those who followed him to succeed . . . Ben-Gurion
  University of the Negev. American Associates. *Israel's Ben-Gurion University
  to Establish Chair after Sid Gillman.* 1983.

"He was tough. But he never expected them to do anything that he wouldn't do
  double." Interview with Bobbe Korbin, March 7, 2011.

CHAPTER 8

Thanks to a contractual arrangement with the other owners, Dan Reeves, the
  team president and one of owners of the squad, was the only one who could
  hire a new coach. Old, John B, "Genius Or Goat—and What Next," *Los
  Angeles Herald and Express,* Jan. 19, 1955.

"The Rams were firing guys left and right." Interview with Melvin Durslag,
  April 20, 2011.

Reeves and Fred Levy were owners when the Rams were in Cleveland . . .
  Quirk, James and Rodney D. Fort. *Pay Dirt: The Business of Professional Team
  Sports.* Princeton, N.J.: Princeton University Press, 1997.

Though it took 39 days between the time Pool choked on his soup and Gillman
  said yes to Reeves's job offer, Reeves was ecstatic in his choice. Furillo, Bud,
  "Ready for Fan Barbs," *Los Angeles Herald and Express,* Feb. 3, 1955.

"With the Rams, it was nothing but football." Massing, Phyllis and Rhoda
  Lewis. Lifestories/A Video Legacy. Jan. 16, 1996.

Lyle looked at the cover of the *Los Angeles Times,* and that's how she discovered her dad had a new job. Interview with Lyle Gillman, March 7, 2011.

As the team entered its first training camp under Gillman in mid-July 1955, the preseason workouts in Redlands were more relaxed than they had been in ages. Finch, Frank, "Sid Gillman Gives Rams New Spirit," *Los Angeles Times*, July 19, 1955.

To Gillman, it made sense because Pool had been undone by the backbiting of his players . . . Burick, Si, "Gillman's Press Problem," *Dayton Daily News*, August 1955.

"I'll never read a sports page as long as I live." Int. with Durslag

In fact, when he needed to make a point, Gillman picked up the chalk and gave the scribes a brief football lesson on his office blackboard. Finch, Frank, "Gillman Cites Shoddy Play of Ram Team," *Los Angeles Times*, Aug. 18, 1955.

The problem with the Rams organization, as Gillman saw it, was there was *too much* offense and not enough defense . . . Murray, James, "Cleveland Won The Title Again But Not Before The Whole NFL Had Come To Appreciate Coach Sid Gillman And His L.A. Rams," *Sports Illustrated*, Jan 2, 1956.

"You not only are the greatest players I've ever been with, but as a group you're the greatest bunch of men." Whorton, Cal, "Gillman Lauded, Game Ball Saved," *Los Angeles Times*, Dec. 12, 1955.

As L.A.'s players walked by Brown in the tunnel after the game and jeered him and his team . . . Murray

But in this game, it was a matter of protection. Zehms, Dick, "In This Corner," *Long Beach Press-Telegram*, Dec. 27, 1955.

"Just remember, it isn't always going to be this easy." Pont, Sally. *Fields of Honor: The Golden Age of College Football and the Men Who Created It.* New York: Harcourt Inc., 2001.

"I wish I could start to describe him. He was a redneck without really being a redneck." Int. with Durslag

In February 1955, just after Gillman took the job . . . Furillo, Bud, "Tells Plans for Rams," *Los Angeles Herald and Express*, Feb. 4, 1955.

"I felt that Van just might not have it after he threw that first pass that was intercepted." Whorton, Cal. "Rams Don't Have No. 1 Quarterback—Gillman," *Los Angeles Times*, Oct. 1, 1956.

Gillman replied that it was easier to let the four coaches in the press box know what play had been called . . . Geyer, Jack, "Ladies Put Sid Gillman on Spot with Hot Barrage of Questions," *Los Angeles Times*, Oct. 26, 1956.

A week later, Gillman said that plays would continue to be—and always be—called from the sidelines. Geyer, Jack, "Sid Says He'll Still Call Plays," *Los Angeles Times*, Nov. 2, 1956.

"When you call signals for Van Brocklin, you're jeopardizing his job." *Washington Star-News*, Nov. 2, 1974.

Afterward, a reporter asked Gillman how many plays had been called from the sideline.

Whorton, Cal, "Gillman Irked by Queries Concerning Play Calling," *Los Angeles Times*, Nov. 5, 1956.

"It's developed into such a tremendous issue." Geyer, Jack. "Wade Due to Open Remaining Games," *Los Angeles Times*, Nov. 9, 1956.

"Dutch, go ahead and get warmed up." Interview with Ron Waller, July 15, 2011.

He never told me why. He just sat me on the bench." Geyer, Jack, "Rams' Van Brocklin Quits Football," *Los Angeles Times*, Jan. 3, 1958.

Before the 1960 season, Van Brocklin announced that it would be his final year before retirement." Didinger, Ray, "Fifty Years Ago, the Eagles Were Champions," *Philadelphiaeagles.com*, Dec. 26, 2010.

And though Wade finished as a two-time Pro Bowler, Gillman blamed himself for not feeding Wade's development because of Van Brocklin. Cronin, Ned, "Cronin's Corner," *Los Angeles Times*, April 10, 1958.

"I was thinking they ought to tighten the goddamn immigration laws in this country." Grizzard, Lewis. *If I Ever Get Back to Georgia, I'm Gonna Nail My Feet to the Ground*. New York: Ballantine Books, 1990.

"Can my husband be happy on the farm? Let me put it this way: pecan trees don't drop touchdown passes." Grizzard

"We were just beginning to understand how moves are made by a receiver." Pont

"If you got one of Sid's videos, you got everything but the touchdowns." Interview with Nick Shundich, March 7, 2011.

As Jack Faulkner—who coached under Gillman at Miami, Cincinnati, L.A. and San Diego—took over the Denver Broncos job . . . Katzowitz, Josh. *Bearcats Rising*. Wilmington, Ohio: Orange-Frazer Press, 2009.

"If we were going to play the Raiders next week, on Sunday night a copy of that game film . . ." Tobias, Todd. "A Bolt From the Past: Sid Gillman as Head Coach in the American Football League" (master's thesis, University of San Diego, 1999).

But he wasn't one of the worst offenders . . . Grosscup, Lee, "Spying in Pro Football," *Sport*, Aug. 1967.

"He was so close to the players and coaches that he could hear 'em talking." Grosscup

Once, when the Chargers prepared for the Bills . . . Reilly, Rick, "Commitment to Honesty," *ESPN.com*, Oct. 14, 2011.

"There have been some funny things happening in our league." Grosscup

"I got him, I caught your man." Underwood, John, "Mile-High Hopes in High Old Denver," *Sports Illustrated*, Oct. 22, 1962.

When the Kansas City Chiefs hired Don Klosterman away from the Chargers
. . . Stram, Hank and Lou Sahadi. *They're Playing My Game.* Chicago: Triumph Books, 1986.

In a conversation long after they were grown, Esther confided that she saw the
two pairs of siblings differently. Pont.

"I would cry from Sunday when we would lose until I got it together again by
Thursday." Interview with Bobbe Korbin, March 7, 2011.

"I didn't care about it." Int. with Lyle Gillman

"We had to elope in 1960, because we never could get Sid to commit to a date."
Interview with Bill Korbin, March 8, 2011.

"After dinner, he would go watch film." Interview with Terry Hill, March 9, 2011.

"Mom and Dad were seriously busier when we were growing up than they were
with Lyle and Bobbe." Interview with Tom Gillman, April 7, 2011.

"Esther is the worst person in the world to sit next to at a football game."
Gregston, Gene, "Chargers Retain Sense of Humor, Keep Busy Too." *San
Diego Evening-Tribune*, April 29, 1961.

"The people who sat in front of the Gillman kids would turn around to my
mother and ask, 'What do you feed your kids? Raw meat?'" Int. with Bobbe
Korbin

"I was probably the only white boy in the world who knew about these high-
low poker games and Jackie Wilson songs." Int. with Tom Gillman

I've been mixed up all my life for 45 years." "Completely Mixed Up, Sid Gillman Admits," *Los Angeles Times*, Feb. 6, 1957.

"Can you imagine going from Cincinnati to Los Angeles?" *Inside Sports*, March
1982.

After the 1956 season mercifully was finished, Esther had seen a stronger version of her husband emerge. Hoffman, Jeane, "Gillman Proved He Can Take
It," *Los Angeles Times*, Dec. 14, 1956.

As one astute writer put it, "To Sid, jazz is the elixir . . ." "The Old Man Is the
Hippest," *San Diego Chargers Game Program*, Dec. 1968.

Or Gillman could sneak out with Esther after curfew to listen to Louis Armstrong . . . Farmer, Sam, "Coach Revolutionized Offenses in Football," *Los
Angeles Times*, Jan 4, 2003.

"The Rams were owned by five guys. Dan Reeves was the principal owner, but
they did a lot by committee." Int. with Tom Gillman

To hear his kids tell it, Gillman wanted to trade for Cardinals standout running back Ollie Matson soon after he arrived in L.A. . . . Int. with Lyle
Gillman

When he turned pro, he was considered the most versatile running back in the
league, more so than Frank Gifford and Jim Brown. Milham, Simon. "Ollie
Matson Remembered." *NFLUK.com*, Feb. 22, 2011.

Quarterback Billy Wade, on his way to the shower . . . Hyland, Dick. "Gillman Doesn't Try to Alibi Ram Defeat," *Los Angeles Times*, Oct. 26, 1959.

That's when Rams ownership began to look at a future without Gillman in charge of the team. Kelley, Bob, "Rams Decided on Change Early in Season," *Long Beach Press-Telegram*, Dec. 15, 1959.

On the Friday before the second Lions game of the season, the Rams' plane took off from the runway . . . Teele, Jack, "Tragedy in 12 Acts: Fall of the Rams," *Long Beach Press-Telegram*, Dec. 14, 1959.

Former Rams halfback Tom Harmon had called the 1959 team "gutless." Finch, Frank, "Gillman 'Quit'; Rams to Buy Up Pact," *Los Angeles Times*, Dec. 13, 1959.

And after the Colts scored three touchdowns in the final 15 minutes of the Rams season to score the win . . . Lewis, Dave, "Injuries Not Key to Rams' Collapse," *Long Beach Independent*, Dec. 15, 1959.

"It was one of the most unhappy decisions that I personally ever have to make." Finch

When the news broke of the AFL owners starting their league . . . *Full Color Football: The History of the American Football League*. NFL Films, 2009.

"Mr. Hunt, I'm very thrilled and honored. I really appreciate it, but I'm not interested in the job." Interview with Carl Peterson, March 21, 2011.

CHAPTER 9

"I think every out-of-work truck driver who ever played football showed up." *Inside Sports,* March 1982.

He applied to become a police officer, but instead, officers threw him in jail. Jenkins, Chris, "Fleet-footed Lowe Got the Chargers Up and Running," *San Diego Union-Tribune*, Feb. 13, 2011.

"When they had tryouts, everybody and their grandmother showed up looking for spots." Jenkins

He didn't make much of an impact on Gillman at first. Zimmerman, Paul, "When Sid Was Caesar," *Sports Illustrated,* Feb. 1, 1988.

Gillman, just like with the Rams five years earlier, was not the organization's first choice to lead the team. UPI, Jan. 8, 1960

"It was a very trying time for him." Interview with Bill Korbin, March 8, 2011

"If he would not have hired Landry or if Landry would have not taken the job . . ." Interview with Gil Brandt, Feb. 2, 2011.

"Isn't that such a bitch?" Interview with Lyle Gillman, March 8, 2011.

Instead, Gillman stayed in L.A., and Hilton met with Gillman to gauge his interest about the Chargers job. Miller, Jeff. *Going Long.* New York: McGraw-Hill, 2003.

When Frank Leahy resigned in July 1960 because of health issues, Gillman took
over his job and his $50,000 a year salary. Dyer, Braven, "Gillman Takes
Leahy's Job with Chargers," *Los Angeles Times*, July 10, 1960.

"We had 50 players coming, 50 going and 50 in mind." Herskowitz, Mickey.
"A Lion in Winter," *Cowboys-Saints Official Game Program*, Sept. 24, 1973.

Today, Mix spends his days in a non-descript building in a non-descript office
park in San Diego's Mission Valley. Interview with Ron Mix, March 10,
2011.

"If you fucked up, Sid was on your ass." Interview with Carl Mauck, April 20,
2011.

But he wasn't quick enough to escape the occasional Gillman barb. Interview
with Bobbe Korbin, March 7, 2011.

Jack Murphy was a man who wanted an answer. Interview with Jerry Magee,
May 18, 2011.

As one of his staff writers penned many years later, "Murphy had a way with
dogs, women readers, and communities." Magee, Jerry, "In the Beginning."
San Diego Magazine, Dec. 2009.

The final realization might have hit home in mid-November 1960 when the
Chargers played host to the Oilers. Murphy, Jack, "Chargers, Houston Clash
Thrills Small L.A. Crowd," *San Diego Union*, Dec. 14, 1960.

A week later, Hilton said his plans were to continue to operating in L.A., but he
also said he'd be willing to listen to offers from other cities. Gregston, Gene,
"'Willing to Listen,' Chargers Owner Replies," *San Diego Evening Tribune*,
Dec. 22, 1960.

A few days after the Chargers lost to the Oilers in the championship game,
Hilton visited San Diego . . . *San Diego Evening Tribune*, Jan. 5, 1961.

"It was similar with the L.A. Rams and L.A. Chargers to the Dallas Texans and
the Dallas Cowboys." Interview with Carl Peterson, March 21, 2011.

The Gillmans were sad to leave L.A., their home for the past six years . . .
Hoffman, Jeane, "Sid Gillmans Packed and Ready to Move Chargers to San
Diego," *Los Angeles Times*, Feb. 7, 1961

Balboa Stadium had been built in 1914 for the Panama-California Exposition
. . . Magee

"He thought it was a piece of shit, basically." Int. with Magee

It wasn't as easy as San Diego and its new tenants thought it might be. Zimmerman, Paul, "When Sid Was Caesar," *Sports Illustrated*, Feb. 1, 1988.

"It's hard to describe," Mix said. "But whatever it is, Jack's got it." Terrell, Roy,
"Supercharged Entry in the AFL," *Sports Illustrated*, Oct. 23, 1961.

"One time he told me, 'You know, Paul, I really like your perspicacity.'"
Gaughan, Mark, "Former Teammates Reflect on the Late Jack Kemp,"
Buffalo News, March 4, 2011.

"He really believed in a lot of social issues." Gaughan

But Kemp didn't impress the Calgary coaches . . . Murphy, Jack, "Grid Talent of Chargers' Kemp Matched Only by His Ambition," *San Diego Union*, April 16, 1961.

Instead of offense, defense was the team's strength . . . Steidel, Dave. *Remember the AFL*. Cincinnati: Clerisy Press, 2008.

Kemp tried to play through the injury, but every time the center snapped the ball against Kemp's hand . . . Shrake, Edwin, "The Bills Come Storming In," *Sports Illustrated*, Jan. 3, 1966.

In those days, the injured reserve list didn't exist. Miller

A dazed Kemp said he wouldn't leave San Diego, but Bills officials threatened to put him on the reserve list and cut off his $1,200 weekly salary. *Sports Illustrated*, Oct. 15, 1962.

You're looking at the only guy who gave away a future President for $100." Anderson, Dave, "The Other League," *The New York Times*, June 7, 1979.

Gillman, though, had set the tone of what he expected from his players and from his owner . . . *Full Color Football: The History of the American Football League*. NFL Films, 2009.

Gillman demanded punctuality, which is why Ron Mix found himself with his face in the dirt one night . . . Mahee, Charles, "A Master of His Art," *Los Angeles Times*, Nov. 13, 1969.

"Things were a little different then." Miller

That's the respect Gillman earned, in part because he never stopped working. Miller

Gillman thought he ran a lackadaisical training camp, and as a result . . . Tobias, Todd. "A Bolt From the Past: Sid Gillman as Head Coach in the American Football League" (master's thesis, University of San Diego, 1999).

"If you have an appointment, keep it." Mix, Ron, "I Swore I Would Quit Football," *Sports Illustrated*, Sept. 16, 1963.

"As if our two practices a day isn't enough." Mix

"This stuff is called Dianabol and it's going to help assimilate protein and you'll be taking it every day." Quinn. T.J. "Pumped Up Pioneers: the '63 Chargers," ESPN.com, Feb. 1, 2009.

"I still remember what it says." Quinn

"Sid doesn't leave a stone unturned." Interview with Keith Lincoln, April 21, 2011.

He first met Roy at a college football coaches conference where Roy gave a presentation about the benefits of lifting weights . . . Quinn

Gillman liked the idea of weight training. Tobias

"I give Sid the benefit of the doubt on that." Int. with Mix

"I think that if dad had been told this is harmful for the body, he never would have done it." Int. with Korbin

"My husband was the doctor, and Buzzie (Malkoff) would yell at Dad and say, 'Stop going to the freaking trainers when something is wrong with you.'" Int. with Lyle Gillman

Gillman did defend himself in 1973, saying, "It was commonly accepted then." "Gillman Provides Ammunition for Union," *Milwaukee Journal*, Aug. 15, 1974.

"I thought they were kicking a dead man, because a dead man can't kick back." Interview with Tom Gillman, April 11, 2011.

"The U.S. weightlifting team used them. Just like high-protein supplements, whatever, to make you stronger and healthier." Feinswog, Lee. "Powerful Impact," *225 Baton Rouge*, Jan. 26, 2009.

"It was too attractive not to take them, because they worked." Int. with Mix

"I do know that Houston at San Diego State was a 210-pound linebacker . . ." Quinn

During the Ridge trial, a lawyer, when questioning Gillman, asked . . . Callahan, Tom, "They're Sure to Have Some Fun in Philadelphia Now," *Washington Star*, April. 24, 1979.

"Oh please, Houston ran into it with his eyes wide open." Int. with Mix

Gillman obviously didn't care. Hoffman, Jeane, "Gillman Doubles in Brass as Charger General Manager, Coach." *Los Angeles Times*, Oct. 11, 1960.

"He wanted that, because he wanted the power." Interview with Tom Bass, March 21, 2011.

Sidney is nothing but a Jekyll and Hyde, and there's a place for people with split personality." Twombly, Wells, "Goodbye, Sidney," *San Francisco Examiner*, Nov. 24, 1971.

Once after a tough negotiation when Gillman wouldn't budge off his original offer . . . Barber, Phil, "To Air was Divine," *Super Bowl XXXII Official Program*, Jan. 1998.

After Dave Kocourek's 1961 season, in which he led the team with 55 catches for 1,055 yards, he asked Gillman for a raise. Zimmerman

"I was very unhappy when our team traded them." Int. with Mix

"You're a professional, and you're doing your job." Int. with Lincoln

Lincoln was a Southern California kid, and since he was a star high school quarterback . . . Int. with Lincoln

With the Chargers leading 7-0, Tobin Rote threw a screen pass to Lincoln on the left sideline . . . NFL Films

In truth, Stratton was scared that Lincoln was going to make him look silly on that play. Maiorana, Sal. *Buffalo Bills: The Complete Illustrated History*. Minneapolis: MVP Books, 2010.

When the game was over, the injured Lance Alworth rose from his seat in the press box . . . Murphy, Jack. "Kemp's Protection Failed Him—Only Against Friendly Mob," *San Diego Union*, Dec. 27, 1964.

"Look at me. I'm still all white." "Pro Football: The Game Nobody Saw," *Time*, Jan. 7, 1966.

CHAPTER 10

When he got to the AFL, though, Gillman's mindset shifted. Tracy, Marc, "The Other League," *Tablet Magazine*, Feb. 3, 2011.

"He was so far ahead of his time, people couldn't totally understand what he was doing." Rappoport, Ken. *The Little League That Could.* Lanham, MD: Taylor Trade Publishing, 2010.

In the 1930s, when Gillman played at Ohio State under Sam Willaman . . . Tobias, Todd. "A Bolt From the Past: Sid Gillman as Head Coach in the American Football League" (master's thesis, University of San Diego, 1999).

In the 1940s, though, coaches like the University of Chicago's Clark Shaughnessy . . . Tobias

Gillman didn't begin using the T-formation at his offensive scheme of choice until 1946 . . . Pont, Sally. *Fields of Honor: The Golden Age of College Football and the Men Who Created It.* New York: Harcourt Inc., 2001.

"Those who say the T is doomed must mean a T without any variations." Howard, Bob. Unpublished article, *Collier's*, 1948.

After the Bearcats beat Tulsa 47–35 in 1951, Gillman was so impressed by his opponent's offense . . . Lawson, Earl, "Football's Man Without Mercy," *Saturday Evening Post*, Oct. 8, 1955.

But Gillman found this too limiting, so he implanted the Spin-T . . . Furillo, Bud, "Tells Plans for Rams," *Los Angeles Herald and Express*, Feb. 4, 1955.

With the Rams, he also began placing his receivers . . . Cronin, Ned, "Cronin's Corner," *Los Angeles Times*, Aug. 13, 1956.

His opponents in L.A. weren't impressed, because, in some ways, he had installed a college-style offense for a professional team. Interview with Ron Waller, July 15, 2011.

"First, we're going to stretch you horizontally." *Inside Sports*, March 1982.

It helped that in the AFL, most teams played a 4-3 defense . . . Interview with Tom Bass, March 21, 2011.

Or as former Texas Tech coach Mike Leach said in 2005: Lewis, Michael, "Coach Lewis Goes Deep, Very Deep," *New York Times Magazine*, Dec. 4, 2005.

The offense grew so complex that when Paul Dietzel . . . Pont

"Everybody had to work like hell to keep up with him." Jaworski, Ron. *The Games That Changed the Game.* New York: Ballantine Books, 2010.

While his counterparts worked like hell to keep up with Gillman, he never stopped tiring of looking for more information. Quinn. T.J., "Pumped Up Pioneers: the '63 Chargers," ESPN.com, Feb. 1, 2009.

Tom Bass was supposed to play football at San Jose State, but a week before the polio vaccine was made public . . . Int. with Bass

"We thought about it, and if you look at (passing) patterns, they are all geometrically designed." Sawchick, Travis, "Clemson Assistant Steele: 'Football All About Angles'," *Charleston Post & Courier*, Oct. 27, 2011.

In the spring of 1964, Gillman sent Bass to meet with a San Diego State mathematics professor . . . Sawchick

"What [Gillman] did was take every pattern and actually measure where was the optimum place to throw the ball, how long the ball should be in the air." Tobias

Gillman, taking the math a step further, divided the football field into seven passing zones across the width of the field. Tobias

"Some guys are just smarter than others, and he was one of them." Interview with Dan Dierdorf, Jan. 11, 2011.

"Everything an offensive coach does is aimed at giving his team an advantage . . ." Klein, Frederick C., "The Coach as Couch Potato," *Wall Street Journal*, Sept. 30, 1995.

With the quarterback taking the snap and dropping back into the pocket . . . Brown, Chris, "Al Davis' strategic legacy," Grantland.com, Oct. 11, 2011.

"He wanted perfection. He wanted absolute perfection." Interview with Dan Pastorini, Aug. 24, 2011.

"No, he never will. There'll always be new horizons." Magee, Jerry, "Gillman, 75, Going Home After Consultation at Pitt," *San Diego Union*, Oct. 11, 1987.

The first time Lance Alworth showed up for work at the San Diego Chargers headquarters . . . Zimmerman, Paul, "When Sid Was Caesar," *Sports Illustrated*, Feb. 1, 1988.

"He was the perfect player for our offense." Buckley, James Jr., "A Weapon Named Bambi," *Super Bowl XXXII Official Program*, Jan. 1998.

"In high school as a basketball player I could never cram the ball into the basket." Shrake

When Ernie Wright entered professional football as an offensive tackle for the Los Angeles Chargers . . . Tobias

"Marshall refuses to use Negro players. He's dead wrong from both a moral and practical standpoint." Murphy Jack, "Racial Bias Makes 'Skins Worst Team in Football—Gillman," *San Diego Union*, Aug. 12, 1961.

"There were very few members of the American Football League who were also members of the NAACP." *Full Color Football: The History of the American Football League*. NFL Films, 2009.

Originally that summer, Gillman wanted a job working street construction so he could spend his days outside doing the heavy work. Interview with Budd Guttman, May 7, 2011.

"He wasn't self-appointed, and he didn't necessarily do it for the whole movement." Interview with Tom Gillman, April 6, 2011.

Even though Alworth had made speeches on behalf of Arkansas governor Orval Faubus . . . Shrake

In the early days of the AFL, the outside world infiltrated the Chargers' racial views. Tobias

"For you to room with a Caucasian player at that time, it was unthinkable." NFL Films

"I didn't hear anybody complain about it." Int. with Mix

CHAPTER 11

"I figured anybody who could run in plays for Paul Brown had to be bright." Anderson, Dave, "San Diego's Super Roots," *The New York Times*, Jan. 25, 1988.

"He was a little bitty shit." Interview with Carl Mauck, April 20, 2011.

The AFL's original deal with ABC paid each team $185,000 per year, but the ratings weren't as high as anticipated . . . Fowler, Bud. *Loser Takes All: Bud Adams, Bad Football and Big Business*. Atlanta; Longstreet Press, 1997.

To contrast, the NFL and CBS had struck a deal in 1962 that brought in $4.65 million annually . . . Miller

Considering none of the new league's teams had made a profit, the league needed to bring in outside money to compete with the NFL *The New York Times*, Aug. 23, 1964.

"At that point, the NFL saw that they were in a war with people that could stay in the war." Rappoport

The Chargers, as Al Davis once said, were the flagship franchise that the rest of the league could emulate. Rappoport

"When Sid came into the AFL, Sid taught the AFL how to do business." Interview with Jerry Magee, May 18, 2011.

"The fact that the Chargers didn't have a big fan base or a great stadium to play in, that was beside the point." Interview with Bill Korbin, March 8, 2011.

"I don't know whose idea that was. But it was a splendid idea." Massing, Phyllis and Rhoda Lewis. Lifestories/A Video Legacy. Jan. 16, 1996.

"The AFL, as you may know, is not a league so much as an exercise in geometric progression." Murray, Jim, "Rented Defenses," *Los Angeles Times*, Jan. 7, 1964.

"He gave the league a strategic tone and a shape." *Full Color Football: The History of the American Football League*. NFL Films, 2009.

Veteran players, like Ernie Ladd and Earl Faison, wanted enormous signing bonuses. Murphy, Jack, "Not a Perfect Deal, But the Only One Acceptable to Sid," *San Diego Union*, Jan. 16, 1966.

During his first day of Chargers training camp, he wolfed down 10 eggs, eight pieces of toast, three glasses of juice, and four cartons of milk. Magee, Jerry, "Ladd Reports—Grocery Bill Up," *San Diego Union*, Aug. 9, 1961.

If he wasn't in the mood for eggs, he'd inhale a dozen pancakes . . . Olderman, Murray, "Big Ladd Fantastic . . . Eating and Playing," *Houston Press*, Nov. 28, 1961.

One day, at the age of 22 when he still had much to prove . . . Associated Press, April 24, 1963.

"I do not like to accuse a man on limited evidence." Murray, Jim, "Ladd the Gourmet," *Los Angeles Times*, April 24, 1963.

Since it wasn't unusual for football players to moonlight as pro wrestlers in the offseason . . . "No Stopping the Big Cat," Steel Belt Wrestling, April 30, 2006.

He began his career as the good guy, but he was too big to elicit much sympathy when he took a beating from his opponent. Litsky, Frank, "Ernie Ladd, Hall of Famer in Football and Pro Wrestling, Dies at 68," *The New York Times*, March 14, 2007.

"I manipulated my Queen into position and said to Ernie, 'Check.'" Funk Jr., Dory, Online World of Wrestling, date unknown.

One day, after signing with the Chiefs, he sauntered into a dorm room while some of his teammates were in the middle of a poker game . . . Steel Belt Wrestling

Making matters worse, Gillman was about to lose the best owner for whom he'd ever worked . . . Tobias

Klein and Schulman restricted the money that could be used to sign the top players of the day . . . Tobias

Klein had begun his career by selling cars in the San Fernando Valley until he made his way into the insurance and theater businesses. Interview with Jerry Magee, May 18, 2011.

"Klein was a good guy, but he was a movie guy." Int. with Mauck

In fact, Syracuse coach Ben Schwartzwalder had said . . . Hyman, Mervin, Arlie W. Schardt and Morton Sharnik, "The Midwest," *Sports Illustrated*, Sept. 18, 1961.

He always believed the Chargers were not satisfied with his play . . . *San Diego Evening Tribune*, Jan. 11, 1967.

"John Hadl to Lance Alworth? Aw man, that was trouble. Trouble." *Top Ten Pass Combos: John Hadl and Lance Alworth,* NFL.com, March 19, 2008.

But eventually, Klein, who had said that Hadl was "no Joe Namath by any stretch of the imagination" . . . Magee, Jerry, "Hadl Looks Back on Seven Seasons," *San Diego Union*, March 30, 1969.

Phillips had spent his entire coaching career in Texas, mostly in the high school ranks . . . Interview with Bum Phillips, June 8, 2011.

"From the time I started, he never let the offensive line work against the defensive line." Int. with Phillips

"Bum, I want you to go back to the 4-3." Int. with Phillips

But Gillman still felt bad, and as was speaking to *San Diego Union* sports editor Jack Murphy, he said, "Sit here with me. I've got this awful pain in my chest." Murphy, Jack, "The Giant Has Toppled and Some Feel a Sense of Loss," *San Diego Union*, Nov. 24, 1971.

Malkoff ordered him to cancel a dinner party he was scheduled to attend and go home and rest.

Murphy, Jack, "Even For a Tough Old Bird Like Sid, It's a Rugged Game," *San Diego Union*, Oct. 9, 1969.

Privately, owner Gene Klein urged him to give up coaching and focus solely on his general manager job . . . Magee, Jerry, *San Diego Union*, Nov. 12, 1969.

"He should quit. He works too hard." Felser, Larry, "AFL," *The Sporting News*, Sept. 13, 1969.

"I was just glad he took my advice." Magee, Nov. 12, 1969

After a staff meeting on Nov. 11, he walked up to Waller . . . Magee, Nov. 12, 1969

"I wanted to stay until the day I dropped." Magee, Nov. 12, 1969

Where else, Klein thought to himself, can I find a better coach? Murphy, Jack, "Turbulent Times for Sidney But Club Owner His Anchor," *San Diego Union*, Oct. 22, 1971.

"Sometimes, you can't see the forest for the trees." Magee, Jerry, "For Gillman It Was a Time to Reflect," *San Diego Union*, Jan. 1, 1971.

"I came out of Sid's office with a good feeling." Murphy, Jack, "Gillman Is More Approachable But He's Still the Emperor," *San Diego Union*, July 15, 1971.

In the midst of that slump, Gillman received a hand-written letter from adolescent siblings Tommy and Karen. . . . Murphy, Oct. 22, 1971

"The saddest thing about it is that Sid pours his blood into it." Smith, Rick, "Sid's Man Alone on Torturous, Long Ride Home," *San Diego Evening Tribune*, Nov. 8, 1971.

"How can I go to my people and tell them I've traded LeVias for a draft choice?" Murphy, Jack, "Dispute Over Deal Triggers Friction Between Sid, Klein," *San Diego Union*, Nov. 28, 1971.

A few weeks later, Gillman knew he needed a confrontation with his boss. Murphy, Jack, Nov. 24, 1971.

"I think it is apparent I've been moving away from one-man rule for some time now." Lockwood, Wayne, "Gillman Calls His Final Play—Resigns," *San Diego Union*, Nov. 23, 1971.

"Dad said, 'If I start making trades in the middle of the season, it looks like I have given up on the season,'" Interview with Lyle Gillman, March 8, 2011.

"Sid went to talk to Gene Klein and he proceeded to hand him his resignation letter and told him . . ." Int. with Phillips

"I have a message for the youth of America. Mitchell, Matt, "Sid Gillman Out! Why?" *The Daily Californian*, Nov. 23, 1971.

"It was a terribly bitter time." Interview with Tom Gillman, April 10, 2011.

"I've got a big rear end. I'm going to spend the rest of my life sitting on it." Zimmerman, Paul, "Screen Gem," *Sports Illustrated*, Sept. 2, 1991.

CHAPTER 12

Two NFL clubs went after Gillman to serve as their offensive coordinator . . . Magee, Jerry, "Gillman Excited Over New Career," *San Diego Union*, Jan. 22, 1972.

Gillman flew to Noll to talk about the position . . . Murphy, Jack, "Sid Returns, This Time with Dallas," *San Diego Union*, March 1972.

"Football must be some game if he needs it so much he's leaving four children and seven grandchildren." Murphy

"What's this all about, Sid?" Interview with Melvin Durslag, April 20, 2011.

Under the NFL-AFL merger rules, Gillman needed one more season in pro football in order to qualify for his pension. Roswell, Gene, "No Bones About It," *New York Post*, June 10, 1972.

"The fact he didn't have an agent killed him financially." Interview with Lyle Gillman, March 7, 2011.

He couldn't do it. He told his daughters he couldn't sleep at the thought. Int. with Lyle Gillman

"He was not a gambler." Interview with Bobbe Korbin, March 7, 2011.

"I told him I wanted him to take over completely." Peebles, Dick, "Bow Tie Traditionalist," *Houston Chronicle*, Feb. 23, 1973.

But in Houston, he was completely in over his head. Marshall, Joe, "After 18 Dry Wells, a Little Gusher," *Sports Illustrated*, Nov. 12, 1973.

When Peterson announced to his team that Gillman would take over the offense . . . Interview with Dan Pastorini, Aug. 24, 2011.

One *Houston Post* reporter wrote that covering the team was like "visiting friends doing eight to 10." Marshall

That, though, is to be expected when a team employs . . . Marshall

In one of his initial team meetings, he warned, "This is not a democracy. This is a dictatorship, and I'm the dick." Int. with Pastorini

"It is people such as Gillman who cause the players to ask for all sorts of freedom they normally wouldn't need . . . Johnson, Chuck, "Gillman Provides
Ammunition for Union," *Milwaukee Journal*, Aug. 15, 1974.

One of the first questions asked by Ogilvie was how Gillman felt about football
players in general. *Washington Star News*, Nov. 2, 1974.

Though Pastorini vehemently disliked Gillman when he chewed out his starting
quarterback in front of the rest of the team . . . Int. with Pastorini

"His ideas on the field are current, but off the field he's not a modern-day coach."
Jacobson, Steve, "The Dictator," *Cleveland Plain Dealer*, Aug. 21, 1974.

Before he accepted Gillman's offer to become the Oilers defensive coordinator,
Phillips told Gillman . . . Interview with Bum Phillips, June 8, 2011.

"Sid was a great guy—one of the best people in the world . . ." Int. with Phillips

After the game, Browns owner Art Modell found Gillman in the Oilers locker
room, stuck out his hand and said, "Congratulations, Sid. Good job,"
Associated Press, Dec. 16, 1974.

"I sought out Sid Gillman to turn the Oilers around, whether it took . . . even
five years. United Press International, Feb. 16, 1975.

"I made it understood that if there were any fines like that this year, it's going to
come out of somebody else's pocket." Associated Press, Dec. 4, 1974.

"It was bad management right to the core." Marshall

One reason for the lack of success was because Adams meddled unnecessarily in
the business affairs of his underlings. Fowler

"Bud knows football, but he doesn't know too much about people." Marshall

"If we win the Super Bowl, we could wind up paying the owner." Kirkpatrick,
Curry, "Hallelujah. He's. Uh. Bum," *Sports Illustrated*, Oct. 27, 1980.

"I don't care what he says: there is no way that $600,000 worth of movies can
make us a better team." Kirkpatrick

Bum Phillips looked at Gillman and saw an immensely talented coach who fit
his offensive schemes and ideas to fit the personnel of his team. Danyluk,
Tom and Paul Zimmerman. *The Super '70s: Memories From Pro Football's
Greatest Era*. Chicago: Mad Uke Publishing, 2005.

His given name was Oail, but he went by Bum because "can't nobody spell it
or pronounce it or anything." Reid, Ron, "Houston Gives 'Em Bum Rush,"
Sports Illustrated, Nov. 3, 1975.

"All he needed was a holster." Kirkpatrick

He also turned down $15,000 to do a beer commercial . . . Fowler

"That was like Camelot for us." Interview with Carl Mauck, April 20, 2011.

"It was like going to Disneyland with Bum." Int. with Pastorini

"I'd make a good one-term politician." Fowler

Gillman offered Phillips a contract which contained a clause that Phillips had
responsibility in the player-personnel and policy-making decisions . . .

Kirkpatrick

"Bud Adams had to let me have it." Kirkpatrick

"Bum wasn't going to be like Bill Peterson." Int. with Pastorini

"We had a tough time getting along with the owner of the club, Bud Adams."
Massing, Phyllis and Rhoda Lewis, Lifestories/A Video Legacy. Jan. 16,
1996.

"I had control of the team." Int. with Phillips

"Bum knew Sid. He knew if they were both there, they weren't going to get
nothing done," Int. with Mauck

In a photo taken at the event, Gillman, clad in a tuxedo, wears a wide grin . . .
Fowler

"It was time to retire." Massing and Lewis

CHAPTER 13

"The last time I was at his house, he became so engrossed in a football discussion he didn't notice that the steaks he had placed on the outside grill had
caught fire." Lawson, Earl, "Football's Man Without Mercy," *Saturday
Evening Post.* Oct. 8, 1955.

"How many kids are so involved in their father's profession?" Interview with
Lyle Gillman, March 7, 2011.

"It was the good news and the bad news. He was very even-keeled, but there was
a degree of absence all the time." Interview with Terry Hill, March 9, 2011.

Gillman was rather narrow-minded on the issue of facial hair as well. Interview
with Tom Gillman, April 6, 2011.

"Marry her. We'll get a parking pass." Interview with Larry Hill, March 9, 2011.

"They are the wandering Jews of the family." Massing, Phyllis and Rhoda
Lewis. Lifestories/A Video Legacy. Jan. 16, 1996.

"I guess I was a tomboy all my life." Beyette, Beverly, "Mrs. Sid Gillman: Football Has Been a Way of Life," *Los Angeles Times,* 1961.

She didn't see football players as brutes who simply looked to pound their
opponents into submission. Peach, Betty, "Mrs. Sid Gillman Feeds Entire
Squad," *San Diego Union,* July 14, 1961.

In truth, Esther was glad her husband was not a 9-to-5 businessman. Hoffman,
Jeane, "Gillman's Glad to Stay in Football Hot Seat," *Los Angeles Times,* Feb.
5, 1960.

So, after dinner, she'd go out with coffee, dessert, and her knitting and sit with
him as he studied the game. Hoffman, Jeane, "Sid Gillman's Wife Watches
Rams Films," *Los Angeles Times,* Aug. 16, 1955.

"She was an angel." Interview with Dan Pastorini, Aug. 24, 2011.

"She could talk about anything and always could talk about football." Interview
with Carl Peterson, March 21, 2011.

While participating in a tennis tournament at the La Costa country club . . . Murphy, Jack, "Speaking of Fischer, Carter, Zimmer and Assorted Topics," *San Diego Union*, June 12, 1972.

"This has been my career." Massing and Lewis

That was made clear one night when the Gillmans went to dinner with Carl Peterson and his wife . . . Int. with Peterson

"Sid was the portrait of the masculine man." Interview with Melvin Durslag, April 20, 2011.

"I didn't expect to live this long." Interview with Tom Gillman, April 11, 2011.

The truth is that when Tommy Jr., was a teenager in the 1970s, he hung around the Dodgers locker room . . . Bean, Billy. *Going the Other Way: Lessons From a Life In and Out of Major League Baseball.* New York: Marlowe & Company, 2003.

"I knew I was gay when I was 5 years old." Int. with Tom Gillman

CHAPTER 14

"I was practically laughing when I phoned Sid." Zimmerman, Paul, "Screen Gem," *Sports Illustrated*, Sept. 2, 1991.

"I wasn't interested in the details." "Sid Gillman: Trading Social Security for Coaching," *College & Pro Football Newsweekly*, 1977.

"I was hired to come in and control the offense, but the way it was finally resolved, I had no control over it on game day, calling plays." Pierson, Don, *Chicago Tribune*, Jan. 4, 2003.

The job appealed to Gillman because he'd been building programs for much of his career . . . Associated Press, Dec. 29, 1978.

Sheppard placed a call to the school and was surprised to learn that he had no trouble reaching Gillman. Interview with Mike Sheppard, Oct. 18, 2010.

Fox originally didn't have any desire for the big time . . . Interview with John Fox, May 10, 2011.

"Why do you keep doing this?" Fox asked Gillman. Int. with Fox

While the USIU receivers ran routes one day, Gillman wandered out of his office to watch . . . Int. with Sheppard

Not all of Gillman's coaching rubbed off on Fox, though. Paige, Woody, "Broncos Coach Fox Wants Winner For Next Ring," *Denver Post*, Feb. 1, 2011.

Dick Vermeil first met Gillman in 1960 at a football clinic in Reno, Nev. . . . Interview with Dick Vermeil, March 17, 2011.

But while he was deciding, hospital employees showed Gillman film of the planned surgery . . . Magee, Jerry, "Sid turns back time." *San Diego Union* Sept. 17, 1979.

"My dad had a hard time figuring out and accepting the health thing and how it prevented him from doing what he wanted to do." Interview with Tom

Gillman, April 10, 2011.

"The greatest thing about Sid is that he's a very opinionated person, a great idea guy with a great work ethic." Litzky, Frank, "When Good Things Happen For Taskmasters." *New York Times*, Jan. 3, 1993.

"He brushed past me for a fleeting moment, and then he was gone." Jaworski, Ron. *The Games That Changed the Game.* New York: Ballantine Books, 2010.

"It was an exercise in the meticulousness of coaching to the nth degree." Interview with Carl Peterson, March 21, 2011.

"Let's see your fingertip control. Shit, Ron, your palm's touching the leather!" Jaworski

Gillman wasn't necessarily coordinating the offense, and he wasn't installing the game plan. . . . Int. with Vermeil

What Gillman did with the scheme in 1980, though, was to sell Vermeil on the philosophy that a two tight end set could help the Eagles offense . . . Didinger, Ray, "Didinger's Mailbag: What's Up with Birds Defense?" Comcast SportsNet Philly, Dec. 5, 2010.

Pastorini walked over to Gillman and said, "You know what, I want to thank you and I want to apologize." Interview with Dan Pastorini, Aug. 24, 2011.

"We figured maybe 50 or 100 guys would show." Didinger, Ray, "Pro Football's Preppie," *The Sporting News*, November 1981.

With his three daughters flanking his wife in the Super Dome stands, they watched the first play from scrimmage . . . Massing and Lewis

"I probably will miss coaching." Forbes, Gordon, "Gillman Turns In His Playbook," *Philadelphia Inquirer*, Jan. 27, 1981.

"I want to take from him as much as possible." Aubrey, Coult, "Young's Not Yet Satisfied," *Allentown Morning Call*, March 10, 1984.

"I'd like for you to come to Pittsburgh for a week and visit with us." Interview with Mike Gottfried, Feb. 24, 2011.

"All too often, people tend to forget that people are still the best research material you can find." Magee

"A lot of the football stuff I owe to Sid." Clark Judge interview with John Harbaugh, Aug. 2011.

CHAPTER 15

Dick Vermeil asked him one day during a Philadelphia session about the first time he had ever seen a quarterback take a shotgun snap . . . Interview with Carl Peterson, March 21, 2011.

His day usually began early in the morning with a four-mile walk on the golf course at La Costa. Zimmerman, Paul, "Screen Gem," *Sports Illustrated*, Sept. 2, 1991.

His pool, naturally, was in the shape of a football, complete with brown tiles on one side that looked like laces . . . Barber, Phil, "To Air Was Divine," *Super Bowl XXXII Official Program*, Jan. 1998.

"If Liberace can shape his pool like a piano, I can have a football." Oates, Bob, "As Others Burn Out, This Coach's Flame Is Going Strong at 71," *Los Angeles Times*, Feb. 6, 1983.

"You're doing a *what*? A history of the American Football League?" Zimmerman

"He was just marvelous to listen to because he was so good and articulate with what he said." Int. with Peterson

"It was fascinating." Interview with Steve Mariucci, March 18, 2011.

"I watched him one time go through the film, and it was like a little kid seeing a movie for the first time." Interview with Dan Pastorini, Aug. 24, 2011.

Because those old Fox and RKO film reels didn't show teams playing successful defense, Gillman studied only the plays that resulted in offensive triumph. Interview with Tom Bass, March 21, 2011.

"It would disturb the daylights out of me if someone were to call me up and say, 'What about this? What about that?'" . . . Barber

"I try to keep up with what everybody is doing, so if the phone rings, I'll be ready." Wolf, Bob, "Under Sid Gillman, the Charger Era Came to Pass," *Los Angeles Times*, Aug. 16, 1989.

That was how Gillman spent nearly every late morning, and after a day of watching film with Gillman . . . Zimmerman

"He found his true love in life." Interview with Phil Simms, Jan. 11, 2011.

As soon as Schottenheimer saw Gillman, he said, "Sid, it's great to see you." Int. with Peterson

"Film is the coach's best friend, you know." Klein, Frederick C., "The Coach As Couch Potato," *Wall Street Journal*, Sept. 30, 1995.

In fact, Gillman later believed he made one mistake with his induction. Interview with Tom Gillman, Feb. 14, 2012.

"It was the greatest experience I ever had." Massing and Lewis

"It was young guys with clipboards, saying, 'Mr. Ditka, could you please get behind Mr. Davis?'" Interview with John McClain, July 21, 2011.

"Miami was known for its coaches. Cradle of Coaches, they call it." Massing and Lewis

"There was a very strong flavor for his induction." Int. with Parseghian

"Dear John: In recent conversations with members of the Miami football team of 1947, it was brought to our attention that Mr. Sid Gillman has not received the honor of being inducted in the Miami Hall of Fame." Miami University archives

"It shows you just how weak a football coach can be." Channel 39 NBC interview, 1991, KNSD.

"Don't eat that. It's so bad for you." Interview with Bill Korbin, March 8, 2011.

"Talk about the center-to-quarterback exchange." Interview with Lyle Gillman, March 8, 2011.

But while working out with a personal trainer at his La Costa home on Aug. 3, 2000, Gillman collapsed. Interview with Lyle Gillman, Dec. 9, 2011.

A week before he passed out in his home, Gillman had attended a Pro Football Hall of Fame celebration. Magee, Jerry, "San Diego and NFL Owe a Huge Debt to Gravely Ill Gillman," *San Diego Union-Tribune*, August 20, 2000.

"He's adjusting. He watched a few football games yesterday; three of them, to be exact—morning, noon, and night." Associated Press, Oct. 10, 2000.

"I don't know if he remembered. But he had a smile on his face." Interview with Ike Belem, Dec. 17, 2011.

"Bobbe, I think he's gone." Interview with Bobbe Korbin, Dec. 10, 2011.

"She had my dad's survival instincts." Int. with Lyle Gillman, March 8, 2011

The holiday card she wrote in 2007 stated, "Had my 95th with my whole family." Nick Shundich files

Once a month, Dick Vermeil would be sitting on his couch watching football, and he'd call Esther to say hello. Interview with Dick Vermeil, March 17, 2011.

"With some of them, football is a vocation. With some, it's an avocation." Zimmerman

When the Packers played the Steelers in Super Bowl XLV, the two combined for 36 running plays, the lowest in any Super Bowl before it. Battista, Judy, "NFL's Shift to Pass Goes Into Higher Gear," *The New York Times*, Oct. 6, 2011.

"I fear we may be losing the essence of what makes this game special." Billick, Brian, "Passing Game Is Changing Football; But May Not Be For Better," NFL.com, Sept. 29, 2011.

"I think the reason it wasn't as prevalent before because if you have a 6-6 Gronkowski-type guy, guess what, I'm putting him at defensive end and have him rush the quarterback." Interview with Tony Gonzalez, Feb. 2, 2012.

"You kidding me, *this* is Sid Gillman's NFL." Interview with Pete Prisco, Nov. 18, 2011.

"Sid was describing the slant pattern." Barber

Like Gillman's offense, Walsh's scheme was based on timing patterns, where the receiver had to reach a certain spot on the field in an exact time. Harris

Gillman wasn't a big fan of the West Coast offense . . . Int. with Vermeil

"He's always believed in controlling the ball with those short passes." *Inside Sports*, March 1982.

"You've changed a hell of a lot," Massing and Lewis

ABOUT THE AUTHOR

Josh Katzowitz is an award-winning sports writer who covers the NFL for CBSSports.com. He's also worked for the *Cincinnati Post* and the Augusta (Ga.) *Chronicle* while occasionally contributing to the *The New York Times, Los Angeles Times,* and *Washington Post.* His first book, *Bearcats Rising,* was released in 2009. He lives with his family in Austin, Texas.